Environmental Politics and Theory

Series Editors
Joel Jay Kassiola, Department of Political Science, San Francisco State University, San Francisco, CA, USA
Anthony Burke, School of Humanities and Social Sciences, UNSW, Canberra, Australia

The premise of this series is that the current environmental crisis cannot be solved by technological innovation alone. The environmental challenges we face today are, at their root, political crises involving political values, institutions and struggles for power. Therefore, environmental politics and theory are of the utmost social significance.

Growing public consciousness of the environmental crisis and its human and more-than-human impacts, exemplified by the worldwide urgency and political activity associated with the problem and consequences of climate and earth system change make it imperative to design and achieve a sustainable and socially just society.

The series publishes inter- and multi-disciplinary scholarship that extends the theoretical dimensions of green political theory, international relations, philosophy, and earth system governance. It addresses the need for social change away from the hegemonic consumer capitalist society to realize environmental sustainability and social justice.

Charlotte Hulme

Corporate Climate Action, Transnational Politics, and World Order

palgrave
macmillan

Charlotte Hulme
United States Military Academy
West Point, NY, USA

ISSN 2731-670X   ISSN 2731-6718   (electronic)
Environmental Politics and Theory
ISBN 978-3-031-34114-4   ISBN 978-3-031-34115-1   (eBook)
https://doi.org/10.1007/978-3-031-34115-1

© The Editor(s) (if applicable) and The Author(s), under exclusive license to Springer
Nature Switzerland AG 2023

This work is subject to copyright. All rights are solely and exclusively licensed by the
Publisher, whether the whole or part of the material is concerned, specifically the rights
of translation, reprinting, reuse of illustrations, recitation, broadcasting, reproduction on
microfilms or in any other physical way, and transmission or information storage and
retrieval, electronic adaptation, computer software, or by similar or dissimilar methodology
now known or hereafter developed.
The use of general descriptive names, registered names, trademarks, service marks, etc.
in this publication does not imply, even in the absence of a specific statement, that such
names are exempt from the relevant protective laws and regulations and therefore free for
general use.
The publisher, the authors, and the editors are safe to assume that the advice and information in this book are believed to be true and accurate at the date of publication. Neither
the publisher nor the authors or the editors give a warranty, expressed or implied, with
respect to the material contained herein or for any errors or omissions that may have been
made. The publisher remains neutral with regard to jurisdictional claims in published maps
and institutional affiliations.

Cover illustration: Evandro Maroni/Stockimo/Alamy Stock Photo

This Palgrave Macmillan imprint is published by the registered company Springer Nature
Switzerland AG
The registered company address is: Gewerbestrasse 11, 6330 Cham, Switzerland

This book is for my parents, Diana and Sandy, with gratefulness for everything.

ACKNOWLEDGMENTS

The research in this book was made possible by generous funding from Yale University, the Smith Richardson Foundation, and the Europa-Kolleg Hamburg and Federal Chancellor Helmut Schmidt Foundation. I thank each interviewee who kindly shared their time and insights; special gratitude is owed to Shikhar Malhotra and Siddharth Dixit for helping arrange interviews in India. Detlef Sprinz, Tyler Pratt, and Frances Rosenbluth each gave important advice and support to my doctoral research, where this project began. Tom Visel helped solve my thorniest emergence challenges (truly a non-repayable debt!), and the book would not be what it is without him.

It is impossible to capture the importance for this book of someone who has been indescribably helpful, provided immeasurable encouragement, and made countless contributions every step of the way, no days off, for seven years. I will rely on Meister Eckhart's good advice that if the only prayer you ever say in your life is "Thank you," that would be enough. Dad: thank you.

CONTENTS

1   Introduction — 1
The Private Sector as Climate Actor — 1
Transnational Politics and Corporate Climate Action — 3
The Emergent Corporate Climate Consensus — 8
  Identifying Climate Convergence — 8
Identifying and Explaining Emergent Outcomes — 12
  Hypothesis 1 (H1) — 16
  Hypothesis 2 (H2) — 17
  Hypothesis 3 (H3) — 18
Corporate Climate Action as a Window on World Order — 21
Roadmap for the Book — 25
References — 27

2   Change of Players, Change of Game — 33
Introduction — 33
Part I: International Context for Corporate Climate Action — 34
  Kyoto to Copenhagen: 1997–2009 — 35
  The Road to Paris: 2010–2013 — 40
  The Paris Conference: 2014–2015 — 42
Part II: Germany — 49
  Germany and the Climate Agenda — 49
  The "Ambition-Action" Gap and the Potential
  for Misperception — 51
Part III: India — 55

ix

x CONTENTS

The Prevailing Logic of Co-benefits	56
The "Ambition-Action" Gap and the Potential for Misperception	61
Part IV: The United States	64
Misaligned Climate "Games" and the Potential for Misperception: The Clinton Presidency	64
Climate Partisanship and the Potential for Misperception: The Obama Presidency	66
Conclusion	71
References	72

3 The Train Has Left the Station: Automotive and Energy-Intensive Industries — 83

Introduction	83
Part I: The Automotive Industry	85
Automakers' Behavior, 2010–2017	90
Identifying New Climate Practices	92
Industry-Level Foundations of the Emergent Climate Consensus	96
Part II: Energy-Intensive Industries	100
Energy-Intensive Companies' Behavior, 2010–2017	102
Identifying New Climate Practices	106
Industry-Level Foundations of the Emergent Climate Consensus	109
Conclusion	116
References	117

4 Climate Influencers: Technology — 123

Introduction	123
Part I: Climate Action, 2010–2017	127
Technology Companies' Behavior, 2010–2017	127
Identifying New Climate Practices	130
Part II: The Logic of Emergence	134
Conclusion	142
References	143

5 "The Earth Is Shifting Beneath Their Feet": Finance — 147

Introduction	147
Part I: The Old Dominant Design Comes Under Pressure	149
Part II: Climate Action, 2010–2017	153

Finance Companies' Behavior, 2010–2017		153
Identifying New Climate Practices		155
Part III: Patterns of Emergent Action		161
Conclusion		166
References		168

6 **The Emergent Corporate Climate Consensus** 173
Introduction 173
Part I: The Development of a Corporate Climate Consensus 178
   Corporate Behavior, 2010–2017 178
Part II: Private Sector Responses to State Abdication
of Leadership 184
Part III: Corporations' Climate Action and Ambition 193
   Hypothesis 2: Industry Type 193
   Hypothesis 3: Headquarter Country 195
Inadvertent Change in the Climate Game 202
References 203

7 **Superpowers, Inc.: Lessons on World Order** 205
Introduction 205
Lesson 1: Corporations May Be Better Than States
at Recognizing New "Games" 205
Lesson 2: Corporations Can Shape New Arenas for State
Behavior, Including Great Power Competition 211
Lesson 3: Corporations Have the Potential to Become Grand
Strategic Actors 216
Lesson 4: Corporations Have the Potential to Outperform
States in Tackling Twenty-First Century Problem Sets 220
Conclusion 224
References 225

Appendix 231

Index 249

List of Figures

Fig. 6.1	Percentage of companies adopting specific climate practices, 2010–2017	182
Fig. 6.2	Percentage of companies deeply invested in specific climate practices, 2010–2017	183
Fig. 6.3	Perceived high-impact risks and opportunities related to climate change, 2010–2016	185
Fig. 6.4	Divergence between companies' climate action and perceptions, 2010–2017	188
Fig. 6.5	Emergent climate consensus by time period, 2010–2016	190
Fig. 6.6	Prevalence of emergent action by industry, 2010–2016	194
Fig. 6.7	Country comparison of emergent action in the automotive industry, 2010–2016	196
Fig. 6.8	Country comparison of emergent action in energy-intensive (EI) industries, 2010–2016	198
Fig. 6.9	Country comparison of emergent action in the technology industry, 2010–2016	199
Fig. 6.10	Country comparison of emergent action in the finance industry, 2010–2016	200
Fig. 6.11	Cumulative change in emergent action by headquarter country, 2010–2016	201

LIST OF TABLES

Table 3.1	Automaker types, 2010–2017	91
Table 3.2	Breadth and depth of automakers' climate action, 2010–2017	92
Table 3.3	Perceived high material impact of climate change among automakers, 2010–2016	97
Table 3.4	Perceived high material impact of climate change for automakers increasing climate performance sufficiently to change types, 2010–2016	98
Table 3.5	Energy-intensive company types, 2010–2017	104
Table 3.6	Breadth and depth of energy-intensive companies' climate action, 2010–2017	106
Table 3.7	Perceived high material impact of climate change among energy-intensive companies, 2010–2016	110
Table 3.8	Perceived high material impact of climate change for energy-intensive companies increasing climate performance sufficiently to change types, 2010–2016	113
Table 3.9	Perceived high material impact of regulation and changing consumer behavior for energy-intensive companies increasing climate performance sufficiently to change types, 2010–2016	114
Table 4.1	Technology company types, 2010–2017	129
Table 4.2	Breadth and depth of technology companies' climate action, 2010–2017	130
Table 4.3	Perceived high material impact of climate change among technology companies, 2010–2016	135

xvi   LIST OF TABLES

Table 4.4	Perceived high material impact of climate change for technology companies increasing climate performance sufficiently to change types, 2010–2016	137
Table 5.1	Finance company types, 2010–2017	154
Table 5.2	Breadth and depth of finance companies' climate action, 2010–2017	156
Table 5.3	Perceived high material impact of climate change among finance companies, 2010–2016	162
Table 5.4	Perceived high material impact of regulation, changing consumer behavior, and physical impacts for individual finance companies, 2010–2016	164
Table 6.1	Company types, 2010–2017	179

CHAPTER 1

Introduction

THE PRIVATE SECTOR AS CLIMATE ACTOR

In a 2019 interview, ex-Shell Oil President John Hofmeister was asked why oil majors like Shell, BP, and Exxon opposed the Trump administration's rollback of methane emissions regulations. He explained that such environmental regulations "are essential for the [fossil fuel] industry to be successful down the road. That's changed in the last 20 years. And so[,] it's necessary for the industry to recognize that this is the way it's going to be, and it is the way it should be" (Hofmeister 2019). What would have seemed like a surprising statement just a decade prior was unexceptional by the late 2010s. By the end of a decade opening in the aftermath of the Great Recession, a growing cohort of leaders of the world's largest companies characterized climate change as a long-term challenge demanding private sector responses. For example, in his 2020 letter to CEOs, Larry Fink, the CEO of BlackRock—which, with $10 trillion in assets under management, is the world's largest asset manager—announced that climate change "has become a defining factor in companies' long-term prospects," and that "we are on the edge of a fundamental reshaping of finance" (Fink 2020). That same year, Microsoft CEO Satya Nadella warned that if companies fail to factor environmental sustainability into their growth plans, capitalism "will fundamentally be in jeopardy" (Clifford 2020).

© The Author(s), under exclusive license to Springer Nature
Switzerland AG 2023
C. Hulme, *Corporate Climate Action, Transnational Politics, and World Order*, Environmental Politics and Theory,
https://doi.org/10.1007/978-3-031-34115-1_1

2   C. HULME

Their words were not just "cheap talk." Throughout the 2010s, private sector climate action gained momentum as companies pursued emissions reductions exceeding what regulation required (Stevens 2019), generated demand for renewable energy in regions governed by fossil fuel-friendly regulation (Vandenbergh and Gilligan 2017b), and converged around the idea that failing to treat climate change as a relevant issue no longer was an option for any serious global actor. As the president of the World Resources Institute put it in 2014,

> America's smartest business leaders are pursuing a strategy unheard of a few short years ago: they are building economic growth while tackling climate change at its source. We believe this is one of the true mind-shifts in modern commerce, as U.S. business leaders see the opportunity of investment in a low-carbon economy and the risk of following a business-as-usual, high-carbon path. (Steer 2014)

What explains the corporate "mind-shift" on climate change, evident not only among US-based corporations but also among a diverse range of firms globally? What accounts for the private sector's perception, as an expert from the Berlin-based Stiftung 2 Grad (the 2° Foundation) described it in an interview for this book, that "the train of transforming the economy has left the station and is not going to return," and that businesses that are "not compliant" with a low-carbon economy "will, in the end, have to transform or even will disappear" (Berlin, November 13, 2018)?

This book examines why and how a growing cohort of private sector actors that might not be expected to adopt certain climate-related behaviors became increasingly invested in them. In particular, it explores the origins and significance of a new corporate climate consensus, or norm about the need for certain types of behavior in an issue area characterized by a "profound lack of international consensus" (Haufler 2001, 114), or agreement among states about how to respond in a concerted, ambitious, and effective fashion. Many observers perceived the 2015 Paris Climate Agreement as signifying a "historic breakthrough on an issue that has foiled decades of international efforts to address climate change" (Davenport 2015), and as marking a watershed in corporate climate action. But this book argues that corporations began to coalesce around a new climate approach well before Paris and that their behavior was grounded in the perception—which the Paris Agreement only strengthened—that states could not be counted on to play their traditional role vis-à-vis a transnational issue poised to shape future global trends.

In recent years, the corporate climate action phenomenon, and especially the growing gap between the level of corporate and government action, has attracted increased attention. In 2022, for example, in the wake of COP26 (the 26th Conference of the Parties to the UN Framework Convention on Climate Change), scholars noted that "the sheer size of the private-sector turnout... suggested that industry was no longer prepared to stand by and wait for government action," proposing that the most significant outcome of the conference "may not have been the formal agreement hammered out by diplomats but the momentum that emerged from the meetings and conversations among global business leaders that took place along the sidelines" (Yanosek and Victor 2022). This book explains how, in a relatively short span of time, from the private sector's perspective the center of gravity in the climate change issue area shifted away from national governments and toward other players, including corporations themselves. It shows why the process by which states increasingly appeared to be the "junior partners" and no longer "the natural problem-solving unit" (Mathews 1997, 63, 65) in an issue area of mounting importance to international security was hard to have anticipated in advance, reflective of an emerging private sector norm, and indicative of how the state system is becoming progressively "embedded in a broadening and deepening transnational arena" (Ruggie 2004, 499).

TRANSNATIONAL POLITICS AND CORPORATE CLIMATE ACTION

For decades political scientists, building on classic theories of the tragedy of the commons in environmental issue areas, framed climate change as a quintessential collective action problem calling for cooperation through international organizations, which could help states reduce emissions by supplying selective incentives (Olson 1965), generating shared norms and applying group sanctions for violations (Ostrom 1990), or providing platforms for altruistic actors to be first movers, producing a cascade effect (Stern 2002). The failure of the 2009 Copenhagen Climate Conference threw into sharp relief the ongoing inability of international organizations to supply adequate selective incentives or generate sufficiently powerful norms to achieve collective action on the most intractable climate change issues. In the wake of the conference, Keohane and Victor's influential

4   C. HULME

work on the "regime complex for climate change" described the range of actors—including UN legal regimes and specialized agencies, bilateral initiatives, "clubs" of states like the G-20, multilateral development banks, subnational actors like California, and private actors like industry—populating the "loosely coupled" array of "narrowly-focused regulatory regimes" that had emerged in the wake of perennial failures by states "to craft a strong, integrated and comprehensive regulatory system for managing climate change" (2010, 2).

The 2010s saw a burgeoning literature on the transnational governance of climate change, including on the proliferation of subnational and market-based initiatives that "cut across traditional state-based jurisdictions, operate across public–private divides," and perform regulatory functions (Bulkeley et al. 2014, 1). The accelerating interest in governance in the private sphere, specifically, reflected not only an appreciation that the processes and services that generate greenhouse gases "are often diffuse, transnational, and frequently beyond direct state control" (Bulkeley and Newell 2015, 6), but also an understanding that even if all key states had the will to address climate change, the magnitude of the problem now is such that they lack the ability to do so on their own. As some experts have noted, considerable additional efforts by private actors are required to "substantially reduce the risk of catastrophic climate change" (Vandenbergh and Gilligan 2017a). The corporate sector is especially critical given its contribution to global greenhouse gas emissions. Citing data from the Climate Accountability Initiative, Bulkeley and Newell highlighted that 63% of emissions of industrial CO_2 and methane from 1751 through 2010 "could be traced to 90 major economic actors in the fossil fuel and cement industries, with half of these emissions having been produced since 1986" (2015, 2–3). Meanwhile, a 2017 study by CDP (formerly the Carbon Disclosure Project) found that 100 companies are responsible for 70% of emissions since 1988 (Griffin 2017).

Scholarship focused on the climate governance function of private actors has considered their role in performing transnational regulatory functions (Eberlein et al. 2014), reformulating the problem of climate change in politically tractable ways, and supplying new institutional avenues for diffusing public rules (Auld and Green 2017). In an important contribution to the field, Green theorized conditions under which private actors may create authoritative rules and standards in environmental issue areas, proposing that they can use either "delegated private authority," which states can confer upon them, or "entrepreneurial private authority," which they can claim in the absence of an international organization serving as a focal point for an issue and homogenous policy preferences among powerful states (2013, 28). Private authority concerns only those situations in which "nonstate actors make rules or set standards that other actors in world politics adopt"; it does not include private efforts to influence states through lobbying or agenda-setting, nor does it encompass creation of norms (Green 2013, 6). Thus, like Bulkeley et al., who approached transnational climate governance in the sense of defined groups of actors concerned with establishing formal and authoritative instruments like carbon markets, certification standards, emissions registries, and carbon labeling (2014, 14), Green examined the role of non-governmental organizations (NGOs) in creating the Greenhouse Gas Protocol (2013, 19).

Anticipating Green, Haufler (2001) theorized situations in which private actors seek rules that states have not provided. With its focus specifically on industry, her book, *A Public Role for the Private Sector: Industry Self-Regulation in a Global Economy*, responded to an important gap in some of the first-generation literature on transnational relations. As Ruggie noted, despite its obvious "global reach and capacity" and ability to make and implement "decisions at a pace that neither governments nor international agencies can match," in the 1970s the field of international relations largely overlooked the corporate sector given that multinational corporations were "not in the same business as states"; in the 1980s, meanwhile, whatever roles they played in the context of international regimes "were filtered through the prisms of their influence on governmental and intergovernmental policy processes" (2004, 501, 514). Yet, in the early 2000s, Cutler observed that in certain transnational issue areas, "firms are basically functioning like governments" (2002, 32).

Haufler argued that industry "self-regulation," or a situation in which "those regulated design [and] enforce the rules themselves," arises from "gaps in global governance that stem from the lack of overarching, comprehensive regulation of corporations at the international level" (2001, 3). She contended that the "risk that governments will intervene, either nationally or internationally, to enforce rules on industry" is an "overwhelming force" driving such behavior (Haufler 2001, 41). In short, industry acts preemptively, when there are both gaps in global regulation *and* widespread expectations that states soon will act to ameliorate those gaps. By voluntarily raising their own standards in issue areas such as the environment and labor practices, industry seeks to ward off, or at least slow down, regulatory action; in the process, if it can develop a reputation for being a "good corporate citizen," it becomes "more likely that government will be willing to delegate authority to the industry, or make them more accepting of industry self-regulation as an alternative to traditional command-and-control regulation" (Haufler 2001, 27). Like Green, Haufler's focus was on the creation of formal and authoritative rules and standards, such as the International Organization for Standardization (ISO) 14,000 environmental management system and the Coalition for Environmentally Responsible Economies (Ceres) Principles.

More recent work by Vandenbergh and Gilligan offered a different perspective on what private actors, including corporations, seek to achieve by adopting practices relevant for addressing climate change. Considering the United States context, they argued that the private sector can "buy time" for the federal government to overcome domestic political obstacles to marshaling a robust climate response; corporations are among the private actors that can "bypass 'solution aversion'—the resistance to climate change [action] that arises from concerns about a big government response." In contrast to Haufler, they argued that in adopting voluntary climate action private actors do not preempt the state in order to stave off unwanted regulation, but rather to pave the way for "a more comprehensive government response" (Vandenbergh and Gilligan 2017b). These actors, including corporations, *want* government action, perceiving climate change as an issue with potentially significant impacts for their interests. In another departure from Haufler and Green's approach, which focused on private actors' coordinated efforts to construct formal rules and standards, many of the corporate climate initiatives of interest and importance in Vandenbergh and Gilligan's work—from carbon neutrality goals adopted by select Big Tech companies to a supply chain emissions reduction initiative piloted by Walmart—"occurred in a one-off, uncoordinated way" (2019, 5).

Each of these contributions to the field of transnational climate governance, and specifically to theorizing the private sector as a climate actor in situations marked by governance gaps left by states, addresses a certain type of private action (formal and coordinated rules, in Haufler and Green, versus informal and uncoordinated actions, in Vandenbergh and Gilligan) and reflects a particular understanding about private actors' expectations for state action (state action is expected in Haufler, as well as in Vandenbergh and Gilligan, but is not expected in Green). This book examines informal, uncoordinated corporate climate action occurring in a context in which corporate actors did not expect robust state climate action, though most desired it. Adopting certain climate practices in the absence of high expectations for state action, and without necessarily intending to behave as climate leaders in a traditional sense, select companies shaped, responded to, and reinforced an emergent "steering mechanism," to borrow a term from Rosenau (1995, 14), governing the climate change issue area: a corporate climate consensus.

As the next section considers, what makes this consensus particularly worthy of examination is that while corporate climate action is considered mainstream from the vantage point of the early 2020s, it represents a remarkable development, one that would not have been anticipated given the private sector's position at the turn of the 2010s and most corporations' individual assessments of the material relevance of climate change during that decade. In addition, the corporations that joined in adopting new climate practices were dispersed across countries and industries and not necessarily operating within networks in which "persistent patterns of association" created structures that "define[d], enable[d], or restrict[ed]" their behavior (Hafner-Burton et al. 2009, 562). Networks feature prominently in the latest generation of scholarship examining the role of transnational actors in governing global issues. For example, Kahler and Lake theorize networked international governance as "based on shared or pooled authority and on repeated, enduring, and reciprocal relationships among actors in different national jurisdictions," and as often including "public–private networks or purely private networks with substantial regulatory authority" (2009, 248–249). Meanwhile, in *The New Power Politics: Networks and Transnational Security Governance*, Avant and Westerwinter emphasize how actors in a network shape their "relational position" to enhance their power and use their relationships "to affect governance outcomes" (2016, 2). While some of the corporations featured in this book may belong to shared networks encompassing their industries or other cross-sections of the private sector, ultimately the book is concerned less with how actors in existing networks intentionally seek to enhance their power or deliberately attempt to affect governance outcomes, and more with how uncoordinated actors dispersed across a vast ecosystem like the private sector may come to converge around certain practices and ideas despite an apparent absence of inclination to do so at an individual level.

8   C. HULME

The Emergent Corporate Climate Consensus

Identifying Climate Convergence

During the 2010s, a growing cohort of corporations adopted climate-relevant practices reflecting a perceived narrowing of possible future directions of the global energy system and the kinds of behavior they should adopt as a result. As the former director of strategy and energy policy for a major European power company reflected in an interview for this book,

> If you go back ten years, there was a variety of views as to where the energy system was going in the long term. That variety of views was driven by different views on technology, how real the threat of climate change was, and how politicians may or may not react to it. What we've seen over [the last] ten years is that diversity of views disappearing. (London, November 12, 2018)

Companies gradually recognized a certain suite of climate change-related practices as part of a new paradigm for success in a changing global environment—and specifically, one in which a low-carbon future increasingly was perceived as very likely due to climate-driven pressures. In business parlance, effectively they came to recognize a new "dominant design," which conventionally refers to a product that is treated as the de facto standard-setter in an industry, thereby leading alternatives to fall away, spurring its entrenchment.

One example of a climate practice that proliferated in the 2010s and that reflected a certain understanding about the future is internal carbon pricing, which "places a monetary value on greenhouse gas emissions, which businesses then can factor into investment decisions and business operations," directing "finance away from high-emitting activities" (Bartlett et al. 2017, 4). According to a Brussels-based energy and climate policy expert interviewed for this book, among various corporate climate practices, internal carbon pricing has special significance as an indicator that a company has not siloed climate change as one "corporate social responsibility" issue among many, but rather is assessing it in terms of its future potential impact on the bottom line (Düsseldorf, Germany, October 6, 2018). An internal carbon price is an indicator of what sort of future a company anticipates, given that it "ensures long term capital investments don't become too costly, or even obsolete, in an environment where greenhouse gas emissions carry a price." In the early 2010s, internal carbon pricing was rare; by 2014, only 150 global companies reported having adopted this practice. However, by 2017, it had become "the new normal for major multinationals," with roughly 1400 companies using an internal carbon price—including "more than 100 Fortune Global 500 companies with collective annual revenues of US$7 trillion"—which represented "an eight-fold leap in take up in the last four years" (CDP 2017).

CDP disclosure is a second key example of a corporate climate practice proliferating during the 2010s. The non-profit CDP conducts annual surveys of thousands of companies worldwide concerning climate-relevant aspects of their activities. A central purpose in collecting this data is providing investors with information about how companies perceive and manage climate-related impacts. The increase in the number of companies participating in CDP disclosure during the 2010s suggests a growing appreciation of the business relevance of climate issues (Das 2012, 248). As of 2010, approximately 2900 companies participated in CDP disclosure on climate change; by 2015, this number was over 5500, and in 2020, there were over 9500 companies disclosing climate data—a 228% increase in ten years (CDP n.d.).

This book examines select climate-related practices of 34 corporations representing four industry groups—automotive, energy-intensive, technology, and finance—and three primary headquarter countries: Germany, India, and the United States.[1] As Chapter 3 introduces and the appendix describes, to systematically evaluate changing patterns of climate activity the book employs three metrics: *product*, capturing the extent to which a company addressed its emissions; *alignment*, gauging the degree to which a company made its activities more coherent with a low-carbon future; and *investment*, assessing a company's allocation of resources to support a low-carbon future. It demonstrates that across industry groups and headquarter countries, the level and ambition of climate activity increased in the 2010s, with certain practices becoming more broadly adopted and

---

[1] For several industries, a major company was headquartered in a country other than Germany, India, or the United States (Japan-based Toyota for automotive, Netherlands-based Shell for oil and gas, and South Korea-based Samsung for technology). Including such companies enhanced the potential to capture as fully as possible how pivotal actors in the case study industries behaved vis-à-vis the climate change issue.

10   C. HULME

firms becoming more deeply committed to them. The book argues that early movers shaped, while others progressively reinforced, a new corporate consensus, or norm, about the kind of behavior necessary to adopt to succeed in a low-carbon future. A key condition spurring such "normative convergence and consensus" (Lascurettes 2017, 3) was the perception that states had failed to provide clear and predictable "rules of the game" for preparing for such a future and that corporations must behave differently as a result. To demonstrate the prevalence of this perception, the book marshals CDP data showing that in the 2010s, corporations increasingly discounted prospects for high-impact climate policy and regulation, reflecting their loss of confidence in state leadership.

In proposing that companies converged around a climate "norm," this book claims that they arrived at a new shared understanding of how they should act, aligning with a classic definition of norms as ideas about "appropriate behavior for actors with a given identity" (Finnemore and Sikkink 1998, 891). The argument is that the broadening and deepening of climate activity during the 2010s reflected a new shared understanding of appropriate behavior for corporations in a changing global environment. This development unfolded at the collective level, arising through what some constructivist international relations scholarship would describe as "social interaction" (Hoffman 2017), as at the individual level corporations often did not perceive serious material risks from adhering to status quo climate behavior or major material benefits from changing their behavior. How and why such a norm, or shared idea about a standard of behavior, arose when many of the initiatives and actions contributing to its development occurred in an uncoordinated and diffuse fashion is the central puzzle that this book addresses.

* * *

Given its use of data from corporate disclosures, including annual reports, sustainability reports, and reports to CDP, this book is attentive to concerns about greenwashing, "communication that misleads people into holding overly positive beliefs about an organization's environmental performance, practices, or products"—the focus of a growing literature. For example, observing that corporate "claims about environmental performance—at both the product level and the corporate level—have increased rapidly in recent years," Lyon and Montgomery proposed a typology of greenwashing drivers and strategies (2015, 223). Noting that much of the greenwash literature "has focused on the pressures placed on an organization by its external environment, suggesting greenwash is a reactive response," they highlighted the empirical finding that the "most important antecedent of greenwash is lax and uncertain government regulation, which creates a low chance of being punished for greenwash." A weak regulatory environment "allows firms to manipulate consumer and investor demands for green products, services, and firms." Meanwhile, the *threat* of heightened regulation also can spur greenwashing, highlighting how firms can engage in this practice to stave off government intervention through rhetoric and symbolic action with marginal behavioral change (Lyon and Montgomery 2015, 234).

In this book, self-reported data on aspects of environmental performance was supplemented by external sources wherever possible (e.g., in Chapter 5, data on finance companies' climate practices was gathered from NGOs like BankTrack, which focuses on increasing transparency surrounding private finance and sustainability). Despite the unavoidable limitations of corporate environmental data, examples in the empirical chapters of "business as usual" companies—firms that either did not seek to hide poor climate performance in their corporate reporting or were unsuccessful in their attempts at greenwashing—coupled with the fact that the empirics do not show a smooth upward trajectory toward heightened climate performance and ambition even within some relatively "climate-progressive" companies, should bolster confidence in the overall picture painted by the data.

In leveraging CDP data concerning companies' perceptions of the regulatory environment, this book provides a snapshot of how these firms publicly assessed the risks and opportunities of adopting new climate approaches or of failing to do so. While it is possible that companies were motivated to misrepresent their beliefs about the present and future regulatory environment, data collected during interviews with industry experts and representatives from companies, conducted on a confidential basis to encourage frank responses, suggests that such misrepresentation was not a common occurrence.

12   C. HULME

Identifying and Explaining Emergent Outcomes

In 1995, Rosenau contended that to "anticipate the prospects for global governance in the decades ahead" was to "look for authorities that are obscure, boundaries that are in flux, and systems of rule that are emergent," arising out of "the activities of other types of actors" besides states (1, 25). An emergent system is one arising unexpectedly or inadvertently from the interactions of actors, generating a situation in which the whole is *different* from, not just greater than, the sum of the parts (Jervis 1997, 12–13). An emergent system is self-organizing. An example of such a system found in the natural world is the V-shaped flight pattern of migrating geese, which comes about "spontaneously from the way geese interact with one another, trying to find the best possible energy reduction and sensory information during flight. In addition to there not being a pre-specified flight pattern in geese, there is also no flight commander goose telling his subordinates to follow him... in the form of a V-pattern" (van Geert 2017, 23).

This book argues that the new corporate climate consensus was emergent, an instance of unexpected self-coordination in a diffuse system of actors. Corporations acted, in effect, much like a flock of geese, "seemingly leaderless, sensing some shift in conditions, sensing each other's intuitions, and smoothly shifting direction *en masse*" (Brooks 2020). Coherence came about through the recognition of an interest at the collective level. The shared idea that climate change was an issue demanding a new approach was not a function of how individual companies perceived the material importance of climate change; as the empirical chapters demonstrate, during the 2010s, at the individual level companies, including what became some of the most ambitious in climate action, did not become appreciably more concerned about significant material impacts flowing from climate-related developments. The new interest recognized at the collective level and spurring a corporate consensus, or normative convergence, was that in an issue area characterized not only by a lack of agreement among states about how to respond in an effective manner but also by declining prospects that states would play their traditional role in governing a transnational issue poised to shape future global trends, corporations must play a different role than in the past.

Amid the array of transnational actors participating in the governance of issue areas like climate change, from the perspective of multinational corporations states long have enjoyed pride of place as the most important governors,[2] or those whose behavior bears most on an issue of paramount concern for the private sector: predictability in the international environment. In the context of issues of transnational importance, states traditionally have performed a specific role in providing corporations with the "rules of the game" in the form of policy and regulation. By indicating how they would respond to these risks, thus signaling how *others*, in turn, should adjust or prepare to adjust *their* behavior, states enhanced predictability in the international environment. But this century, the most powerful states have proven unwilling to provide clear and effective rules vis-à-vis certain challenges; select issue areas, climate change being an especially clear case, have lacked strong state governance. Consistent with Vandenbergh and Gilligan (2019), this book assumes that with a low-carbon future appearing increasingly likely, the private sector would like states to provide clear and predictable policy and regulation concerning climate change and a potential global low-carbon transition. No corporation wants to get left behind, having failed to prepare adequately for a new global climate and energy reality and its attendant economic and geopolitical changes. By the 2010s, the decade of interest in this book, climate change had gained growing international recognition as not just one among many global challenges but as one likely to be a defining issue in the twenty-first century.

However, just because corporate actors were dissatisfied with the climate governance that states provided, it did not follow that they would act. Nature may abhor a vacuum, but it was hardly inevitable that the private sector, including some corporations whose business models were deeply enmeshed in the high-carbon status quo, would adopt behavior that effectively began to address a lacuna left by states: shaping some rules for how corporations should behave to succeed in a changing global environment, specifically, one marked by a growing view that a low-carbon future was a likely prospect given climate-related pressures. Although not inevitable, this book argues that this is what ultimately unfolded in the 2010s. States, despite periodically raising expectations that they would act ambitiously and effectively to clarify the path toward a low-carbon future, did not make the climate issue a high priority. Corporations, seeking

---

[2] There are exceptions to this general rule. For example, automakers in the US market may look to California more than the federal government as the key pace-setter on emissions standards, given the size of its market and the freedom to set its own, tougher standards that it has been afforded by Washington, D.C.

14   C. HULME

confidence in the future context in which they were going to have to function, sought to create more predictable conditions. In an environment in which states could not be counted on to play their traditional role as "rule-writers," corporations adopted climate-relevant practices that they came to recognize as necessary for success in a low-carbon future. In adopting a new paradigm of response, they generated increased certainty and predictability about where they were headed and how they planned to get there.

If the argument is correct that the corporate climate consensus was an emergent outcome, reflecting self-coordination arising from the recognition of an interest at the collective level, what should the data show? Using the broadening and deepening of climate activity as an indicator of consensus, or as evidence of the "invisible hand" of the consensus steering mechanism at work, there should be an inverse relationship between the breadth and depth of corporate climate action, on the one hand, and the prevalence of the view among individual companies that climate change was becoming a more pressing material concern, on the other. This counterintuitive mismatch between company-level perceptions of the material importance of the climate change issue and a new corporate climate approach is the relationship that the concept of emergence helps to illuminate.

* * *

This book's approach to identifying and explaining an emergent outcome, which reflects the development of an interest at the collective level, producing change that can be difficult to anticipate in advance but that often seems inevitable in hindsight, is captured by Granovetter's threshold model of collective behavior. This model theorizes how collective goods can be achieved by uncoordinated actors if a certain group of actors have particular "thresholds" for action at a given moment (Granovetter 1978). As Kuran (1991) demonstrated in his application of the threshold model to democratic revolutions, a domino effect is generated only if, in a given context, there is a first mover with a revolutionary threshold of zero (i.e., they will protest on the streets regardless of whether anyone else is protesting) existing alongside an individual with a threshold of one (i.e., they will join the pro-democracy protest if there is one other protester), existing alongside an individual with a threshold of two (i.e., this individual will join the protest if they see two other protesters), and so on. What matters for realizing the collective outcome is that the "right" individuals (given their particular revolutionary thresholds) coexist at a certain time in a given context.

The threshold model underscores that a collective outcome can be achieved that does not reflect the importance accorded to that outcome based on the individual interest sets of the participating actors. As actors gather new information in their environment, they may or may not reprioritize a particular interest within their interest set—and even if they *do* reprioritize a certain interest, it still might not be ranked particularly high. The following set of ten numbers represents a cohort of actors, each with a different threshold for a certain action (represented by a number ranging from zero to ten): {0, 1, 2, 3, 4, 5, 6, 7, 8, 10}. Most of the actors do not have a particularly low threshold for joining the activity in question; yet, as theorized by the threshold model, nine will join in the behavior (actors with thresholds zero through eight). In such a situation, in which a collective outcome is achieved despite it not being of particularly high importance for many actors, or not ranked very high in their interest sets, the outcome is emergent, or a second-order effect flowing from actors' interactions as opposed to individual attributes. By contrast, the following set of numbers represents a cohort of actors whose behavior also will generate a collective outcome, but one not emergent in nature: {0, 1, 2, 2, 2, 2, 2, 2, 2, 2}. In this case, the collective outcome (all ten actors joining in the behavior) is not emergent; it easily could be anticipated on the basis of the attributes (the low thresholds for action) of the individual actors.

Importantly, actors' thresholds for action are not fixed and can change based on factors ranging from the easing of external sanction for participation to a growing sense that actors participating in the behavior are "on the winning side." Perceptions are crucial; dispersed, decentralized, uncoordinated actors always find themselves in situations of imperfect information, never entirely sure to what extent there is support for the action that they are contemplating. An actor's perception that others are on the brink of acting, or that the tide is turning and that failing to join in the behavior now will disadvantage them later, can spur an actor into participating in a behavior where it previously had been unwilling or simply uninterested.

This book argues that the development of a corporate climate consensus was emergent, a collective outcome that was achieved despite most companies not ranking climate change very high in their interest

16   C. HULME

sets. In fact, as the consensus strengthened throughout the 2010s, in many cases individual companies' assessments of the material importance of climate change not only did not increase but actually *declined* significantly.

What explains when and why certain companies joined in the process that produced the climate consensus—and why some of those companies were first movers (i.e., with action thresholds of 0)—while others stayed on the sidelines? The hypotheses below articulate this book's general expectations about the timing of the broadening and deepening of climate action, as well as about the types of corporations primarily driving this development.

Hypothesis 1 (H1)

Corporate climate action will broaden and deepen when prospects in the international landscape for ambitious and concerted state-led climate action are low.

H1 articulates the expectation that the broadening and deepening of corporate climate action accelerated during the 2010s. The international policy context is used as a proxy for states' appetite for taking action to address an issue calling for a transnational response. H1 captures the argument that the clearer it became that the 2009 Copenhagen Climate Conference signified the unraveling of prospects for concerted international action on an issue that is not amenable to "go-it-alone" solutions—confirmed by the 2015 Paris Climate Conference—the more that the private sector viewed states as abdicating their traditional role and the stronger the perceived need to act on its own. In short, H1 proposes that waning prospects for concerted international action on a transnational issue that the private sector appreciates will inform future trends and entail potentially significant implications for its activities will lead to a higher level of corporate climate action, even if individually companies do not yet see strong material reasons to act. H1 anticipates that if there *are* reasonable prospects for concerted state-led climate action, corporations would lack a strong incentive to become climate active prior to perceiving pressing material reasons for doing so. They would expect that states would continue to play their traditional role, paving the way for companies to succeed in a changing environment.

This claim stands in contrast to influential arguments in the literature. Haufler, for example, maintained that the prospect for industry "self-regulation" in an issue area is lowest when there are no ongoing negotiations over a formal, binding international regime (2001, 41). Thus, there should not have been significant levels of climate-related self-regulation during the 2010s, a decade opening in the wake of the Copenhagen Conference, whose collapse dashed hopes for such a regime. Demonstrating that it was in this context that companies intensified their self-regulation, this book explains this development as a function of the emergent consensus mechanism "steering" uncoordinated actors in a certain direction.

While H1 addresses the condition in which the emergent pattern of action came about (a perceived absence of adequate state climate governance), it does not address which actors became part of the process that produced it, including which were the first movers. No company, no matter how powerful, commands consensus or compels others to follow its lead. Yet, action by well-positioned first movers can act as an accelerant of consensus by spurring a narrowing of the debate about whether joining in a certain behavior will be advantageous, thus potentially altering individual companies' thresholds for action. But the influence of a first mover is not a given; as the threshold model captures, just because there is a prominent actor willing to take a risk and bet on a certain future, it does not mean that others necessarily will agree with its bet or be willing to assume the risks that following its lead might entail.

Below are two hypotheses on industry- and country-level factors making it more likely that corporations will increase their level of climate activity seemingly absent strong individual incentives to do so. These hypotheses expect that certain corporations, depending on their industry or headquarter country, will be more inclined not just to recognize the need for a new approach to an unconventional issue poised to impact the future global landscape, but to seize the initiative and embrace a new role vis-à-vis this type of challenge.

Hypothesis 2 (H2)

Compared to a company in an industry that is strongly tied to the fossil fuel-centered status quo, a company in an industry that is not strongly tied

18   C. HULME

to the fossil fuel-centered status quo will be more likely to broaden and deepen its climate activity prior to perceiving a strong material incentive to do so.

Companies whose business models are based on fossil fuel-centered activities are less likely than companies whose business models are not based on fossil fuel-centered activities to undertake actions with the potential to alter the status quo without perceiving powerful material incentives to do so. The logic of H2 is that even if such fossil fuel-centered companies accept that a low-carbon transition is likely, and even if they anticipate certain costs of waiting to adjust their approach, their preference will be to remain committed to a favorable status quo as long as possible. In contrast, companies with business models that are not based on fossil fuel-centered activities are more likely to take action on climate change— an issue of transnational importance that states have proven unwilling to address effectively—prior to perceiving strong material incentives to do so.

If H2 correctly anticipates the relationship between the corporate climate consensus and industry type, the data should show companies in the technology industry broadening and deepening their climate activity in the context of low expectations either of high-impact material risks from inaction or of significant material opportunities tied to climate-active policies. The data also should show companies in automotive, finance, and energy-intensive industries either not participating or participating to a lesser extent in adopting more climate-active approaches amid limited perceptions of high-impact risks and/or opportunities linked to climate change.

Hypothesis 3 (H3)

Compared to a company whose headquarter country historically has been climate active, a company whose headquarter country historically has not been climate active will be more likely to broaden and deepen its climate activity prior to perceiving a strong material incentive to do so.

Companies headquartered in a country in which the government historically has been active in addressing climate change would not have a powerful incentive to become climate active prior to perceiving strong material reasons for doing so; companies would expect continued leadership and action from the state that anchors their activities.[3] In contrast, if the government has a record of relative inactivity on the climate change issue, companies may take action on their own prior to perceiving significant material incentives to do so.

As Chapter 2 examines, the three main case-study countries—Germany, India, and the United States—represent varying degrees of historical federal government activity in the climate change issue area, with Germany at the higher end of the activity continuum and India and the United States at the lower end. If H3 correctly anticipates the relationship between a company's pattern of climate activity and its headquarter country, then within any given industry India- and US-based companies should account for most instances of broadening and deepening levels of climate activity amid a limited sense among individual actors that climate change was becoming a more pressing material issue; Germany-based companies should account for fewer. In addition, if the overall prevalence of such behavior trends upward, as H1 anticipates, then H3 expects that India- and US-based companies primarily will account for the upward trend (i.e., they will register more marked relative increases in this type of behavior compared to Germany-based companies).

In a preview of the findings, among the main case-study industry groups, technology was most responsible for the pattern of broadening and deepening climate activity amid low expectations for strong state governance of the issue area; during the 2010s, titans of technology like Apple and Google took more climate action, even becoming global leaders in certain practices, while their outlook for robust state action declined. Within most industries, US companies undertook the highest absolute level of action that "ran ahead of," or outpaced, their individual expectations for costly climate-related material risks or high-yield opportunities. However, German companies contributed most significantly to the upward trend in this type of behavior—an especially notable finding given that traditionally they have operated in a context of strong state

---

[3] As discussed in footnote 2, in certain cases a subnational polity potentially is the more relevant frame of reference than the national government. For example, according to the logic of H3, US automakers, for whom a crucial frame of reference is California (historically very climate active), might be less likely to adopt climate activity prior to perceiving a strong incentive to do so compared to US cement or steel companies that lack a California equivalent.

leadership in the climate issue area.[4] This suggests that while select US companies played an especially key role as early movers in shaping what became the corporate climate consensus, and although US companies overall consistently responded to its "invisible hand," to an unexpected degree it increasingly steered German companies over time.

* * *

What are the main alternative explanations for the new private sector pattern of response to climate change? The first is that the key explanatory factor that this book proposes (companies' declining confidence in states' willingness to act) is based on a misinterpretation of what developments in the 2010s conveyed about states and the climate issue area. Some have argued that the 2015 Paris Agreement in fact was a watershed, representing a major step forward in international climate policy (Falkner 2016, 1107). Following this logic, the collapse of the 2009 Copenhagen Conference was not the death knell for states' climate leadership; rather, it signified the abandonment of an unworkable approach. According to this alternative explanation, the new pattern of response would best be explained as a function of corporations being spurred to action due to states undertaking a new climate strategy in the context of the Paris Agreement. As the following chapters show, however, there is little evidence to suggest that the private sector interpreted the trajectory of international climate policy in this way. Rather, the data shows that the pattern of corporate climate action developed specifically in the context of diminishing confidence in states' willingness to address the issue.

A second alternative explanation is that the key factor in corporations altering their climate approach was consumer pressure, and specifically the perception of increasingly serious impacts from failing to adjust to changing consumer demands for low-carbon, climate-friendly products. However, each empirical chapter presents CDP data conveying that most companies did not, in fact, see climate-related changing consumer practices becoming a more urgent concern, as well as marshals data from interviews with corporate representatives confirming the gap between what consumers often say about the importance of climate change, on

---

[4] This book assumes that German companies, given the unique regulatory capabilities of host states, focus most on the regulatory environment in Germany, as do Indian and US companies vis-à-vis the Indian and US environments, respectively.

the one hand, and their willingness to prioritize low-carbon products, on the other.

CORPORATE CLIMATE ACTION AS A WINDOW ON WORLD ORDER

Beginning with the end of the Cold War, prominent scholars began to argue that profound transformations in the international system, often either barely perceptible or overlooked, were underway. In the late 1990s, for example, Mathews wrote that the "steady concentration of power in the hands of states that began in 1648 with the Peace of Westphalia is over, at least for a while." Observing states and NGOs "collaborating ad hoc in large-scale humanitarian relief operations that involve both military and civilian forces," she pointed out that almost "unnoticed, hybrids like these, in which states are often the junior partners, are becoming a new international norm." Further, she noted, the "clash between the fixed geography of states and the nonterritorial nature of today's problems and solutions, which is only likely to escalate, strongly suggests that the relative power of states will continue to decline. Nation-states may simply no longer be the natural problem-solving unit" (Mathews 1997, 50).

By the early 2000s, Ruggie heralded the early days of "a fundamental reconstitution of the global public domain—away from one which equated the 'public' in international politics with states and the interstate realm to one in which the very system of states is becoming embedded in a broader, albeit still thin and partial, institutionalized arena concerned with the production of global goods." Transnationalization, Ruggie contended, was "transforming the world polity" in ways that such pioneers of the field of transnational relations as Nye and Keohane had anticipated, "albeit in ways they could barely imagine at the time" (2004, 499). Indeed, in the early 1970s, these scholars, while identifying new actors in global politics, argued not so much that they would supplant states as that their interactions would "increase the sensitivity of societies to one another and thereby alter relationships between governments" (Nye and Keohane 1971, 336).

By the mid-2010s, the idea that the state-centered system was giving way to a "multi-actor system" whose most powerful actors were not only or even principally states had become increasingly mainstream (Khanna 2016a, 30). In 2016, for example, a *Foreign Policy* article proposed that the Pew Research Center, which regularly asks respondents whether

22   C. HULME

states like China will eclipse the United States as a superpower, should consider "widening its scope of research—for corporations are likely to overtake all states in terms of clout" (Khanna 2016b). That year, one study found that of the world's 100 wealthiest entities, less than one-third were states (Inman 2016). The rest were corporations like Shell, whose annual revenue is higher than the gross domestic product (GDP) of over 80% of states (Worldometer 2017; Macrotrends n.d.); Walmart, the world's third-largest employer after the US Defense Department and the Chinese People's Liberation Army (Stimage 2018); and Apple, whose market capitalization hit $3 trillion in 2022 (Leswing 2022). But these firms are not simply ultra-wealthy—they also have a broader reach or scope of influence than most states, 150 of which have populations of 10 million or less, on par with the smaller of the world's megacities (Khanna 2016a, 68). Corporations are not alone in gaining economic ground on states, including major regional powers; in 2018, California pulled ahead of the UK as the world's fifth-largest economy and in 2021, Texas overtook Brazil as the ninth-largest (Segarra 2018; Texas Economic Development Corporation 2021).

That certain actors beyond states (hereafter, non-state actors) have outsized resources and that they engage in global affairs is not new. At the subnational level, for example, since 1953, when New York City launched its first mission abroad, more than 200 US states and cities have followed suit. Over 24,000 companies elect the executives of the governing body of London, or the City of London Corporation, whose lord mayor "travels like a statesman from Brazil to China securing financial arrangements, all with the full support of the U.K." (Khanna 2016a, 58–59). In a 1993 article entitled, "California's Foreign Policy," *Foreign Affairs* captured the immense capabilities and the global scope of interests of a subnational heavyweight arguably in a class of its own, observing, "California in many ways is not a state, but a nation" (Goldsborough 1993, 88). Meanwhile, as Mathews observed in 1997, nearly "all 50 American states have trade offices abroad, up from four in 1970, and all have official standing in the World Trade Organization" (61–62).

What is new, however, is that non-state actors, whether subnational or corporate, are becoming increasingly active in issue areas of importance to international security, long perceived as "the sphere of 'high politics' among nation-states" (Haufler 2016, 224). Equally striking is that today, these actors sometimes adopt policy stances that either contradict those of their own governments or conspicuously exceed them in their ambition. In the climate change arena, a policy-focused group, We Are Still In—which launched in 2017 and counted among its members 4000 US businesses, along with 300 cities and 10 states, representing $9.5 trillion in GDP—committed to abide by the terms of the Paris Agreement regardless of the US withdrawal announced by the Trump administration.[5] In 2020, US corporations, states, and cities effectively bypassed what they perceived to be an inadequate federal response to the COVID-19 pandemic, devising their own "rules of the game" for responding (Collinson 2020). Following Russia's 2022 invasion of Ukraine, "scores of major multinational corporations... divested from Russian business interests," often exceeding the level of divestment required by the sanctions levied by their governments. These businesses acted "as a private sector army of sorts," as one *Forbes* commentator described it, "effectively weaponizing commerce" and having the potential to "influence the political calculus in this war as much as or more than traditional diplomacy coupled with government sanctions" (Mainwaring 2022).

What also is new is that unconventional issues, from climate change and pandemic disease to irregular migration and threats in cyberspace, are becoming more salient in the international security environment. While their relevance today widely is taken for granted, the mainstreaming of unconventional security issues, or those that are non-military and not centered around Great Power dynamics, is a relatively recent development. Even scholarship appreciating that non-state actors increasingly play a role in the governance of security issues has tended to overlook climate change; for example, the index to a 2016 volume on the subject of non-state action in the international security domain contains no reference to "climate" or "environment" (Avant and Westerwinter 2016).

By exploring the phenomenon of corporate action in an issue area that has proven intractable for states and that is poised to significantly impact international security, this book responds to a call to treat firms "as important actors in security affairs" (Haufler 2016, 242). By examining the process by which select "corporate nations" (Francis 2016) with resources and reach exceeding that of most states became more climate active during the 2010s, it also demonstrates the need for a reappraisal of the conditions under which such actors may take on new roles in the

---

[5] The United States formally rejoined the Paris Agreement in February 2021.

24   C. HULME

international security landscape. Specifically, this book proposes that if states are perceived as abdicating leadership on the type of complex new challenge that climate change typifies—and that, as Council on Foreign Relations President Richard Haas has projected, "will probably define this era of history far more than the more familiar great power competition" (2020)—others may attempt to fill the vacuum, ultimately reshaping the landscape and context in which states will have to advance their interests.

* * *

For scholars addressing the corporate climate action phenomenon through a more critical lens than those with a relatively high degree of optimism about corporations' ability to play a meaningful role in reducing emissions, a key premise is the observation that in "a global economy based on economic growth and fossil fuel-based energy, corporations have limited incentives to undertake radical decarbonization, and have resisted attempts to legislatively restrict emissions" (Wright and Nyberg 2017, 1637). Scholars like Wright and Nyberg, for example, contend that the underlying incentive structures underpinning profit-maximizing corporations, coupled with the quarterly or yearly timeframe guiding their decision-making, render these actors "particularly ill-suited to address climate change" (2017, 1635). Importantly, this book does not argue that corporations are the actors best suited to address climate change. In examining to what extent 34 corporations adopted certain practices during the 2010s, it seeks simply to capture and explain behavioral change in a key decade—one whose opening was marked by divergent perspectives on climate change in the private sector but whose close was characterized by an apparent crystallization of a consensus on the issue's importance. While Chapter 7 considers tentative lessons about what these developments may signify about the private sector's future role in unconventional issue areas like climate change, the book recognizes, consistent with the points underscored by Wright and Nyberg, that much remains to be seen in terms of whether these developments prove to be sustainable and provide decisive support to a global low-carbon transition.

In addition, this book examines corporate efforts to fill a perceived leadership vacuum in the sense of firms assuming an increasingly prominent role in the issue area, particularly relative to states, without claiming that their activity is adequate to surmount the problem of climate change itself. Le Prestre rightly observes that the state "remains the indispensable [climate] actor," as "only it has the necessary regulatory authority" to enact the scope and scale of change needed to mitigate the problem (2017, 41), while Vandenbergh and Gilligan correctly emphasize that climate change "will not be solved without government responses" (2017b). But amid perennial failures by states to perform the role that only they can, this book contributes to a literature seeking to explain how, why, and with what impacts others—even seemingly the most unlikely—may undertake certain courses of action in their stead. When Haufler observed that the "character of international relations has changed in the past 50 years from one in which the global agenda was established by the most powerful countries, to one in which powerful commercial and activist groups shape the debate and often determine outcomes," the point was not that such groups necessarily would shape the debate in a desirable way or determine positive outcomes, but rather that they had a growing ability and interest to play a dominant role on the global stage (2001, 121). That understanding represents the point of departure for how this book approaches the subject of corporate climate action.

Roadmap for the Book

The remainder of the book applies the insights from this chapter to demonstrate how (by broadening and deepening their climate activity) and why (amid a perceived abdication of state leadership) members of a cohort of 34 of the world's largest corporations adopted a new approach to certain climate-relevant practices during the 2010s. Chapter 2 sets the context for the empirical chapters, exploring the climate policy landscape at the international level, as well as domestically in Germany, India, and the United States. The chapter analyzes the messages states assumed they were conveying through their policies and behavior, while considering alternative ways that corporations might have interpreted that behavior. It proposes that states failed to recognize that although they saw themselves as having made considerable strides in climate governance, the private sector did not necessarily interpret their behavior in such a favorable light. While the chapter addresses multiple milestones in the history of international climate policy, the 2015 Paris Conference is a particular focus given its significance within the book's timeframe of interest.

If the corporate climate consensus led certain companies progressively to take up new climate practices despite the apparent lack of individual

26   C. HULME

material incentives to do so, which, specifically, were part of the process shaping that consensus, or norm? To answer this question, Chapters 3–5 examine patterns of climate activity in four industry groups: automotive and energy-intensive (Chapter 3), technology (Chapter 4), and finance (Chapter 5). Chapter 6 draws together the empirical findings, presenting aggregate data on the extent to which the 34 corporations reduced their emissions, made their activities more coherent with a low-carbon future, and allocated resources to support such a future. It analyzes the hypotheses introduced in this chapter about industry- and country-level factors making it likelier that certain corporations will increase their level of climate activity despite climate change being ranked relatively low in their interest sets. Chapter 6 then explores conditions under which companies altered their behavior, showing that climate activity broadened and deepened amid a significant decline in their outlook for climate-related regulation and little change in their consistently limited concern with climate-driven changes in consumer behavior. The chapter analyzes what the data suggests about the proposition, which Chapter 2 introduces, that corporations perceived policy developments in a different way than states intended and that the conventional wisdom often has assumed.

Chapter 7 concludes by examining what lessons the corporate climate action phenomenon offers about the changing global role of powerful non-state actors. By better understanding when, how, and why the private sector became less willing to wait for states' leadership in the climate change issue area, we can better appreciate how non-state actors might become increasingly ambitious and assertive in bypassing conventional centers of authority and crafting their own responses to issues poised to shape the twenty-first century, from pandemic disease to Great Power clashes over world order. While it is premature to say that states are in absolute decline, they are becoming relatively less influential in the global landscape than they have been for the last 375 years—since the birth of the Westphalian, state-centered world order—partly due to having proven unwilling or unable to address some of the most pressing challenges on the horizon. Arguably, nowhere is states' relative decline more apparent, or its ramifications more evident, than in the climate change issue area, the subject of this book.

References

Auld, Graeme, and Jessica Green. 2017. Unbundling the regime complex: Effects of private authority. *Transnational Environmental Law* 6 (2): 259–284. https://doi.org/10.1017/S2047102516000121.

Avant, Deborah, and Oliver Westerwinter. 2016. Introduction: Networks and transnational security governance. In *The new power politics: Networks and transnational security governance*, eds. Deborah Avant and Oliver Westerwinter, 1–18. New York: Oxford University Press.

Bartlett, Nicolette, Hannah Cushing, and Sara Law. 2017. Putting a price on carbon: Integrating climate risk into business planning. CDP. October 2017. https://cdn.cdp.net/cdp-production/cms/reports/documents/000/002/738/original/Putting-a-price-on-carbon-CDP-Report-2017.pdf?1507739326.

Brooks, David. 2020. Biden's rise gives the establishment one last chance. *The New York Times*, March 5, 2020. https://www.nytimes.com/2020/03/05/opinion/joe-biden-2020.html.

Bulkeley, Harriet, Liliana Andonova, Michele Betsill, Daniel Compagnon, Thomas Hale, Matthew Hoffmann, Peter Newell, Matthew Paterson, Charles Roger, and Stacy VanDeveer. 2014. *Transnational climate change governance*. New York: Cambridge University Press.

Bulkeley, Harriet, and Peter Newell. 2015. *Governing climate change*, 2nd ed. New York: Routledge.

CDP. 2017. More than eight-fold leap over four years in global companies pricing carbon into business plans. October 12, 2017. https://www.cdp.net/en/articles/media/more-than-eight-fold-leap-over-four-years-in-global-companies-pricing-carbon-into-business-plans.

CDP. n.d. Companies' scores. https://www.cdp.net/en/companies/companies-scores.

Clifford, Tyler. 2020. Capitalism "will fundamentally be in jeopardy" if business does not act on climate change, Microsoft CEO Satya Nadella says. CNBC. January 16, 2020. https://www.cnbc.com/2020/01/16/microsoft-ceo-capitalism-is-in-jeopardy-if-we-do-not-act-on-climate-change.html.

Collinson, Stephen. 2020. As Trump refuses to lead, America tries to save itself. CNN. July 16, 2020. https://www.cnn.com/2020/07/16/politics/donald-trump-coronavirus-leadership/index.html.

Cutler, A. Claire. 2002. Private international regimes and interfirm cooperation. In *The emergence of private authority in global governance*, eds. Rodney Hall Bruce and Thomas J. Biersteker, 23–42. New York: Cambridge University Press.

Das, Tarun. 2012. Climate change and the private sector. In *Handbook of climate change and India*, ed. Navroz Dubash, 246–253. New York: Earthscan.

28   C. HULME

Davenport, Coral. 2015. Nations approve landmark climate accord in Paris. *The New York Times*, December 12, 2015. https://www.nytimes.com/2015/12/13/world/europe/climate-change-accord-paris.html.

Eberlein, Burkard, Kenneth Abbott, Julia Black, Errol Meidinger, and Stepan Wood. 2014. Transnational business governance interactions: Conceptualization and framework for analysis. *Regulation & Governance* 8 (1): 1–21. https://doi.org/10.1111/rego.12030.

Falkner, Robert. 2016. The Paris agreement and the new logic of international climate politics. *International Affairs* 92 (5): 1107–1125. https://doi.org/10.1111/1468-2346.12708.

Fink, Larry. 2020. A fundamental reshaping of finance. BlackRock. January 14, 2020. https://www.blackrock.com/americas-offshore/en/larry-fink-ceo-letter.

Finnemore, Martha, and Kathryn Sikkink. 1998. International norm dynamics and political change. *International Organization* 52 (4): 887–917. https://doi.org/10.1162/002081898550789.

Francis, David. 2016. The top 25 corporate nations. *Foreign Policy*, March 15, 2016. https://foreignpolicy.com/2016/03/15/these-25-companies-are-more-powerful-than-many-countries-multinational-corporate-wealth-power/.

van Geert, Paul. 2017. Constructivist theories. In *The Cambridge encyclopedia of child development*, eds. Brian Hopkins, Elena Geangu, and Sally Linkenauger, 19–34. Cambridge, UK: Cambridge University Press.

Goldsborough, James. 1993. California's foreign policy. *Foreign Affairs* 7 (2): 88–96. https://doi.org/10.2307/20045527.

Granovetter, Mark. 1978. Threshold models of collective behavior. *The American Journal of Sociology* 83 (6): 1420–1443. https://doi.org/10.1086/226707.

Green, Jessica. 2013. *Rethinking private authority: Agents and entrepreneurs in global environmental governance*. Princeton, NJ: Princeton University Press.

Griffin, Paul. 2017. The carbon majors' database. CDP. July 2017. https://cdn.cdp.net/cdp-production/cms/reports/documents/000/002/327/original/Carbon-Majors-Report-2017.pdf?1501833772.

Haas, Richard. 2020. How will coronavirus pandemic change the way we see the world? NPR. May 14, 2020. https://www.npr.org/2020/05/14/855855714/how-will-coronavirus-pandemic-change-the-way-we-see-the-world.

Hafner-Burton, Emilie, Miles Kahler, and Alexander Montgomery. 2009. Network analysis for international relations. *International Organizations* 63 (3): 559–592. https://doi.org/10.1017/S0020818309090195.

Haufler, Virginia. 2001. *A public role for the private sector: Industry self-regulation in a global economy*. Washington, D.C.: Carnegie Endowment for International Peace.

Haufler, Virginia. 2016. Corporations, governance networks, and conflict in the developing world. In *The new power politics: Networks and transnational security governance*, eds. Deborah Avant and Oliver Westerwinter, 224–244. New York: Oxford University Press.

Hoffman, Matthew. 2017. Norms and social constructivism in international relations. International Studies Association and Oxford University Press. December 22, 2017. https://oxfordre.com/internationalstudies/display/10.1093/acrefore/9780190846626.001.0001/acrefore-9780190846626-e-60.

Hofmeister, John. 2019. Former Shell Oil president John Hofmeister weighs in on rollback of emissions rules. NPR. August 29, 2019. https://www.npr.org/2019/08/29/755555482/former-shell-oil-president-john-hofmeister-weighs-in-on-rollback-of-emissions-ru.

Inman, Phillip. 2016. Study: Big corporations dominate list of world's top economic entities. *The Guardian*, September 12, 2016. https://www.theguardian.com/business/2016/sep/12/global-justice-now-study-multinational-businesses-walmart-apple-shell.

Jervis, Robert. 1997. *System effects: Complexity in political and social life*. Princeton, NJ: Princeton University Press.

Kahler, Miles, and David Lake. 2009. Economic integration and global governance: Why so little supranationalism? In *The politics of global regulation*, eds. Walter Mattli and Ngaire Woods, 242–276. Princeton, NJ: Princeton University Press.

Keohane, Robert, and David Victor. 2010. The regime complex for climate change. Harvard Project on International Climate Agreements. https://www.belfercenter.org/sites/default/files/legacy/files/Keohane_Victor_Final_2.pdf.

Khanna, Parag. 2016a. *Connectography*. New York: Random House.

Khanna, Parag. 2016b. These 25 companies are more powerful than many countries. *Foreign Policy*, March 15, 2016. https://foreignpolicy.com/2016b/03/15/these-25-companies-are-more-powerful-than-many-countries-multinational-corporate-wealth-power/.

Kuran, Timur. 1991. Now out of never: The element of surprise in the East European revolution of 1989. *World Politics* 44 (1): 7–48. https://doi.org/10.2307/2010422.

Lascurettes, Kyle. 2017. The concert of Europe and great-power governance today. RAND Corporation. https://www.rand.org/content/dam/rand/pubs/perspectives/PE200/PE226/RAND_PE226.pdf.

Le Prestre, Philippe. 2017. *Global ecopolitics revisited: Toward a complex governance of global environmental problems*. London: Routledge.

Leswing, Kif. 2022. Apple becomes first U.S. company to reach $3 trillion market cap. CNBC. January 3, 2022. https://www.cnbc.com/2022/01/03/apple-becomes-first-us-company-to-reach-3-trillion-market-cap.html.

30   C. HULME

Lyon, Thomas, and A. Wren Montgomery. 2015. The means and ends of greenwash. *Organization and Environment* 28 (2): 223–249. https://doi.org/10.1177/1086026615575332.

Macrotrends. n.d. Royal Dutch Shell revenue 2010–2022. https://www.macrot rends.net/stocks/charts/SHEL/shell/revenue.

Mainwaring, Simon. 2022. Russian aggression triggers unprecedented response and what it means for brand leadership. *Forbes*, March 7, 2022. https://www.forbes.com/sites/simonmainwaring/2022/03/07/russian-aggression-triggers-unprecedented-response-and-what-it-means-for-brand-leadership/?sh=35bec4a374f3.

Mathews, Jessica Tuchman. 1997. Power shift. *Foreign Affairs* 76 (1): 50–66. https://doi.org/10.2307/20047909.

Nye, Joseph, and Robert Keohane. 1971. Transnational relations and world politics: An introduction. *International Organization* 25 (3): 329–349. https://doi.org/10.1017/S0020818300026187.

Olson, Mancur. 1965. *The logic of collective action*. Cambridge, MA: Harvard University Press.

Ostrom, Elinor. 1990. *Governing the commons: The evolution of institutions for collective action*. Cambridge, UK: Cambridge University Press.

Rosenau, James. 1995. Governance in the twenty-first century. *Global Governance* 1 (1): 13–43. https://doi.org/10.1057/9780230245310_2.

Ruggie, John Gerard. 2004. Reconstituting the global public domain—Issues, actors, and practices. *European Journal of International Relations* 10 (4): 499–531. https://doi.org/10.1177/1354066104047847.

Segarra, Lisa Marie. 2018. California's economy is now bigger than all of the U.K. *Fortune*, May 5, 2018. https://fortune.com/2018/05/05/california-fifth-biggest-economy-passes-united-kingdom/.

Steer, Andrew. 2014. Seeing U.S. business opportunity in a low-carbon economy. World Resources Institute. October 14, 2014. https://www.wri.org/ins ights/seeing-us-business-opportunity-low-carbon-economy.

Stern, Paul. 2002. New environmental theories: Toward a coherent theory of environmentally significant behavior. *Journal of Social Issues* 56 (3): 407–424. https://doi.org/10.1111/0022-4537.00175.

Stevens, Pippa. 2019. Behind Walmart's push to eliminate 1 gigaton of greenhouse gases by 2030. CNBC. December 15, 2019. https://www.cnbc.com/2019/12/15/walmarts-project-gigaton-is-its-most-ambitious-climate-goal-yet.html.

Stimage, Kaityn. 2018. The world's largest employers. World Atlas. https://www.worldatlas.com/articles/the-world-s-largest-employers.html.

Texas Economic Development Corporation. 2021. Texas enters 2021 as world's 9th largest economy by GDP. Texas Economic Development Corporation.

January 27, 2021. https://businessintexas.com/news/texas-enters-2021-as-worlds-9th-largest-economy-by-gdp/.

Vandenbergh, Michael, and Jonathan Gilligan. 2017a. Government action isn't enough for climate change. The private sector can cut billions of tons of carbon. *The Conversation*, June 21, 2017. https://theconversation.com/government-action-isnt-enough-for-climate-change-the-private-sector-can-cut-billions-of-tons-of-carbon-79728.

Vandenbergh, Michael, and Jonathan Gilligan. 2017b. Why private "actors" are taking center stage on climate change. GreenBiz. December 9, 2017. https://www.greenbiz.com/article/why-private-actors-are-taking-center-stage-climate-change.

Vandenbergh, Michael, and Jonathan Gilligan. 2019. *Beyond politics: The private governance response to climate change*. Cambridge, UK: Cambridge University Press.

Worldometer. 2017. GDP data by country. https://www.worldometers.info/gdp/gdp-by-country/.

Wright, Christopher, and Daniel Nyberg. 2017. An inconvenient truth: How organizations translate climate change into business as usual. *Academy of Management Journal* 60 (5): 1633–1661. https://doi.org/10.5465/amj.2015.0718.

Yanosek, Kassia, and David Victor. 2022. How big business is taking the lead on climate change. *Foreign Affairs*, February 3, 2022. https://www.foreignaffairs.com/articles/world/2022-02-03/how-big-business-taking-lead-climate-change.

CHAPTER 2

Change of Players, Change of Game

INTRODUCTION

In "Hypotheses on Misperception," Jervis argued that in developing images of others to try to predict their behavior, an actor "may, for a number of reasons, misperceive both others' actions and their intentions" (1968, 454). Two hypotheses are especially salient for appreciating why signals that seem clear to senders may be misinterpreted by receivers. First, Jervis argued that "when people spend a great deal of time drawing up a plan or making a decision," and since "they are aware of what is to them the important pattern in their actions," they "tend to think that the message about it that they wish to convey will be clear to the receiver," and "that the pattern will be equally obvious to others" (1968, 474). Second, he observed that in situations in which actors are not trying to conceal their intentions, "they tend to assume that others accurately perceive these intentions"; only rarely "do they believe that others may be reacting to a much less favorable image of themselves than they think they are projecting" (Jervis 1968, 477).

This chapter proposes that misinterpreted signals may be important in explaining why the private sector unexpectedly became a key climate actor during the 2010s, assuming a different role in the issue area than it had historically. Through developments in their climate approach, states sent what they thought was a clear signal about their intentions; corporations

---

© The Author(s), under exclusive license to Springer Nature Switzerland AG 2023
C. Hulme, *Corporate Climate Action, Transnational Politics, and World Order*, Environmental Politics and Theory,
https://doi.org/10.1007/978-3-031-34115-1_2

33

may not have interpreted the signal as intended. This chapter establishes the basis for this possibility by exploring the climate policy landscape at the international level, as well as domestically in Germany, India, and the United States, analyzing the messages that states intended to convey through their behavior and considering alternative ways that corporations might have interpreted that behavior. Chapters 3–6 explore whether the data supports the argument that corporations perceived developments in a different way than states intended and that observers often have assumed.

Part I of this chapter focuses on developments at the international level between the 1992 Rio Climate Conference and the 2015 Paris Climate Conference. It explores the signals that states intended to send others, including the private sector, by shifting from a "top-down" model of climate action, based on mandatory emissions reductions negotiated at the international level, to a "bottom-up" approach, premised on voluntary national contributions to a shared emissions reduction goal. Drawing on Jervis' insights into the roots of misperceived behavior and intentions, Part I advances an alternative interpretation of how corporations may have perceived policy developments that to states manifestly demonstrated their growing commitment to—and indicated considerable progress toward—bold climate action.

Parts II, III, and IV trace developments in the policies of Germany, India, and the United States, respectively, analyzing how states' policy activity defined the context in which corporations interpreted their commitment to addressing climate change and spurring a low-carbon transition. The chapter's main insight is that if corporations indeed interpreted signals in a manner that was different from what states intended, then states inadvertently helped to precipitate a change in the climate game, whose key players and dynamics looked very different by the turn of the 2020s compared to the previous three decades.

PART I: INTERNATIONAL CONTEXT FOR CORPORATE CLIMATE ACTION

Since the early 1990s, when the Intergovernmental Panel on Climate Change (IPCC) warned that climate change was a global threat requiring international cooperation (Intergovernmental Panel on Climate Change, n.d.), climate change has commanded growing worldwide recognition and heightened concern, with states periodically raising expectations that they will act to address it. Ultimately, however, they have failed to do so effectively. By the end of 2018, three years after world leaders at the Paris Conference achieved an unprecedented consensus about the need for *all* states to contribute to cutting greenhouse gas (GHG) emissions, just seven states had undertaken actions consistent with the less ambitious of two scenarios under the Paris Agreement (limiting global warming to 2°C above pre-industrial levels); of these, only Morocco and The Gambia had adopted behaviors consistent with the more ambitious scenario of 1.5°C (Erickson 2018). Recognizing the limited progress that had been made to date, in 2018, the IPCC issued a special report underscoring the persistent gap between what states had said they would do and what they actually had done to address climate change. The report noted that limiting global warming to 1.5°C above pre-industrial levels would require that "net human-caused emissions of carbon dioxide ... fall by about 45 percent from 2010 levels by 2030, reaching 'net zero' around 2050." Achieving this objective, remarked one IPCC Working Group co-chair, "is possible within the laws of chemistry and physics," but "would require unprecedented changes" (Intergovernmental Panel on Climate Change 2018).

The following three sections analyze key developments in the international community's climate approach from the late 1990s to the mid-2010s, focusing particularly on the potential disjunction between what states sought to convey through their behavior and how corporations interpreted that behavior.

Kyoto to Copenhagen: 1997–2009

The 1992 Rio Climate Conference, or Earth Summit, the first United Nations (UN) Conference on Environment and Development, was highlighted by the signing of the UN Framework Convention on Climate Change (UNFCCC), the agreement forming the basis for most subsequent international climate agreements. The UNFCCC, noting that human activities had "substantially" increased the level of GHGs in the atmosphere, acknowledged that "the global nature of climate change calls for the widest possible cooperation by all countries and their participation in an effective and appropriate international response, in accordance with their common but differentiated responsibilities and respective capabilities and their social and economic conditions" (United Nations 1992, 1). To support the "ultimate objective" of stabilizing "greenhouse gas concentrations in the atmosphere at a level that would prevent dangerous

36   C. HULME

anthropogenic interference with the climate system," the UNFCCC called on developed countries to "take the lead in combating climate change" through a variety of mitigation and adaptation measures (United Nations 1992, 4).

Following the UNFCCC's entry into force in 1994, the 1997 Kyoto Protocol operationalized the convention by "committing industrialized countries and economies in transition" to reduce greenhouse gas emissions "in accordance with agreed individual targets" (United Nations Climate Change, n.d.). It set binding GHG emissions reduction targets for developed countries, imposing on them a more significant burden of responsibility in alignment with the principle of "common but differentiated responsibilities" (CBDR). Enshrined in the UNFCCC, which stressed "the legitimate priority needs of developing countries for the achievement of sustained economic growth and the eradication of poverty," CBDR was premised on the rationale that while all states should contribute to addressing climate change, developed countries should shoulder the vast majority of the burden, given both their resources and outsized historical contribution to current levels of GHGs in the atmosphere (United Nations 1992, 6).

The Kyoto Protocol embedded the CBDR architecture by separating "Annex I" from "non-Annex I" countries. Annex I countries faced binding emissions reduction targets and were responsible for submitting regular reports about "net changes in greenhouse gas emissions … measured as verifiable changes in carbon stocks" to ensure that their aggregate emissions did not "exceed their assigned amounts" (United Nations 1998, 3). Non-Annex I countries, in contrast, faced no binding targets and were responsible for reporting "in more general terms" (and less frequently) on mitigation and adaptation efforts than Annex I countries (United Nations, n.d.). Most importantly, by setting binding emissions reduction targets for only 38 states (including industrialized economies and select economies in transition), the Kyoto Protocol excluded such critically important developing countries as China and India from mandatory emissions reductions.

The CBDR approach, while necessary in 1997 to secure support from developing countries, institutionalized a certain mindset and gave standing to a particular perspective that colored the approach that these countries took going forward, which effectively amounted to a "you broke it, now you buy it" mentality. As they did not create the problem of climate change, developing countries were not going to be involved in solving it at the expense of other priorities, most importantly economic development. The CBDR approach also sowed the seeds for a future split in the developed world. The European Union (EU), for example, while ultimately supporting a revision of Kyoto's "strong differentiation" between Annex I and non-Annex I countries, remained committed to the Kyoto process (Ohliger 2015, 6). The United States, meanwhile, having signed the Kyoto Protocol during the Clinton administration, reconsidered its commitment shortly after George W. Bush took office, when the recently inaugurated president unsigned the agreement, reflecting "the domestic concern that middle-income developing countries [most importantly, China] were not required to take action" to curb their rapidly increasing emissions despite their growing resources (Climate Nexus, n.d.). Given that the United States accounted for nearly one-quarter of global emissions in the late 1990s, its failure to ratify the Kyoto Protocol sealed its fate as an inadequate global response to climate change (Ritchie and Roser, n.d.)

Following the Kyoto Protocol's entry into force in 2005, the key question was how to increase its effectiveness following the 2012 expiration of its first commitment period. In particular, states had to grapple with whether the protocol should be extended for a second commitment period with new emissions reduction targets for industrialized countries or whether instead there should be a comprehensive new agreement covering emissions of both developed and developing countries. States determined that questions about the nature of a post-2012 climate regime would be addressed by the 2009 Copenhagen Climate Conference, a deadline creating "enormously high expectations" for the summit, "much higher than for any previous [Conference of the Parties to the UNFCCC] except perhaps the Kyoto meeting" (Bodansky 2010, 234).

In the run-up to the conference, working groups met to attempt to bridge differences not only between developed and developing countries but also among developing countries. As Bodansky observed in a "postmortem" of Copenhagen, developing countries, having "succeeded during the Kyoto process in establishing what amounts to a 'fire wall' between Annex I and non-Annex I parties ... are unwilling to give that up now, by replacing the Protocol with a new legal instrument." However, while increasingly powerful developing countries like China and India rejected the possibility of the "adoption of a new legal agreement addressing their own emissions," other developing countries, including Small Island Developing States, supported a complementary agreement

38   C. HULME

"that would be more comprehensive in coverage," including not only the United States but also "major developing countries such as Brazil, China, and India." Multiple meetings of various working groups failed to resolve these differences; by the final preparatory meeting it was clear that "the conference would be able to produce, at best, a political agreement rather than a full-fledged legal instrument" (Bodansky 2010, 233–234).

Indeed, negotiations at Copenhagen reached a stalemate until the last day of the conference, when a coalition of heads of state, led by US President Barack Obama, hammered out a brief, milquetoast document that recognized that "deep cuts in global emissions are required according to science," and reported, "We decide to pursue various approaches ... to promote mitigation actions" (United Nations 2009). The Conference of the Parties merely "took note" of the non-binding Copenhagen Accord (Walker and Biedenkopf 2018, 36). Ultimately, as the director of global climate solutions for World Wildlife Fund International summarized in the wake of the conference, "The negotiations in Copenhagen ended without a fair, ambitious or legally binding treaty to reduce greenhouse gas emissions" (Vaughan and Adam 2009).

Yet, some stakeholders maintained that the meeting achieved meaningful outcomes. For example, the climate change rapporteur for the Council of Europe noted, "I've read a lot about so-called Brokenhagen and the failure to get a legally binding agreement. Frankly we were never going to get one .... What you need is a statement of principle. At Copenhagen this was a final admission that we cannot let temperature rise 2C above pre-industrial levels." He highlighted as particularly "remarkable" the fact that 192 countries signed the Copenhagen Accord—an effective consensus (Vaughan and Adam 2009). Similarly, in a 2017 interview for this book, a lead climate negotiator for the United States prior to and at the Paris Conference reflected,

> We saw Copenhagen as much more of a success than probably anybody else. It was chaotic and kind of a mess at the end; there was very nearly a complete collapse with nothing to show for it. Certainly it fell way short of what were always unrealistic expectations on the part of many around the world. But from our point of view, it moved the ball forward in a number of ways. It planted seeds that bore fruit later at Paris. (New Haven, Connecticut, November 13, 2017)

However, the overwhelming message coming out of the Copenhagen Conference was that states had failed to move forward meaningfully to address a challenge requiring cooperative action. Indeed, during the decade following the conference a consensus emerged that it marked "the low point" in the history of the global climate regime (Ivanova 2017, 17). As Nicholas Stern, author of the influential *Stern Review on the Economics of Climate Change*, observed, "The Copenhagen meeting was a disappointment, primarily because it failed to set the basic targets for reducing global annual emissions of greenhouse gases from now up to 2050, and did not secure commitments from countries to meet these targets collectively" (Vaughan and Adam 2009). Ian Bremmer, president of the Eurasia Group, remarked that there "was not nearly enough common ground among the leading established and emerging players to reach a deal that would have required sacrifice from all sides," and "no single country or bloc of countries had the clout to impose a solution" (2012, 9). The language of the Copenhagen Accord itself captured the failure to make meaningful progress, underscoring that states continued to defer addressing specific details pertaining to the most significant issues, including the relative contributions of developed and developing countries to reducing emissions. Despite their consensus that "deep cuts in global emissions are required according to science," states merely noted, "We should cooperate in achieving the peaking of global and national emissions as soon as possible, recognizing that the time frame for peaking will be longer in developing countries" (United Nations 2009).

To corporations observing the outcome of the Copenhagen Conference—a truncated "political rather than … legal document" leaving "many details to be filled in later," laying out no global emissions reduction goal, and ignoring the question of emissions reductions for major developing economies (Bodansky 2010, 235)—a plausible conclusion was that states had failed to make significant progress in addressing climate change in a concerted fashion, much less resolve the most challenging outstanding questions concerning the future of the global climate regime. While the empirical chapters explore the degree to which corporations actually arrived at this conclusion, it is worth highlighting here that some observers perceived during the conference and in its aftermath that it had become clear that "the private sector is not waiting for a government consensus to develop." Indeed, while much of the attention during the conference itself focused on inter-state gridlock, during the negotiations there was "no shortage of business leaders agitating for business to do its part, whether a political agreement was reached or not." For example, Richard Branson, CEO of Virgin Group, declared from his "War on Carbon" headquarters in Copenhagen that if "governments do not come to a resolution then I think it's up to businesses to actually force through resolutions to this issue" (Teitelbaum 2010). In fact, *Forbes* noted, during the Copenhagen Conference, "unlike many other businessmen who were waiting for their world leaders to take the lead, Branson had already realized what now seems quite obvious: Politicians are not going to offer real solutions—instead, it will be the private sector" (Burkart 2010).

The Road to Paris: 2010–2013

In 2010, the 16th Conference of the Parties to the UNFCCC (COP16) was held in Cancun, Mexico, where states, against the backdrop of "modest" expectations following the collapse of talks at Copenhagen, "studiously avoided – or tried to avoid – the contentious issue of assigning emissions reductions commitments," focusing instead on such relatively non-controversial areas as creating a new Green Climate Fund and Technology Mechanism for facilitating knowledge-sharing on low-carbon technologies, with an emphasis on developing countries (Hultman 2010). However, even as they punted on outstanding questions concerning the future of the Kyoto Protocol and the climate regime more broadly, delegates at Cancun sowed the seeds for an underlying shift in how states would approach climate action at the international level; in key respects, the "Paris model," or the germ of the idea for the model, emerged in Cancun. A Brookings analyst described the shift this way: "Instead of a Kyoto-like approach where all countries negotiated specific reduction amounts, the Cancun approach allowed countries to publicly state their domestic emissions reduction commitments and then allowed those commitments to be reviewed by the international community" (Hultman 2011).

While delegates at Cancun left it to subsequent COPs to address how voluntary emissions reduction commitments would be reported, monitored, and enforced, they began the international community's pivot toward "a new era of international cooperation on climate change." As Rajamani wrote in a post-COP16 analysis, while "few, if any, of the disagreements that led to the collapse of [the Copenhagen Conference] … have been authoritatively resolved, the Cancun Agreements clearly indicate the path the post-2012 climate regime is likely to take" (2011, 499–500). It increasingly was evident, for instance, that the "less politically palatable elements of the Kyoto Protocol," including "quantified emission limitation and reduction objectives," would "fall by the wayside" (Rajamani 2011, 512).

If COP16 foreshadowed that the future of international climate action would depart from the Kyoto model, COP17 in Durban, South Africa, confirmed it. Three COP17 outcomes in particular point to a potential disjunction between what states intended to signal about how their climate approach had evolved post-Copenhagen and the signal that corporations may have perceived.

First, Durban dissolved the firewall between developed and developing countries. Indeed, the conference outcome document, the Durban Platform, "was built explicitly on the promise that the framework convention would not again produce a treaty that was not symmetrical, applying to all parties under the Convention" (Light 2011). In fact, "the Durban Platform contains no reference to developing, developed, Annex I or non-Annex I parties," the categories that had "dominated" the pre-2012 climate regime, representing "a significant shift in how the Durban Platform decision frames the new round of negotiations" (Bodansky 2012). Notably, however, while the platform made no reference to CBDR, signaling the end of the bifurcated structure of the climate regime up to that point, in fact it paved the way for a modified version of CBDR to be the rationale upon which the Paris Agreement ultimately was founded. Durban opened the door, in effect, to *all* states applying the CBDR rationale to *themselves*, with each state determining its individual capabilities and responsibilities, relative to the common objective of emissions reduction.

Second, while Durban provided the mandate for the negotiations leading up to the 2015 Paris Conference, it failed to address the substance of those negotiations. As Bodansky assessed, the Durban Platform "is an empty vessel that can be filled with whatever content the parties choose." The "laundry list" of issues it listed as relevant for consideration was "pretty thin gruel," he argued, as "it provides no guidance as to how any of these issues should be addressed, or even that they ought to be included in the final outcome. As a result, everything is, in effect, on the table" (Bodansky 2012).

Third, although Durban extended the Kyoto Protocol for a second, post-2012 commitment period, the United States remained outside the

42   C. HULME

fold, with major economies like Japan, Russia, and Canada opting out of a second commitment period (Hultman 2011). In short, the second Kyoto commitment period would be even weaker than the first.

While for states Durban represented a step forward, setting in motion a pivot away from the Kyoto model and toward the possibility of a more workable approach, COP17 potentially communicated something very different to corporations. Jervis' second hypothesis on misperception is especially salient; with actors tending "to assume that others accurately perceive [their] intentions," only rarely accounting for the fact that "others may be reacting to a much less favorable image of themselves than they think they are projecting" (1968, 477), states failed fully to appreciate that what to them appeared a significant step in the right direction might well have been interpreted by the private sector as confirming their fecklessness. For corporations, the most salient takeaway from Durban may not have been that states had begun to pivot from an unworkable approach toward the possibility of a more effective one, but rather that they had dissolved the firewall between developed and developing countries—opening the door to the possibility that *no* states would be subject to mandatory emissions reduction targets—while offering no substantive roadmap forward, *and* in the context of a weakened Kyoto regime. In fact, while Durban might simply have confirmed corporations' unfavorable image of states as unable to "get their act together," it also might have worsened it. For instance, by eliminating the differentiation between developed and developing countries, the Durban Platform suggested that states were headed toward a new, "lowest common denominator" approach, sacrificing ambition in the quest to get all key players on board, including China and India, states that for decades had conveyed unambiguously their refusal to prioritize emissions reduction over economic development.

The Paris Conference: 2014–2015

In the post-Durban run-up to the 2015 Paris Conference, an important breakthrough occurred in November 2014, bolstering hopes that a new approach, premised on nationally determined contributions to a shared emissions reduction goal, signified a watershed in the dim history of international efforts to address climate change. That month, US President Barack Obama and Chinese President Xi Jinping unveiled the US-China

Joint Announcement, which, according to Gallagher and Xuan, "surprised and delighted most in the global community," with several world leaders later pointing to the announcement "as being a key turning point that led to the Paris Agreement" (2019, 7). Jointly announcing the Intended Nationally Determined Contributions (INDCs) for the United States and China, or the emissions reduction targets to which they would commit as the basis for post-2020 action, Obama and Xi jumpstarted the INDC announcement process; by the beginning of COP21 in Paris in December 2015, 180 countries representing 95% of global emissions had unveiled their targets. As Lewis noted, the Obama-Xi announcement was crucial in "setting an example and paving the way for the Paris Climate Agreement a year later" (as cited in Ruwitch 2021).

The US-China Joint Announcement marked both the first time that China had announced its climate targets in such an early and ambitious fashion and the first time that the United States and China had made such a joint statement. The United States committed to "achieve an economy-wide target of reducing its emissions by 26%-28% below its 2005 level in 2025," making "best efforts" to achieve the 28% level. China, meanwhile, planned to "achieve the peaking of CO_2 emissions around 2030 and to make best efforts to peak early," with the intention of increasing the share of renewables in its energy mix "to around 20% by 2030" (The White House 2014). China's commitment received particular notice; its plan "to strive for peak carbon by 2030 surely is significant compared to its stance to date," noted one Brookings expert, even accounting for the "unknown" of where that peak would be (Boersma 2014). Both countries announced their intention "to continue to work to increase ambition over time." Whereas the Durban Platform made no reference to CBDR, the US-China Joint Announcement explicitly stated that both sides were committed "to reaching an ambitious 2015 agreement that reflects the principle of common but differentiated responsibilities and respective capabilities, in light of different national circumstances" (The White House 2014). Obama and Xi confirmed that CBDR remained integral to the post-2012 climate regime; the announcement modeled the novel concept—a marker of the "age of Paris"—of each state unilaterally applying the principle to itself.

While its basic approach was established before the 2015 conference, Paris was tasked with addressing some major outstanding questions. For example, would states' Nationally Determined Contributions (NDCs) be situated in a legally binding context? Would states have the power to accept or reject one another's level of ambition? What strategies would be employed to close the gap between what states brought to the table at the Paris Conference in terms of their INDCs and what was required to limit global warming to 2°C above pre-industrial levels? The question of closing the "ambition gap" was particularly urgent; prior to the negotiations in Paris, one thing was "already certain," as *Carbon Brief* noted: the outcome of the deal "will not succeed in limiting temperatures" to 2°C (Yeo 2015). The INDCs that states submitted did not add up to keeping global temperatures at the level that they had identified as the objective of international climate negotiations since 2010; in fact, the research group Climate Action Tracker calculated that if states followed through on their INDCs the world would be on track for a rise in temperature of 2.7°C (Yeo 2015). Indeed, recalled the lead US climate negotiator previously cited, the "perfectly understandable" initial resistance by some states to an NDC-based model rested on the fact that "if you let everyone decide for themselves, there is going to be a gap"; their contributions would not add up to the reductions required to achieve the international community's 2°C (much less 1.5°C) goal. From his perspective in 2017, however, there was "not a great answer that says, 'Here's how we are going to get where we need to go'" (New Haven, Connecticut, November 13, 2017).

The Paris Agreement enshrined a "hybrid model of international climate policy," blending voluntary substantive action with legally binding process-related requirements (van Asselt and Hale 2016). The INDC pledges were not legally binding; requirements pertaining to reporting on those pledges and on progress toward achieving targets were (United Nations 2016). States were not required to take into account peer feedback on their level of ambition; in essence, Paris hinged on a "take it or leave it" mindset, with the priority being getting everyone on board—not criticizing what they brought to the table.

With no mechanism to mandate targets, the Paris Agreement integrated the idea of ratcheting up levels of ambition over time, or what has been called the "ambition mechanism," to address the gap between what states pledged to do and what was required to achieve global mitigation goals (Yeo 2015). The expectation was that every five years, as states fulfilled the requirement of submitting revised NDCs, their national climate action plans and emissions reduction targets would become progressively more ambitious, thus helping to close the gap, so evident prior to the Paris Conference, between states' commitments and what was needed to achieve their shared objective.

* * *

World leaders and diplomats claimed that the Paris Agreement sent the private sector a decisive signal about states' commitment to addressing climate change in an ambitious, concerted fashion. For example, UN Secretary-General Ban ki-Moon, describing it as a "monumental triumph," said that Paris demonstrated that governments "have agreed to binding, robust, transparent rules of the road to ensure that all countries do what they have agreed across a range of issues." Ban remarked that markets "now have the clear signal they need to unleash the full force of human ingenuity and scale up investments that will generate low-emissions, resilient growth" (United Nations 2015). Likewise, US Secretary of State John Kerry, who characterized the agreement as "the strongest, most ambitious climate pact ever negotiated" (Hollingsworth 2016), remarked, "Paris's importance is that even without the fixed number [mandatory emissions reductions] and the legal shell, we are going to see an enormous amount of movement without creating political obstacles that prevent us from being able to send that signal. I have absolute confidence in the ability of capital to move where the signal of the marketplace says 'go' after Paris" (Cama 2015). Christiana Figueres, UNFCCC Executive Secretary, calling Paris "an agreement of conviction," stated, "The Paris Agreement … sends a powerful signal to the many thousands of cities, regions, businesses and citizens across the world already committed to climate action that their vision of a low-carbon resilient future is now the chosen course for humanity this century" (United Nations Climate Change 2015).

Paris *did* send a signal—but not necessarily the one that states assumed or intended. Jervis' hypotheses on misperception shed light on why the private sector might have interpreted signals differently than states intended, ultimately spurring select corporations to assume a new role in the climate change issue area.

First, states, having spent "a great deal of time drawing up a plan [and] making a decision" about the nature of the post-2012 climate regime, assumed that the message they sought to convey was clear; understanding what to them was "the important pattern in their actions," they thought that the pattern would be "equally obvious to others" (Jervis 1968, 474). From states' perspective, the most important pattern in their actions, including abandoning the Kyoto-style model and pivoting toward a bottom-up approach, was that they had made substantial progress

46   C. HULME

since Copenhagen. Paris might not have solved every challenge, but it set a trajectory for success and "changed the game"—and, crucially, by enabling states to decide for themselves what to contribute, got *everyone* to play. Indeed, by giving themselves the freedom to determine at the domestic level what to contribute to global mitigation objectives, thus establishing "the primacy of domestic politics in climate change" and thereby breaking free from the gridlock that had plagued international climate politics for decades, states demonstrated a commitment to a "new logic of international climate politics" (Falkner 2016, 1107). They assumed that corporations would interpret such a commitment as having the potential to transform global progress on addressing climate change.

Yet, accountability ultimately is what matters to the private sector; it is unlikely that good intentions alone would have been sufficient to convince corporations that the game really had changed. In the Paris Agreement, the only accountability in terms of legally binding requirements concerned process, not substance; what was important was whether states were reporting what they were doing, not what they were doing per se. In addition, what they were promising was insufficient to urgently mitigate climate change and accelerate a low-carbon transition. Even scholars arguing the merits of the Paris Agreement, including Falkner, who wrote that its grounding in domestic politics offered "the chance of more durable international climate cooperation," conceded that it was unclear "whether the treaty can actually deliver on the urgent need to de-carbonize the global economy" (2016, 1108). By 2018, states already were failing to implement the level of action to which they had fulsomely committed themselves at the Paris Conference. As a *New York Times* article observed, highlighting the degree to which states were falling short of the emissions reduction commitments contained in their NDCs, even "if every country did manage to fulfill its individual pledge, the world would still be on pace to heat up well in excess of 2 degrees Celsius ... over preindustrial levels, the threshold that world leaders vowed to stay 'well below' in Paris because they deemed it unacceptably risky" (Plumer and Popovich 2018).

In short, inadequate results that were unlikely to be strengthened over time, coupled with good intentions not matched by serious accountability mechanisms, meant that what seemed to states the obvious pattern in their behavior from Copenhagen to Paris—that they had made remarkable progress in a short period of time, demonstrating a renewed commitment to, and ability to deliver, effective climate leadership—was by no means obvious to the private sector.

Second, states themselves acknowledged the inadequacy of the Paris Agreement by including the ambition mechanism within its framework, assuming that others would accept inadequacy today for the commitment to heightened ambition tomorrow. States assumed, consistent with Jervis' second hypothesis on misperception, that their pioneering of the novel ambition mechanism would be positively perceived, failing to recognize the prospect of others reacting "to a much less favorable image of themselves" than they thought they were projecting (Jervis 1968, 477). The White House reflected such an assumption. Calling the Paris Agreement "the most ambitious climate change agreement in history," it underscored that the deal established "a framework to ratchet up ambition"; in laying "the foundation for countries to work together to put the world on a path" to keeping global warming "well below" 2°C, the agreement "sets an ambitious vision to go even farther than that" (The White House 2015).

But rather than seeing the ambition mechanism as a meaningful tool to close the gap between states' initial commitments and prospects for achieving the objectives of Paris, the private sector had compelling reasons to interpret such a mechanism as an admission by states that after decades of effort, and despite the breakthrough that Paris was supposed to signify, they still did not agree on how to "get where we need to go," as the US negotiator put it (New Haven, Connecticut, November 13, 2017). Indeed, the problem with an approach centered around an expectation for increased ambition became increasingly obvious by October 2021, when states were supposed to submit new NDCs in accordance with the commitment enshrined in the Paris Agreement to enhance emissions reduction targets every five years (the initial submission deadline of 2020 had been revised due to the COVID-19 pandemic). As the World Resources Institute reported, 140 states, accounting for 57% of global emissions, had submitted updated NDCs; such vital states as China and India, collectively accounting for 31% of global emissions, had not. Of those states that had submitted updated NDCs, "around 58% increased their ambition. Fourteen percent either made no change or decreased

48 C. HULME

their ambition" (Fransen 2021).[1] In short, it soon became clear that Paris simply masked those unresolved collective action problems that for decades had plagued global climate efforts. With states choosing their own emissions reduction targets, and with no legally binding provision ensuring that they actually increased their ambition over time, the agreement was attractive to free-riders seeking the benefits of membership without having to contribute anything costly. [2]

* * *

Between 1997 and 2015, the international community's approach to addressing climate change evolved from a top-down model, with emissions reduction targets for developed countries negotiated at the international level, and with developing countries exempt from mandatory reductions, to a bottom-up model, premised on all states choosing for themselves what to contribute to a shared emissions reduction target. For states, it was difficult to imagine how this evolution could be interpreted as anything other than significant progress in a short period of time, or be perceived as something different than a heightened commitment to address climate change and nurture conditions to encourage a global low-carbon transition. However, as this part of the chapter explored, the private sector plausibly may have interpreted states' behavior very differently; rather than perceiving the arc of their policies from Kyoto to Paris as indicative of an intensifying commitment to climate action, it may have perceived Paris as confirming what it long had suspected: that states did not have a credible plan for getting the world where it needed to go to avoid global warming exceeding 2°C above pre-industrial levels and, importantly for corporations, for providing the type of policy and regulatory regime needed to support their transition to, and success in, a low-carbon future.

---

[1] For the remaining countries, it was not possible to compare the ambition levels of the new and updated NDCs with the original NDCs due to a lack of data in the original NDCs.

[2] On free-riding see Olson (1965, 21) and Reisman (1990, 46). On limitations to international agreements posed by the least ambitious party see Esty and Moffa (2012, 783).

Part II: Germany

Examining the evolution of the German government's activity in the realm of climate-related policy, this part of the chapter appraises the context for climate action by some of Germany's largest corporations. It explores the possibility of a disjunction, similar to the one that potentially existed in the international context, between how the state perceived itself and interpreted its pattern of behavior and how corporations perceived the state and interpreted its behavior. The first section provides a brief sketch of Germany's approach to the climate change issue area since the 1990s, while the second looks in greater detail at areas that illustrate the distinction between how Germany has tended to perceive itself (as a standout climate leader) and the results it has achieved in practice.

Germany and the Climate Agenda

During the 1980s, climate change became an increasingly important political and public issue in Germany, but it was not until 1990 that Berlin unveiled its First Climate Policy Programme, which issued a target for reducing emissions by 25% by 2005 compared to 1987 levels (Weidner and Mez 2008, 361). Its early adoption of such a target led Germany, the highest emitting EU Member State, to emerge as the de facto climate leader within the EU, which, as the world's third-largest emitter, was an early mover in the issue area (Tiseo 2021; Boasson and Wettestad 2013, 37). Indeed, at the 1992 Rio Conference the EU pushed (ultimately unsuccessfully) for "binding commitments for industrialized countries in the international negotiations, seeking to get them to commit to stabilize CO_2 emissions at 1990 levels by the year 2000" (Boasson and Wettestad 2013, 36). Following the 1997 Kyoto summit, with the EU having agreed to an overall 8% reduction in GHGs compared to a 1990 base-line for the first commitment period (2008–2012), Germany assumed the largest share of the burden, committing to reducing emissions 25% during that period (Weidner and Mez 2008, 363). Reflecting its Kyoto commitments, Germany's Fifth Climate Policy Programme of 2000 "differed significantly" from its earlier targets both in terms of the time horizon (2008–2012) "and the scope of the commitment, which shifted from CO_2 to the six greenhouse gases that were regulated by the Kyoto Protocol" (Matthes 2017, 8).

50   C. HULME

The late 2000s and early 2010s represented a high-water mark for Germany's climate action, including efforts to raise others' level of ambition. In 2007, for example, with the launch of its Integrated Energy and Climate Programme, which for the first time set a domestic emissions reduction target for 2020, Germany attempted to spur the EU to more ambitious action in its 2020 climate targets, with Berlin announcing that it would ratchet up its target from 30% to 40% should the EU endorse a 30% target (Matthes 2017, 9). In 2009, the EU adopted a "hugely complex package of climate and energy measures" that was "the most ambitious in the world at that time" (Jordan et al. 2010, 6; Walker and Biedenkopf 2018, 36); its ambition was particularly notable given that Europe was in the thick of the global financial crisis. Ultimately, however, its "20-20-20" package did not meet Germany's proposed level of ambition, including a 20% as opposed to 30% emissions reduction target (European Commission, n.d.).

During this period, Germany's reputation for a high level of climate action was burnished further by the acceleration of the Energiewende, the "planned transition to a low-carbon, nuclear-free economy" that dates to the 1970s but that gained traction following the 2011 Fukushima Daiichi nuclear disaster (Clean Energy Wire, n.d.). Angela Merkel developed a global reputation as the "Climate Chancellor," a nickname conferred in 2007 by the German press following her G-8 climate diplomacy efforts and advocacy for EU emissions reduction targets (Thalman and Wettengel 2019). Even as the political winds in Berlin shifted in 2009 with the coming to power of a government of two pro-business parties and the dissolution of the "Red-Green" coalition (Ladrech 2019, 18), which since the late 1990s had launched and sustained influential policies supporting the Energiewende's vision of a low-carbon and nuclear-free Germany (Wehrmann 2017), Berlin remained committed to supporting ambitious climate action, including the EU's 20-20-20 package.

Following the Copenhagen Conference, which dealt a fatal blow to the top-down model of climate action for which the EU historically had been the strongest advocate, climate change diminished in importance on the EU's agenda, especially as the global recession deepened. Consistent with the broader international community's move toward letting states select their own emissions reduction targets, prior to the 2015 Paris Conference the EU set forth a 2030 framework that, while presenting ambitious targets (Walker and Biedenkopf 2018, 39), had "fewer binding national targets, no 'sub-targets' such as exist to 2020 for transport, and greater flexibilities for Member States to choose what is right for them" (Delbeke et al. 2015, 87). In this context, as the EU grappled with slowing momentum in the climate issue area, Germany appeared to stay the course, forging ahead with characteristically ambitious targets; in 2016, for example, it released its Climate Action Plan 2050, which presented the medium-term target of cutting GHG emissions by at least 55% by 2030 compared to 1990 levels (Government of Germany 2016).

The "Ambition-Action" Gap and the Potential for Misperception

To Berlin, the important pattern in its climate-related behavior since the 1990s was unmistakable: amid changes in government, a global financial crisis, and the EU retreating from its historical level of climate activity and ambition, Germany had demonstrated constancy and commitment as a global climate leader. Berlin's unchanging image of itself as consistently willing—when so few other key countries were—to make politically tough decisions for the sake of addressing climate change was captured by Weidner and Mez's observation that Germany had "not shied away from strong regulatory and tax policies that impose significant costs on industry and the general population" (2008, 364).

To others, however, the key pattern or message in Germany's behavior was not necessarily so obvious; by the mid- to late 2010s, in fact, with ever-clearer gaps between Germany's stated ambitions and the results it had achieved, observers increasingly called into question Berlin's claims to climate leadership, while predicting that it would miss its 2020 climate targets, set in 2007, by significant margins. For example, in 2017, the Berlin-based think tank Agora Energiewende projected that Germany would miss its 40% emissions reduction target by 10%—"not a little bit off, but a huge miss," in the words of its director (Reuters 2017). In 2018, Germany's environment ministry announced that the 2020 target was unachievable due to emissions from coal-fired power plants and the transport sector, and warned that missing the 2020 target by what it projected to be 8% would amount to "a significant blow to Germany's climate policy" and "a disaster for Germany's international reputation as a climate leader" (Apparicio 2018). While the government blamed the failure on unanticipated growth in the population and economy, experts pointed to Berlin's refusal to confront politically fraught questions surrounding a coal phase-out, as well as its efforts to shield companies in energy-intensive industries from the Energiewende's actual costs through, for example, generous tax exemptions (Pescia and Ichiyanagi 2017, 21).

Meanwhile, by the mid-2010s, the so-called Energiewende paradox—that Germany's "rapid development of renewable power has barely dented CO_2 emissions" (Amelang 2016)—had become all too obvious. The paradox resulted from renewable energy having edged out nuclear power but neither renewables nor natural gas supplanting coal. In 2010, coal generated 43% of Germany's electricity (Renewable Energy World 2011); by 2015, that number essentially was unchanged (44%); and by 2017, it still was 40% (Pescia and Ichiyanagi 2017, 16). Indeed, as of 2018, Germany was responsible for one-third of the EU's total coal consumption and was one of only five European states in which coal power stations accounted for 25% of total emissions (Jones and Gutmann 2015, 7).

In fact, a key reason that questions emerged about Germany's ability to achieve the targets in its Climate Action Plan 2050 was that the plan lacked a deadline for a coal phase-out yet included the aim of "almost halving emissions from the power sector between 2014 and 2030," which, according to some experts, "can only be achieved with closure or drawdown" of coal-fired power plants (Rocha et al. 2017, 30). In 2019, following protracted negotiations between Berlin and coal-reliant regions, the government finally announced a coal phase-out date of 2038, confirming Berlin's gradualist approach vis-à-vis this most politically challenging of decisions, while throwing into sharp relief the fact that, whatever ambitious targets it has set since the mid-2000s with an eye toward a low-carbon future, Germany has lacked a political and societal consensus about the timing of this future. One result is that emissions from the power sector, which is highly dependent on coal and accounts for 40% of Germany's emissions (Pescia and Ichiyanagi 2017, 15), decreased less than 4% between 2000 and 2015, according to a Climate Analytics report (Rocha et al. 2017, 23).

In short, by the late 2010s, the gap between what Germany *said* about its commitment to addressing climate change and what it had *done*, or its achievements in terms of decarbonizing its economy, was increasingly obvious. This gap was not entirely new, even if it had become significantly more pronounced. In the 1990s, for example, Berlin's stance toward emissions trading, which would become the "linchpin of EU climate policy" (van Asselt 2010, 125), captured its readiness to walk away from lofty rhetoric about bold climate action when it conflicted with industry preferences. Among the various EU Member States that strenuously opposed such a market-based mechanism, Germany, whose own climate policy "mixed traditional regulation with voluntary agreements and eco-taxes," was "the prime sceptic to emissions trading" (Boasson and Wettestad 2013, 59). Voluntary agreements were the clear preference of German industry, which includes such European heavyweights as Thyssenkrupp, BASF, E.ON, and RWE. Ultimately, the EU pursued the emissions trading route; the 2003 Emissions Trading Directive set an emissions cap covering 10,000 installations in select sectors (including energy-intensive industries), which was aligned with the EU's emissions target under the Kyoto Protocol (van Asselt 2010, 128). Yet, Member States retained the authority to determine both the total allowances allocated to installations and their distribution, and, reflecting the preferences of select industries and powerful Member States (like Germany), allowances were not auctioned but were distributed for free (van Asselt 2010, 136). The Emissions Trading System (ETS) soon failed, with Member States having overallocated allowances. While key Member States, including Germany, had become more amenable to "a more harmonized ETS" by mid-2008, Germany remained "something of a champion" for continued free allowances for energy-intensive industries (Boasson and Wettestad 2013, 64, 65).

Germany's approach to the automotive industry—responsible for roughly 800,000 German jobs and over 400 billion euros in annual revenue (Sauerbrey 2019)—especially sheds light on what has been a disjunction between the government's rhetoric and behavior in crucial moments when "the rubber meets the road." In 2013, for example, after five years of negotiations had produced agreement among EU Member States about a new round of emissions standards for automobiles, Chancellor Merkel intervened "at the last minute by calling the Irish EU Council President, asking him to take the subject off the agenda." The process was delayed another year and ultimately led to "watered-down rules" (Thalman and Wettengel 2019). In part due to this type of behavior, emissions in Germany's transport sector have climbed 20% since 1995 "and are rising with no end in sight," according to a *Yale Environment 360* article. The same article reported that, expressly "in the face of auto industry opposition," Berlin, after initially strengthening its support for the Energiewende following the 2011 Fukushima Daiichi nuclear disaster, had "backed off decarbonizing the transportation sector." It also

54   C. HULME

failed to support a meaningful carbon price, "dragged its feet on [renewable energy] grid expansion," and failed to implement "significant parts of its 2050 climate program" (Hockenos 2018).

* * *

Since the 1990s, Germany, a pathbreaker in renewable energy and early mover in the climate change issue area, has perceived its behavior through a particular lens: its image of itself as a climate leader. In the late 2010s and early 2020s, it more explicitly acknowledged the serious gaps existing between its ambitious targets and its ability to achieve them. In 2020, for example, an analysis commissioned by Berlin concluded that the "comprehensive 2030 climate package" announced in 2018 "will likely fail to reach its objective and not bring about the desired carbon emissions reduction" (Wehrmann 2020). Yet, in contrast to, for example, the United States during the Trump administration, Germany has not consciously abdicated climate leadership; rather, it has wavered in enforcing tough climate-related rules when those rules concern prized industries, including, perhaps most clearly, automotive.

Drawing on Jervis' hypotheses on misperception, this section has considered how the private sector might have perceived the government's behavior and how that perception might have differed appreciably, specifically by the mid- to late 2010s, from Berlin's self-image. The empirical chapters evaluate whether the data support the argument that such misperception, whereby the government misjudged how the private sector would interpret and react to its policies, is important to explain the process by which select Germany-based companies came to adopt a new climate approach and assume a different role than in the past. In fact, in 2018, one German newspaper, reporting that Berlin seemed "in no hurry to repair the country's tarnished reputation on climate change, let alone take the lead in battling global warming," and noting that Germany's "corporate titans have climate goals that are more ambitious than their government's," observed, "Instead of waiting for action at the top, [Germany-based] big businesses are practically falling over themselves to cut emissions in line with the Greenhouse Gas Protocol" (Carbon Pricing Leadership Coalition 2018).

Part III: India

Evaluating how and why the Indian government became increasingly active in the climate change issue area starting in the mid-2010s, this part of the chapter considers the context for climate action by select Indian corporations. The first section addresses how, despite recently increasing levels of climate action, the rationale for India's climate approach in fact has been consistent since the 1990s; its guiding principle has been that addressing climate change must not come at the expense of advancing economic development and alleviating poverty—"primordial policy preoccupations for Indian policymakers," as one scholar has described it (Michel 2009, 2). Its prevailing commitment to a policy of "co-benefits," with development, not climate change mitigation, as the primary objective of climate-relevant behavior, is not incompatible with mitigating climate change. Yet, the co-benefits logic had the potential to affect how the private sector perceived the government's commitment to creating conditions for a low-carbon future. Drawing on Jervis' insights into potential sources of misperception, for the government the key takeaway from its behavior—the "important pattern" that it assumed to be "equally obvious to others" (1968, 474)—was that during the 2010s it began burnishing its global climate leadership credentials while maintaining its priority focus on development. There was the potential, however, for the private sector to interpret its behavior in a very different light. From the private sector's perspective, the climate co-benefits policy may have been interpreted as indicative of New Delhi's commitment not to establishing "rules of the game" for a low-carbon future but rather to creating a more favorable environment for development (including, importantly, fossil fuel-based development).

The second section examines an additional source of potentially divergent perceptions, namely, that while New Delhi had a certain image of itself in the context of announcing bold renewable energy targets and making instrumental contributions to the Paris Conference, it failed fully to anticipate how others might respond "to a much less favorable image" (Jervis 1968, 477). New Delhi's ambitious target-setting was one thing; the private sector may have viewed its ability and will to execute policies—including by securing acceptance and implementation by India's influential states—as a very different matter given its longtime record of "failures of implementation" (Frankel 1978, 156).

This part of the chapter sheds light on an alternative interpretation of New Delhi's growing level of activity in the climate issue area, examining how developments that widely have been viewed as indicative of its commitment to turning the page on its reputation as a "climate holdout" (Ayres 2018, 167), and as evincing its intention to become a serious player in shaping a low-carbon future, could be interpreted in a much different light. Exploring the possibility of a disjunction between how the government perceived itself and interpreted its pattern of behavior and how the private sector perceived the government and interpreted its behavior, it offers insights into potentially key features of the context in which the private sector increased its level of climate activity during the 2010s.

The Prevailing Logic of Co-benefits

For decades after the UNFCCC enshrined the principle of "common but differentiated responsibilities" (CBDR), establishing that "all states are responsible for addressing global environmental destruction yet not equally responsible" given different historical contributions to the problem and resource disparities (Epstein 2013), India's primary focus was "preserving the 'differentiated' architecture of the climate regime that it helped to embed within the UNFCCC" (Sengupta 2012, 307). The CBDR principle strongly appealed to India, aligning with the G-77 bloc's position, of which it was an absolutist champion, that developing countries had a right to pursue economic development regardless of the industrialized world's newfound interest in reducing emissions. With the CBDR architecture embedded in the 1997 Kyoto Protocol, separating Annex I from non-Annex I countries, thus excluding India from mandatory emissions caps, the G-77 position became the "centerpiece" of New Delhi's position at international climate negotiations (Jha 2009, 33). As Das has considered, New Delhi's "defensive negotiating strategy" at the international level sent a strong signal to industrial players that "they would be insulated from climate measures" (2012, 247).

The global CBDR principle dovetailed with India's domestic logic of "co-benefits," enshrined in its 2008 National Action Plan for Climate Change (NAPCC), which underscored that India's climate policies were grounded in the "overriding priority of economic and social development and poverty eradication." The NAPCC stated, "In view of the large uncertainties concerning the spatial and temporal magnitude of climate change impacts, it is not desirable to design strategies exclusively for responding to climate change. Rather, the need is to identify and prioritize strategies that promote development goals but also serv[e] specific climate change objectives" (Government of India 2008, 13). The NAPCC announced plans for eight national missions designed to "launch the economy on a path that would progressively and substantially result in mitigation through avoided emissions" (Government of India 2008, 6). Consistent with the NAPCC's framework, these missions, including the flagship National Solar Mission (NSM) and National Mission on Enhanced Energy Efficiency (NMEEE), were oriented toward the overriding goal of advancing development through expanded use of renewable energy and more efficient utilization of existing power capacity—not toward addressing climate change per se.

Following the launch of the NAPCC, regulatory measures under the aegis of the new missions were unveiled, including the NMEEE's Perform Achieve Trade (PAT) scheme, established in 2012, which set "mandatory, specific targets for energy consumption" for designated companies in energy-intensive industries. Companies saving more energy than was required were issued Energy Savings Certificates that could be traded with underperformers; renewable energy usage was one way that companies could meet their targets (International Energy Agency 2019). But it was not until 2014, when Prime Minister Narendra Modi announced the target of achieving 100 gigawatts (gw) of solar energy capacity by 2022—at the time, India had only 3 gw of solar and just under 34 gw of total renewable capacity—that India appreciably ramped up its ambition in the climate arena. Its pledges in the run-up to the Paris Conference—to reduce the emissions intensity of its GDP by at least 33% by 2030 compared to 2005 (Singh and Kamal 2015) and to ensure that non-fossil fuels represented 40% of its energy generation capacity by 2030 (Goswami 2016)—appeared to confirm its heightened level of commitment to becoming a more serious climate actor.

In fact, its bold renewable energy target, coupled with what appeared to be an unusually cooperative stance toward the negotiations at the Paris Conference, led some observers to conclude that India had not simply retreated from its decades-long intransigence on the need to contribute to addressing climate change given its small historic responsibility for global emissions and low per-capita emissions, but had outright assumed the mantle of climate leadership. Ayres, for example, contended that instead of "an India resisting a perceived agreement imposed by the West, an

India actively shaping the global agenda emerged" at the Paris Conference (2018, 167). The climate division head at the World Resources Institute, speaking in the context of India's assurance of its commitment to the Paris Agreement regardless of the announced US withdrawal by the Trump administration, remarked, "This is proof of India's decisive leadership on climate change as they embrace the clean energy revolution to power their homes and create jobs" (Mathiesen 2017). Meanwhile, the UN Secretary-General singled out India (along with China) for "assuming the leadership in climate action to make sure that we don't suffer the dramatic and devastating impacts of climate change," particularly in "a moment when others are failing" (Indian Express 2018).

While its behavior in the Paris "moment" was interpreted by some observers as a watershed for India, ultimately it was underpinned by the longstanding co-benefits logic.[3] As a leading Indian negotiator at the Paris Conference recalled in an interview for this book, India's emphasis on renewable energy and energy efficiency "had begun earlier," prior to Paris, "for non-climate reasons" (New Delhi, August 1, 2018). Similarly, a PricewaterhouseCoopers consultant who worked with the government of Prime Minister Manmohan Singh in 2013 to craft the 100 gw solar target never mentioned climate change in discussing the factors behind the renewable energy push. Instead, he underscored India's efforts to compete in the renewables space with China, which had announced ambitious solar targets of its own (Gurugram, India, August 1, 2018).

Since the mid-2010s, the government was unambiguous about its overriding priority of development, including that driven by fossil fuels; in a revealing 2014 speech, Energy Minister Piyush Goyal announced that India would become a "renewables superpower," while also emphasizing that coal-fired power generation would see "very rapid expansion" (Carrington 2014). Policies that could be interpreted as indicative of a renewed commitment to a low-carbon transition, such as the government's closure of 37 coal mines in 2017, primarily were a function of

---

[3] A leading US negotiator at the Paris Conference expressed skepticism that it marked a turning point in India's approach, reporting that India "didn't suddenly start cooperating with us in some visible way, nor have they changed their tune all the way into the Bonn meeting [COP23, held in November 2017] right now." New Haven, Connecticut, November 13, 2017.

insufficient infrastructure to handle additional coal-generated power.[4] As the Paris negotiator explained,

> We've always seen climate change as being a co-benefit, and macroeconomic stability and urban air quality as being the main benefits. We've typically thought that the world has inverted the benefits by saying that climate is the main benefit and there are other co-benefits. We think it's the other way around. Yes, climate change is becoming higher in priority as more and more of it happens, but that still doesn't take away from the fact that you need to provide electricity to everybody. (New Delhi, August 1, 2018)

Prior to the conference, he noted that the government was feeling "blindsided by the extreme reaction to the increased usage of coal in India," explaining,

> We were blindsided because yes, coal use was going to double, but renewables use was going to increase ten-fold. That surprised us because even when we doubled our coal use, it would still be less, for example, than the coal use in the US or China, with the reductions they were looking at. So it surprised us—why is this an issue? That's when we decided we would keep on focusing on renewables. This is our policy goal. We are going to increase coal—there's no doubt about it. But our emphasis is that we move to a price regime where renewables become more attractive. (New Delhi, August 1, 2018)

There were three key development-oriented reasons for India's energy efficiency and renewable energy "push" beginning in the mid-2010s. First, there were significant macroeconomic impacts from India's reliance on imported energy. In fact, due to the poor quality of its domestic coal reserves, India relied on imported coal and oil for over 80% of its energy supply at the turn of the 2010s (Noronha 2009, 9). According to the International Energy Agency (IEA), by raising its energy efficiency ambition India "could save some USD 190 billion per year in energy imports by 2040 and avoid electricity generation of 875 terawatt hours per year," roughly half of its current annual power generation (International

---

[4] As a Reliance Power executive explained, India's problem is not one solely of energy availability, but also "capacity to pump to the last consumer. Our distribution sector has been a problem." Gurugram, India, August 6, 2018.

Energy Agency 2020, 16). With India's power requirements growing and "limited alternatives available," the government wanted to reduce coal dependence, and the price of renewables made it a more attractive option than nuclear power. Meanwhile, large hydroelectric power plants were "totally unviable" due to growing public awareness of "the environmental challenges and the resettlement issues associated with it" (international development consultant, Noida, India, August 3, 2018).

Second, India doubled down on renewable energy to tackle air pollution, which had become an impediment to economic development. A 2021 report by The Energy and Resources Institute (TERI), a New Delhi-based think tank, noted that the "rising trends in population growth and the consequent effects on air quality are evident in the Indian scenario. For example, the megacities of Delhi, Mumbai, and Kolkata combined [hold] a population exceeding 46 million." TERI reported that in 2017, air pollution was responsible for "over 1.1 million premature deaths" in India (Gurjar 2021). Meanwhile, the Public Health Foundation of India (PHFI) reported that in 2019, the "economic loss due to lost output from premature deaths and morbidity from air pollution was 1.4%" of Indian GDP; PHFI also noted that in 2019, the 1.7 million deaths "attributable to air pollution" represented 18% of all deaths in India (2020).

Third, renewable energy helped India address its persistent problem with power distribution, and particularly its weak capacity to deliver power to the estimated 200–230 million people who still lacked access to electricity by the late 2010s (BBC News 2018; Murphy and Daly 2018). Promoting decentralized power generation through rooftop solar offered a solution typically cheaper than building a new grid or integrating more areas, especially rural communities, into existing conventional (coal-powered) transmission and distribution networks (Reliance Power executive, Gurugram, India, August 6, 2018).

For Indian states that had become more engaged on climate issues, they shared the federal government's commitment to a policy based on co-benefits; their primary motivation in coming to the table was not mitigating climate change per se, but rather advancing a host of other priorities. As a Mumbai-based green technology entrepreneur put it, the "whole green thing has penetrated multiple segments—not only urban transportation but also agriculture, energy security, water, and waste management. So, depending on what the issue is in that local state, they would have a higher focus on that particular area. So, I think that everybody has found their own sort of niche where green is interesting for them and supports their cause" (Mumbai, August 16, 2018). The co-benefits logic has been particularly apparent in rapidly industrializing states like Andhra Pradesh and Telangana, for example, which, in their quest to provide access to electricity, "have been proactive when it comes to setting up not only solar power plants but also coal-based power plants" (Schneider Electric renewable energy expert #1, Gurugram, India, August 6, 2018).

As discussed above, a policy motivated by the logic of co-benefits is not incompatible with making meaningful progress in reducing emissions; the policy rationale is far less important than the results. But whereas the government viewed the motivation for its behavior as unimportant—what mattered were results, including that by 2018 renewables made up 21% of India's energy mix, "way ahead of what the IEA scenario had pegged for 2040" (Topping 2018, 3)—to corporations the rationale for climate policy, whether at the national or state level, potentially *did* matter. The private sector might have perceived that a policy principally driven by the immediate needs of development as opposed to a focus on a low-carbon future per se ultimately would fail to supply adequate "rules of the road" guiding the private sector toward such a future. The empirical chapters examine whether the private sector indeed perceived that while the world was headed toward a low-carbon future, the government in India was not necessarily stepping up to shape the rules of such a future, despite growing levels of activity in the climate issue area—and whether this perception spurred certain leading corporations to reevaluate their own approaches.

The "Ambition-Action" Gap and the Potential for Misperception

A second potential source of differing perceptions was that while New Delhi had a favorable image of its ability and will to translate lofty ambition into action, the private sector might not have shared that image. The state in India is weak, often failing to translate policy ambitions into results. Indeed, in 1978, Frankel used the phrase "failures of implementation" to explain India's inability to enact basic social reform in the post-Nehru years (Frankel 1978, 156). Beyond the three-decade period Frankel studied (1947–1977), her phrase could well describe the enduring gap between what the state says it intends to do and what it actually does in the world's largest democracy. In fact, Migdal has noted, social scientists have reassessed their "confidence about the power of

62 C. HULME

the state in the Third World, and elsewhere," partly because they have observed "how infrequently potential strength has been translated into effective action" in countries like India (2001, 42). In the climate domain in particular, observers note that India has lacked a coherent national strategy for translating its ambitious targets into results. As Khandekar has observed,

> Although there have been many individual initiatives in India on climate change, and there has been government support for renewables ... efforts so far have been fragmented. State and national governments, individual departments, businesses, non-governmental organisations, and academics have all worked separately, and sometimes in opposition to each other. (2020)

As Chapter 6 explores, there frequently was a significant gap between the ambitious targets that India announced during the Paris Conference, such as cutting the emissions intensity of its GDP 33% by 2030, and "realities on the ground." For example, three years after the conference, for some crucial sectors, including steel, the government still had not issued sector-specific targets "in line with the big numbers" unveiled at Paris (Tata Steel regulatory expert, New Delhi, August 7, 2018). Likewise, the PAT scheme under the NMEEE, established in 2012, "was very ambitious" and initially had "good momentum," but due to "certain market failures" designated consumers were unable to sell their Energy Saving Certificates at the right price, which "de-motivated the scheme." Failure of "such a big mechanism, covering nearly 65% of primary energy consumption," was not "favorable to a transition to a low-carbon economy" (Dalmia Bharat Cement sustainability expert, New Delhi, August 27, 2018). Similarly, the Renewable Purchase Obligation (RPO) regulatory scheme, which was unveiled in 2003 to induce demand for renewables, suffered partly because regulators did not fully enforce it (UN 2018). As a top executive at Mahindra Susten, the clean technology arm of the Mahindra Group, noted in 2018, the RPO obligations "were there on paper, but even if you talk about it today, the enforceability is still a big question" (Mumbai, August 14, 2018).

In the Indian context, arguably even more challenging than designing, executing, and sustaining a coherent national-level strategy in any policy domain, including climate change, is securing support and commitment from fiercely independent states, whose chief ministers, as Das has written, "are the real rulers of India" (2019). Not only are the states enormously powerful, but their priorities do not necessarily align with those of New Delhi. In the Indian federal system, there typically is a national-level ministry and a counterpart department at the state level. But considering the Ministry of Forests and Climate Change, "very few states have a counterpart department," one expert noted in 2018. "So, everything has been some kind of push from the top. India has a national plan for climate change, but not every state has a state action plan for climate change" (international development consultant, Noida, India, August 3, 2018). To be sure, some states that are not "allies with the central policy" have demonstrated interest in the climate agenda. As the Mumbai-based green technology entrepreneur previously cited observed, "I don't think there's any state that's saying anything so blunt as, 'I don't care about the environment.' Nobody's saying that. The only difference is how active or passive they are. Is it mostly lip service or is it actual action?" (Mumbai, August 16, 2018). Indeed, some states lag behind on basic policies to operationalize their stated objectives for renewable energy. For instance, as one expert pointed out in an interview, in some states "net metering policy is not there, where you can install an offered solar panel on your roof and then sell it to the grid—that policy is missing" (Schneider Electric renewable energy expert #2, Gurugram, India, August 6, 2018).

$$* \quad * \quad *$$

This section has considered two factors that may have led the private sector to view New Delhi's behavior in the climate issue area through a different lens than the government, with possible implications for corporations' understanding of their own approach to climate change and a low-carbon future. First, the private sector might have perceived a different signal from, or drawn different conclusions about, the government's "development-first" climate policy than New Delhi assumed. Whereas the government did not view the motivation for its climate-related behavior as problematic, the private sector might have concluded that even if the government was increasingly active in climate-related issues, that did not necessarily mean that it was concerned with creating conditions nurturing the private sector's journey toward, and success in, a low-carbon future. Second, the private sector might not have shared New Delhi's image of its ability and will to translate bold targets into meaningful—and sustained—action; there was the potential for perceptions of an especially salient ambition-implementation gap in the climate policy domain. The empirical chapters investigate whether these potentially divergent perceptions were important factors in the landscape, translating to enhanced climate action by some leading lights of "India, Inc."

PART IV: THE UNITED STATES

Borrowing Putnam's insight that the politics of international negotiations is akin to a "two-level game" (1988), since the 1990s the United States periodically has made plays at the international level of the climate game that suggested a certain level of commitment at the domestic level, including helping to broker the Kyoto Protocol, rescuing the Copenhagen Conference from abject collapse, and playing a vital role in the process leading to the Paris Conference. Yet, even as certain administrations have seized windows of political opportunity to pursue a more ambitious approach, the domestic foundation for their actions ultimately has been fragile. This part of the chapter examines the weak domestic basis for action in two illustrative contexts, the presidencies of Bill Clinton and Barack Obama, which for different reasons were marked by a limited ability to commit credibly to climate action and leadership. It analyzes the possibility of a disjunction between what to these administrations was the "important pattern in their actions" (Jervis 1968, 474)—that they had moved the climate action "ball" forward in meaningful ways—and what the private sector saw as the key takeaway. Such misaligned perceptions, with Washington having a certain image of itself not shared by the private sector, may have shaped the landscape and context in which leading corporations assumed new roles in the climate change issue area by the late 2010s and turn of the 2020s.

Misaligned Climate "Games" and the Potential for Misperception: The Clinton Presidency

Following the Reagan and George H.W. Bush presidencies, which were marked by "fierce battles with environmental groups," the political winds appeared to shift decisively with the first Clinton administration. With a Democrat in the White House for the first time in 12 years and a Democrat-controlled House of Representatives and Senate, the early 1990s seemed a potential turning point away from a thin national climate agenda, which during the 1980s had consisted only of a few bills with limited legislative prospects. Indeed, it was during the incoming Clinton administration's transition process that the "first serious conversations about imposing costs on carbon pollution" occurred (Mildenberger 2020, 276, 281).

Early on the White House sought to put climate change on the agenda; in the 1993 deficit reduction package, for example, it proposed an energy tax on fuel (the British Thermal Unit [BTU] tax). Given that the BTU tax imposed costs based on energy content rather than carbon intensity, it entailed high costs for low-carbon but high-energy sources (e.g., nuclear reactors and hydroelectric dams), while imposing "fewer costs on coal than a carbon tax" (Mildenberger 2020, 281). Yet, it nonetheless represented a strong early effort to reduce emissions while generating revenue for reducing the deficit. However, as Royden has observed, after the BTU tax failed during budget negotiations, for the White House the lesson was obvious: "a broad-based carbon or energy tax was politically unacceptable in the United States, even with a Democratic Congress. The administration would need to come up with other tools to address climate change" (2002, 420).

The White House soon shifted its attention from the domestic arena to US involvement in international climate efforts. In 1993, it released a 44-point national climate action plan to serve as the basis for US commitments under the UNFCCC, which President George H.W. Bush had signed in 1992 and that established the expectation that by 2000 Annex I countries would make progress toward reducing emissions to 1990 levels. Importantly, however, the Clinton administration's plan did not include any mandatory emissions reductions, a reflection of the fact that the administration sought to "minimize the need for legislative or regulatory action" after its failed opening gambit with the BTU tax (Royden 2002, 421). Thus, Mildenberger has noted, in the run-up to the 1997 Kyoto summit (COP3), while the White House announced that the US would endorse "substantial" commitments, it "struggled to articulate a federal policy vision that could deliver on these commitments," and its efforts were "restricted to plans that were steeped in political symbolism but sidestepped meaningful costs" (2020, 282).

There were stark differences between the administration's preferred policies and self-image as a climate leader—Vice President Al Gore particularly embraced his role in brokering the Kyoto Protocol—and the domestic political reality. Most dramatically, in July 1997, the Senate passed the Byrd-Hagel Resolution 95–0, which characterized developing

66   C. HULME

countries' exemption from mandatory emissions reductions as "inconsistent with the need for global action on climate change," and resolved that the United States should not enter into a treaty requiring mandatory reductions only from developed countries. Thus, even before COP3 began the Senate dispelled any doubt about the prospect of US ratification of what would emerge as the Kyoto Protocol. While the Byrd-Hagel Resolution was not legally binding, to achieve ratification the Clinton administration would have needed to "change the minds of at least 67 senators—a formidable task," as Hovi, Sprinz, and Bang observed (2010, 130).

Yet, even after passage of Byrd-Hagel, with the non-ratification writing on the wall, for the Clinton administration the key pattern in its behavior and the central message that it thought it had conveyed was that the United States had made an unmatched commitment to addressing climate change, played a key role in ensuring the success of the Kyoto negotiations, and provided critical momentum to international climate action. As Vice President Gore put it in a speech delivered during the Kyoto conference, "For our part, the United States remains firmly committed to a strong, binding target that will reduce our own emissions by nearly 30 percent from what they would otherwise be—a commitment as strong, or stronger, than any we have heard here from any country" (The White House 1997). Yet, this was by no means the obvious takeaway for others. For the private sector, the message coming out of Kyoto may have been that whatever international commitments a climate-active administration might make, with a weak domestic basis for action those commitments lacked credibility. The lesson potentially was that, having failed to appreciate that there were not two separate climate games—one international and one domestic—but rather one coherent, two-level game, the Clinton administration actually had done very little to "move the ball forward" in a meaningful fashion.

Climate Partisanship and the Potential for Misperception: The Obama Presidency

During the Clinton administration, the key complicating factor in the United States' ability to make credible international climate commitments was bipartisan opposition to the terms of the Kyoto Protocol, specifically its exemption of developing countries, including China and India, from mandatory emissions reductions while requiring such reductions from developed countries. Climate change was not yet a polarizing issue in Congress nor an intensely partisan issue among Americans. Indeed, research by the Political Psychology Research Group (PPRG) at Stanford University found that the "partisan gap" among Americans in terms of their perceptions about whether global warming has occurred (and if so, whether it has been caused at least partly by human activity) "was only 8 percentage points on average in 1997 and 1998" (Political Psychology Research Group, n.d.). In 2000, meanwhile, Pew found that 78% of Democrats and 64% of Republicans worried about global warming "a great deal" or "a fair amount" (Samuelson 2018).

Early in the George W. Bush administration, in fact, even as the White House announced US non-participation in the Kyoto regime, there appeared to be at least the possibility of an active climate agenda. Indeed, "an emissions trading scheme for carbon pollution remained part of the Bush transition document and early administration planning" (Mildenberger 2020, 282). Further, there appeared to be momentum toward bipartisan climate legislation. In 2003, for example, Republican Senator John McCain and Democratic Senator Joe Lieberman introduced what became a three-part series of "Climate Stewardship Acts" to create a mandatory national cap and trade system (ultimately, in 2007, the final act died in committee). In 2006, Lieberman and Republican Senator John Warner negotiated "a full emissions trading scheme in partnership with industry" and advocates for reform like the US Climate Action Partnership, a coalition of major business and environmental players that included DuPont, Duke Energy, General Electric, the Environmental Defense Fund, the Natural Resources Defense Council, and the Nature Conservancy (Mildenberger 2020, 283).

In early 2009, the new Obama administration and Democrats in Congress sought to capitalize on their "new agenda-setting power"; Democrats held the House of Representatives 257–178 and the Senate 60–40 (as two Independents caucused with the Democrats). Yet, pro-climate legislators "still had to bargain with fellow Democratic officials who championed the concerns of such economic sectors as coal, heavy industry, and agriculture," one result of which was that fossil fuel interests retained "persistent influence over federal climate policy design" (Mildenberger 2020, 283). Nonetheless, in 2009 the House passed the Waxman-Markey Bill, or the American Clean Energy Security Act, which included a comprehensive cap and trade scheme, a clean energy mandate, and support for low-carbon technology—the "closest the U.S. [ever]

68   C. HULME

came to pricing carbon," noted Stokes and Breetz (2020, 290). But the bill, which passed the House with support from 211 Democrats and just 8 Republicans (meanwhile, 44 Democrats and 168 Republicans voted against it), never received a Senate vote, with Harry Reid, the Senate Majority Leader, recognizing it lacked the 60 votes necessary to overcome the filibuster.

While the failure of Waxman-Markey, representing, "by a large margin, the most comprehensive piece of climate legislation to have passed either branch of Congress," throws into sharp relief the increasingly clear partisan divide over the climate change issue in Congress, at the same time Americans were becoming more polarized in their attitudes toward climate change (Mildenberger 2020, 283). For example, PPRG found that the partisan gap on opinions concerning global warming was 30% in 2011—up from just 8% in 1997/1998 (Political Psychology Research Group, n.d.).

Notably, as the climate change issue became more intensely partisan in nature, it also commanded little public concern. In 2008, Pew found that just 30% of American adults said that "dealing with global warming should be a top priority for the president and Congress," a number that remained remarkably steady over the course of the next five years (Funk and Kennedy 2020). During the Obama presidency, therefore, even with Democrats in power—seemingly the "right" party to advance the climate agenda—climate change's lack of political salience created few incentives for action.

Thus, at the December 2009 Copenhagen Conference, when Obama announced that he had achieved a "meaningful and unprecedented" climate deal with China and other key emerging economies, the domestic backdrop to this announcement, coming just months after the failure of Waxman-Markey, was one marked by limited concern with climate change overall and by the increasingly partisan nature of the issue. In short, there was an extremely weak domestic basis for action by the president. But for Obama, the important takeaway from Copenhagen and the non-binding deal that he helped to broker—whose emissions targets, the president admitted, would "not be by themselves sufficient to get to where we need to get by 2050"—was that the United States had moved the world in the right direction, or, as he put it, gotten "that shift in orientation moving" (Henry 2009).

While the president had a certain image of his administration's ability to act as a climate leader on the global stage despite the failures of climate action in the domestic arena, he failed to appreciate fully how the growing politicization of the issue in the United States not only had eroded what bipartisan basis for action had existed in the early 2000s, but also may have nurtured a particular perception among others about the credibility of Washington's global climate commitments. For the private sector, it may have been difficult to give much credence to Obama's claims about the significance of the deal reached at Copenhagen—that "there will be a sense on the part of each country that we're in this together, and we'll know who is meeting and who is not meeting, [sic] the mutual obligations that have been set forth" (Henry 2009)—when in the United States prospects for bridging partisan differences over the climate agenda appeared increasingly dim. Indeed, while Waxman-Markey had failed to overcome the 60-vote filibuster threshold when they *had* 60 senators, following the 2010 midterm election Democrats lost six Senate seats, as well as 63 House seats, which gave Republicans control of the House (which they retained for the remainder of the Obama presidency).

Despite the early failure to establish a national cap and trade system, however, the Obama administration did achieve significant wins for the climate agenda, including the Clean Air Act (CAA), which represented a "major departure from previous federal climate policy proposals," focusing on "cost imposition on carbon polluters without the subsidy or financial support carrots that had been ... part of failed federal emissions trading legislation." In August 2015, under the aegis of the CAA, the administration unveiled the Clean Power Plan (CPP), which "proposed reductions in power sector carbon pollution of 30 percent below 2005 levels by 2030." While the states were given latitude to develop their own policies to achieve Environmental Protection Agency (EPA) targets, the federal government "would develop federal plans for states that refused to comply with the CPP" (Mildenberger 2020, 284). In contrast to Copenhagen, when President Obama's rhetoric about US commitments to climate action contrasted starkly with the recent failure of Waxman-Markey, at the December 2015 Paris Conference the United States had a relatively stronger record on which it could stake its claim to be "a global leader in the fight against climate change" (Somanader 2016).

Yet, the growing problem of "partisan gridlock" and polarization over climate change meant that potentially important developments such as the CPP and US leadership in the Paris process were subject to reversal (Hsueh 2020, 243). Indeed, with climate change becoming a more partisan issue, US climate policy has become more unpredictable, marked by "increasingly large swings from one presidential administration to the next" (Konisky 2020, 5). For example, the EPA during the Obama administration bypassed Congress after its failure to enact emissions reduction legislation, using its CAA authority to mandate reductions; subsequently, Obama-era regulatory measures targeting fossil fuel power plants and vehicles were reversed by the Trump administration (Konisky 2020, 4), which replaced the CPP with the 2019 Affordable Clean Energy rule, which "dramatically weakened requirements on state-level power sectors to manage their carbon pollution" (Mildenberger 2020, 284). Likewise, the US zig-zagged from being one of the critical players lending momentum to the Paris process under the Obama administration (including by encouraging China and India to join) to being a spoiler, announcing its intention to withdraw from the Paris Agreement after Trump took office.

Executive branch zig-zagging has been coupled with gridlock on Capitol Hill. As Konisky has observed in considering environmental policy broadly, because "the two sides of this debate have become so embedded in broader American politics, they typically are unable to find much common ground. As a consequence, current U.S. environmental policy typically involves bitter, partisan and interest group politics, most often leading not just to disagreement, but policy gridlock at the national level" (Konisky 2020, 3). With Congress all too often unwilling to act, presidents increasingly rely on "administrative tools" to advance their policy objectives on environmental issues broadly and on climate change specifically; such reliance further undercuts US credibility, as each administration simply can reverse the actions of its predecessor (Konisky 2020, 5). Such unpredictability on the part of the executive branch, coupled with legislative branch fecklessness, makes it difficult for even climate-active administrations to commit credibly to climate action, much less to leadership.

* * *

From the late 1990s, when the Clinton administration championed the Kyoto Protocol on the global stage but faced bipartisan opposition at home, through the 2010s, when Obama administration efforts to forge ahead on the climate agenda unfolded in the context of climate change becoming an increasingly partisan issue, periodic US efforts at climate leadership have suffered from a perennially weak domestic basis for action. This section has considered the possibility of a misalignment between what to the Clinton and Obama administrations was the key pattern in their behavior—that despite certain domestic circumstances complicating their ability to address climate change in a robust fashion, they had advanced (and indeed helped hold together) the global climate agenda at watershed moments (e.g., Kyoto, Copenhagen, and Paris)—and what the private sector potentially understood as the important message in their behavior: that, absent firm domestic political foundations, Washington's periodic attempts at climate leadership were, in the end, seriously limited in their impact. Chapters 3–6 explore whether the private sector failing to share Washington's favorable self-image as being willing and able to lead in the climate issue area in critical moments shaped the landscape in which it became a key climate actor in the 2010s, assuming a significantly different role in the issue area than it had historically.

CONCLUSION

From the late 1990s through the 2010s, while states periodically sent what they thought were clear signals about their intentions to address climate change and support a low-carbon transition, the private sector may not have interpreted them as intended. Drawing on Jervis' hypotheses on misperception, this chapter considered how, in shifting from a top-down model of international climate action (the Kyoto model), premised on mandatory emissions reductions for industrialized countries and select economies in transition, to a bottom-up approach (the Paris model), premised on nationally determined contributions to a shared emissions reduction goal, states assumed that others would appreciate what to them clearly was the "important pattern in their action" (Jervis 1968, 474): that, by giving themselves the latitude to determine at the domestic political level what to contribute to global mitigation objectives, they had set a trajectory for success, sowing the seeds for transformative progress on addressing climate change after decades of gridlock. For the private sector, however, the takeaway potentially was that states still lacked answers about how to get where they needed to go in terms of realizing shared mitigation objectives in a concerted, ambitious, and effective fashion.

72 C. HULME

Likewise, in each country case, the government assumed that its behavior conveyed a certain signal: for Berlin, that it was an exceptional climate leader; for New Delhi, that in the mid-2010s it turned the page on its reputation as a climate holdout; and for Washington, that it gave indispensable momentum to the international policy process at such key moments as Kyoto, Copenhagen, and Paris. But in each case, the private sector did not necessarily receive the signal as intended. German companies potentially saw a growing gap between the government's historically climate-active behavior and its present commitment to paving the way toward a low-carbon future. In India, whereas the government did not see the development-driven motivation for its climate-related behavior as problematic, the private sector may have concluded that its growing level of climate activity did not necessarily mean that New Delhi was concerned with nurturing the private sector's journey toward a low-carbon future. Further, the frequent gap between New Delhi's ambitious target-setting and its implementation challenges, including securing acceptance among India's states, may have undercut the private sector's confidence that it really had become a more serious player in the climate change issue area. The US private sector, meanwhile, may have perceived that whatever efforts at climate leadership certain administrations made on the global stage, a perennially weak domestic basis for action severely undercut their ability to commit credibly to climate action.

If misperception indeed was a factor in the landscape, with states misjudging how the private sector would interpret their commitment to addressing climate change and spurring a low-carbon transition, then states inadvertently may have precipitated a change in the key players and dynamics of the climate game. They assumed, particularly throughout the 2010s, that they were becoming more effective and ambitious in their approach to climate change; the empirical chapters explore whether the private sector perceived a much less positive image than states thought they were projecting, and in *this* context assumed a different role in the issue area.

References

Amelang, Sören. 2016. When will Germany finally ditch coal? *Clean Energy Wire*, December 16, 2016. https://www.cleanenergywire.org/factsheets/when-will-germany-finally-ditch-coal.

2 CHANGE OF PLAYERS, CHANGE OF GAME 73

Apparicio, Soila. 2018. Germany to miss 2020 climate target, government concedes in official report. *Climate Home News*, December 6, 2018. https:/ /climatechangenews.com/2018/06/12/germany-miss-2020-climate-target-government-concedes-official-report/.

van Asselt, Harro. 2010. Emissions trading: The enthusiastic adoption of an "alien" instrument? In *Climate change policy in the European Union: Confronting the dilemmas of mitigation and adaptation?*, eds. Andrew Jordan, Dave Huitema, Harro van Asselt, Tim Rayner, and Frans Berkhout, 125–144. Cambridge, UK: Cambridge University Press.

van Asselt, Harro, and Thomas Hale. 2016. Maximizing the potential of the Paris Agreement: Effective review in a hybrid regime. Stockholm Environment Institute. https://www.jstor.org/stable/pdf/resrep02776.pdf?ref reqid=excelsior%3A0b0ec74e84e379a8bb3ec7383a295100&ab_segments=& origin=&initiator=&acceptTC=1.

Ayres, Alyssa. 2018. *Our time has come: How India is making its place in the world*. Oxford, UK: Oxford University Press.

BBC News. 2018. India says all villages have electricity. BBC. April 30, 2018. https://www.bbc.com/news/world-asia-india-43946049.

Boasson, Elin Lerum, and Jørgen Wettestad. 2013. *EU climate policy: Industry, policy interaction and external environment*. London: Routledge.

Bodansky, Daniel. 2010. The Copenhagen climate change conference: A postmortem. *American Journal of International Law* 104 (2): 230–240. https:/ /doi.org/10.5305/amerjintelaw.104.2.0230.

Bodansky, Daniel. 2012. The Durban Platform Negotiations: Goals and Options. Harvard Project on Climate Agreements. July 2012. https://www.belfercen ter.org/publication/durban-platform-negotiations-goals-and-options.

Boersma, Tim. 2014. U.S.-China joint announcement on climate change is a big deal. Brookings. November 13, 2014. https://www.brookings.edu/blog/pla netpolicy/2014/11/13/u-s-china-joint-announcement-on-climate-change-is-a-big-deal/.

Bremmer, Ian. 2012. *Every nation for itself: Winners and losers in a G-Zero world*. New York: Penguin.

Burkart, Karl. 2010. Richard Branson's war on carbon. *Forbes*, February 23, 2010. https://www.forbes.com/2010/02/22/carbon-climate-copenhagen-technology-ecotech-branson.html?sh=683ad84e1d36.

Cama, Timothy. 2015. Kerry says he's looking to the private sector to solve climate change. *The Hill*, December 7, 2015. https://thehill.com/policy/ energy-environment/262314-kerry-private-sector-is-key-in-climate-fight/.

Carbon Pricing Leadership Coalition. 2018. German businesses outpace politicians on carbon issues. February 27, 2018. https://www.carbonpricingleade rship.org/blogs/2018/2/27/german-businesses-outpace-politicians-on-car bon-issues.

Carrington, Damian. 2014. India will be renewables superpower, says energy minister. *The Guardian*, October 1, 2014. https://www.theguardian.com/environment/2014/oct/01/india-will-be-renewables-superpower-says-energy-minister.

Clean Energy Wire. n.d. Germany's Energiewende in brief. https://www.cleanenergywire.org/germanys-energiewende-brief.

Climate Nexus. n.d. Common but differentiated responsibilities and respective capabilities (CBDR-RC). https://climatenexus.org/climate-change-news/common-but-differentiated-responsibilities-and-respective-capabilities-cbdr-rc/.

Das, Gurcharan. 2019. Strong state, strong society: The reforms India needs Prime Minister Narendra Modi to courageously undertake. *The Times of India*, May 31, 2019. https://timesofindia.indiatimes.com/blogs/men-and-ideas/strong-state-strong-society-the-reforms-india-needs-prime-minister-narendra-modi-to-courageously-undertake/.

Das, Tarun. 2012. Climate change and the private sector. In *Handbook of climate change and India*, ed. Navroz Dubash, 246–253. New York: Earthscan.

Delbeke, Jos, Ger Klaassen, and Steffan Vergote. 2015. Climate-related energy policies. In *EU climate policy explained*, eds. Jos Delbeke and Peter Vis, 61–91. New York: Routledge.

Epstein, Charlotte. 2013. Common but differentiated responsibilities. *Britannica*, March 11, 2013. https://www.britannica.com/topic/common-but-differentiated-responsibilities.

Erickson, Amanda. 2018. Few countries are meeting the Paris climate goals. Here are the ones that are. *The Washington Post*, October 11, 2018. https://www.washingtonpost.com/world/2018/10/11/few-countries-are-meeting-paris-climate-goals-here-are-ones-that-are/.

Esty, Daniel, and Anthony Moffa. 2012. Why climate change collective action has failed and what needs to be done within and without the trade regime. *Journal of International Economic Law* 15 (3): 771–791. https://doi.org/10.1093/jiel/jgs033.

European Commission. n.d. 2020 Climate & energy package. https://climate.ec.europa.eu/eu-action/climate-strategies-targets/2020-climate-energy-package_en.

Falkner, Robert. 2016. The Paris Agreement and the new logic of international climate politics. *International Affairs* 92 (5): 1107–1125. https://doi.org/10.1111/1468-2346.12708.

Frankel, Frances. 1978. India's political economy, 1947–1977: The gradual revolution. Princeton, NJ: Princeton University Press.

Fransen, Taryn. 2021. Making sense of countries' Paris Agreement climate pledges. World Resources Institute. October 22, 2021. https://www.wri.org/insights/understanding-ndcs-paris-agreement-climate-pledges.

Funk, Cary, and Brian Kennedy. 2020. For Earth Day 2020, how Americans see climate change and the environment in 7 charts. Pew Research Center. April 21, 2020. https://www.pewresearch.org/fact-tank/2020/04/21/how-americans-see-climate-change-and-the-environment-in-7-charts/.

Gallagher, Kelly Sims, and Xiaowei Xuan. 2019. *Titans of the climate: Explaining policy process in the United States and China.* Cambridge, MA: MIT Press.

Goswami, Urmi. 2016. India's renewable energy targets catch the attention of global investors, still need ground work. *The Economic Times,* July 2, 2016. https://economictimes.indiatimes.com/news/politics-and-nation/indias-renewable-energy-targets-catch-the-attention-of-global-investors-still-need-ground-work/articleshow/53015707.cms.

Government of Germany. 2016. Climate Action Plan 2050. Federal Ministry for the Environment, Nature Conservation, Nuclear Safety and Consumer Protection. https://www.bmuv.de/en/publication/climate-action-plan-2050-en.

Government of India. 2008. National Action Plan for Climate Change. National Informatics Centre. https://archivepmo.nic.in/drmanmohansingh/climate_change_english.pdf.

Gurjar, Bhola Ram. 2021. Air pollution in India: Major issues and challenges. The Energy and Resources Institute. April 5, 2021. https://www.teriin.org/article/air-pollution-india-major-issues-and-challenges.

Henry, Ed. 2009. Obama announces climate change deal with China, other nations. CNN. December 18, 2009. http://www.cnn.com/2009/POLITICS/12/18/obama.copenhagen/index.html.

Hockenos, Paul. 2018. Carbon crossroads: Can Germany revive its stalled energy transition? *Yale Environment 360.* Yale University School of the Environment. December 13, 2018. https://e360.yale.edu/features/carbon-crossroads-can-germany-revive-its-stalled-energy-transition.

Hollingsworth, Barbara. 2016. Kerry signs "landmark" Paris Climate Change Agreement on Earth Day. *CNS News,* April 22, 2016. https://www.cnsnews.com/news/article/barbara-hollingsworth/kerry-signs-landmark-paris-climate-change-agreement-earth-day.

Hovi, Jon, Detlef Sprinz, and Guri Bang. 2010. Why the United States did not become a party to the Kyoto Protocol: German, Norwegian, and US perspectives. *European Journal of International Relations* 18 (1): 129–150. https://doi.org/10.1177/1354066110380964.

Hsueh, Lily. 2020. Calling all volunteers: Industry-self regulation on the environment. In *Handbook of U.S. environmental policy,* ed. David Konisky, 243–256. Northampton, MA: Edward Elgar.

Hultman, Nathan. 2010. The Cancun Agreements on climate change. Brookings. December 14, 2010. https://www.brookings.edu/opinions/the-cancun-agreements-on-climate-change/.

Hultman, Nathan. 2011. The Durban platform. Brookings. December 12, 2011. https://www.brookings.edu/opinions/the-durban-platform/.

Indian Express. 2018. UN hails India, China for leadership role over climate change. January 13, 2018. https://indianexpress.com/article/world/un-hails-india-china-for-leadership-role-over-climate-change/.

Intergovernmental Panel on Climate Change. 2018. Summary for policymakers of IPCC Special Report on Global Warming of 1.5°C approved by governments. October 8, 2018. https://www.ipcc.ch/2018/10/08/summary-for-policymakers-of-ipcc-special-report-on-global-warming-of-1-5c-approved-by-governments/.

International Energy Agency. 2019. Perform, Achieve, Trade (PAT) scheme. June 5, 2019. Updated May 12, 2021. https://www.iea.org/policies/1780-perform-achieve-trade-pat-scheme.

International Energy Agency. 2020. India 2020: Energy policy review. January 2020. https://www.iea.org/reports/india-2020.

Intergovernmental Panel on Climate Change. n.d. History of the IPCC. https://www.ipcc.ch/about/history/.

Ivanova, Maria. 2017. Politics, economics, and society. In *The Paris Agreement on Climate Change: Analysis and commentary*, eds. Daniel Klein, Maria Pia Carazo, Meinhard Doelle, Jane Bulmer, and Andrew Higham, 17–26. Oxford, UK: Oxford University Press.

Jervis, Robert. 1968. Hypotheses on misperception. *World Politics* 20 (3): 454–479. https://doi.org/10.2307/2009777.

Jha, Prem Shankar. 2009. Indian public perceptions of the international climate change negotiations. In *India climate change booklet*, eds. David Michel and Amit Pandya, 31–35. Washington, D.C.: Stimson Center. https://www.stimson.org/wp-content/files/India%20Climate%20Change%20Booklet%20FINAL.pdf.

Jones, Dave, and Kathrin Gutmann. 2015. End of an era: Why every European country needs a coal phase-out plan. Climate Action Network Europe and Greenpeace. https://www.greenpeace.de/sites/default/files/publications/end-of-era-coal-phase-out-plan-20151204.pdf.

Jordan, Andrew, Dave Huitema, and Harro van Asselt. 2010. Climate change policy in the European Union: An introduction. In *Climate change policy in the European Union: Confronting the dilemmas of mitigation and adaptation?*, eds. Andrew Jordan, Dave Huitema, Harro van Asselt, Tim Rayner, and Frans Berkhout, 3–26. Cambridge, UK: Cambridge University Press.

Khandekar, Nivedita. 2020. India is taking the climate crisis seriously for the "first time." *EcoWatch*, March 18, 2020. https://www.ecowatch.com/india-climate-crisis-2645524391.html.

Konisky, David. 2020. US environmental policy research in uncertain times. In *Handbook of U.S. environmental policy*, ed. David Konisky, 1–10. Northampton, MA: Edward Elgar.

Ladrech, Robert. 2019. Party politics and EU climate policy. In *EU climate diplomacy: Politics, law and negotiation*, eds. Stephen Minas and Vassilis Ntousas, 13–21. New York: Routledge.

Light, Andrew. 2011. Why Durban matters. Center for American Progress. December 19, 2011. https://www.americanprogress.org/article/why-dur ban-matters/.

Mathiesen, Karl. 2017. India reaffirms Paris climate commitments. *Climate Home News*, November 5, 2017. https://www.climatechangenews.com/2017/05/ 11/indian-energy-minister-reaffirms-paris-climate-commitments/.

Matthes, Felix Christian. 2017. Germany's stance on climate and carbon policy instruments for the power generation sector: Current status and perspectives, implications for France and the European Union. Institut français des rela tions internationales. December 2017. https://www.ifri.org/sites/default/ files/atoms/files/matthes_germany_climate_carbon_policy_2017.pdf.

Michel, David. 2009. Introduction. In *India climate change booklet*, eds. David Michel and Amit Pandya, 1–5. Washington, D.C.: Stimson Center. https://www.stimson.org/wp-content/files/India%20Climate%20C hange%20Booklet%20FINAL.pdf.

Migdal, Joel. 2001. *State in society: Studying how states and societies transform and constitute one another*. Cambridge, UK: Cambridge University Press.

Mildenberger, Matto. 2020. The dynamics of federal climate policy conflict. In *Handbook of U.S. environmental policy*, ed. David Konisky, 275–288. Northampton, MA: Edward Elgar.

Murphy, Bruce, and Hannah Daly. 2018. Electricity in every village in India. International Energy Agency. June 1, 2018. https://www.iea.org/commen taries/electricity-in-every-village-in-india.

Noronha, Ligia. 2009. Climate change and India's energy policy: Challenges and choices. In *India climate change booklet*, eds. David Michel and Amit Pandya, 7–11. Washington, D.C.: Stimson Center. https://www.stimson.org/wp-con tent/files/India%20Climate%20Change%20Booklet%20FINAL.pdf.

Ohliger, Tina. 2015. On the way to COP 21 in Paris. European Parlia ment. June 2015. https://www.europarl.europa.eu/RegData/etudes/BRIE/ 2015/542224/IPOL_BRI(2015)542224_EN.pdf.

Olson, Mancur. 1965. *The logic of collective action*. Cambridge, MA: Harvard University Press.

Pescia, Dimitri, and Emi Ichiyanagi. 2017. *The Energiewende* in a nutshell. Agora Energiewende. https://www.agora-energiewende.de/fileadmin/Pro jekte/2017/Energiewende_in_a_nutshell/Agora_The_Energiewende_in_a_n utshell_WEB.pdf.

Plumer, Brad, and Nadja Popovich. 2018. The world still isn't meeting its climate goals. *The New York Times*, December 7, 2018. https://www.nyt imes.com/interactive/2018/12/07/climate/world-emissions-paris-goals- not-on-track.html.

Political Psychology Research Group. n.d. Partisan views. Stanford University. https://climatepublicopinion.stanford.edu/consumer-choices/partisan-views.

Public Health Foundation of India. 2020. Health and economic impact of air pollution in India. December 22, 2020. https://phfi.org/health-and-eco nomic-impact-of-air-pollution-in-india/.

Putnam, Robert. 1988. Diplomacy and domestic politics: The logic of two-level games. *International Organization* 42 (3): 427–460. https://doi.org/10.1017/S0020818300027697.

Rajamani, Lavanya. 2011. The Cancun Climate Agreements: Reading the text, subtext and tea leaves. *The International and Comparative Law Quarterly* 60 (2): 499–519. https://doi.org/10.1017/S0020589311000078.

Reisman, David. 1990. *Theories of collective action: Downs, Olson and Hirsch.* New York: Palgrave Macmillan.

Renewable Energy World. 2011. New record for German renewable energy in 2010. March 25, 2011. https://www.renewableenergyworld.com/baseload/new-record-for-german-renewable-energy-in-2010/#gref.

Reuters. 2017. Germany set to miss 2020 climate goals by far: study. September 2, 2017. https://www.reuters.com/article/us-germany-climatechange/ger many-set-to-miss-2020-climate-goals-by-far-study-idUSKCN1BI1P6.

Ritchie, Hannah, and Max Roser. n.d. United States: CO_2 country profile. Our World in Data. https://ourworldindata.org/co2/country/united-states.

Rocha, Marcia, Paola Yanguas Parra, Fabio Sferra, Michiel Schaeffer, Niklas Roming, Andrzej Ancygier, Ugur Ural, and Bill Hare. 2017. A stress test for coal in Europe under the Paris Agreement: Scientific goalposts for a coor-dinated phase-out and divestment. Climate Analytics. February 2017. https://climateanalytics.org/media/eu_coal_stress_test_report_2017.pdf.

Royden, Amy. 2002. U.S. climate change policy under President Clinton: A look back. *Golden Gate University Law Review* 32 (4): 415–478. https://digitalco mmons.law.ggu.edu/cgi/viewcontent.cgi?article=1842&context=ggulrev;US.

Ruwitch, John. 2021. On climate, U.S. and China pledge cooper-ation, but competition will also be prominent. NPR. April 21, 2021. https://www.npr.org/2021/04/21/989165775/on-climate-u-s-and-china-pledge-cooperation-but-competition-will-also-be-promine.

Samuelson, Robert. 2018. Who's afraid of global warming? *The Washington Post,* April 25, 2018. https://www.washingtonpost.com/opinions/whos-afr aid-of-global-warming/2018/04/25/e8228960-4897-11e8-827e-190efaf1f 1ee_story.html.

Sauerbrey, Anna. 2019. Does Germany's vaunted car industry have long to live? *The New York Times,* December 30, 2019. https://www.nytimes.com/2019/12/30/opinion/germany-cars-tesla-audi.html.

Sengupta, Sandeep. 2012. Climate change and India's national strategy. In *Grand strategy for India: 2020 and beyond,* eds. Krishnappa Venkatshamy and Princy George, 301–313. New Delhi: Institute for Defence Studies and Analyses.

Singh, Jyotsna, and Rakesh Kamal. 2015. India announces its INDC, pledges to cut emissions intensity of its GDP by 33–35 per cent by 2030. *Down to Earth*, September 30, 2015. https://www.downtoearth.org.in/coverage/climate-change/climate-change-package-51338.

Somanader, Tanya. 2016. President Obama: The United States formally enters the Paris Agreement. United States National Archives and Records Administration. September 3, 2016. https://obamawhitehouse.archives.gov/blog/2016/09/03/president-obama-united-states-formally-enters-paris-agreement.

Stokes, Leah, and Hanna Breetz. 2020. States of crisis: Subnational inaction on climate change in the United States. In *Handbook of U.S. environmental policy*, ed. David Konisky, 289–301. Northampton, MA: Edward Elgar.

Teitelbaum, Henry. 2010. Analysts say COP 15 helped bridge the private-public divide. Ecosystem Marketplace. February 16, 2010. https://www.ecosystemmarketplace.com/articles/analysts-say-cop-15-helped-bridge-the-private-public-divide/.

Thalman, Ellen, and Julian Wettengel. 2019. The story of "Climate Chancellor" Angela Merkel. *Clean Energy Wire*, September 23, 2019. https://www.cleanenergywire.org/factsheets/making-climate-chancellor-angela-merkel.

Tiseo, Ian. 2021. Carbon dioxide emissions in the European Union 2000–2020, by country. Statista. July 22, 2021. https://www.statista.com/statistics/1171389/co2-emissions-european-union/.

Topping, Nigel. 2018. Progress report: India is powering towards a low-carbon future. We Mean Business Coalition. July 30, 2018. https://www.wemeanbusinesscoalition.org/blog/progress-report-india-powering-towards-low-carbon-future/.

United Nations. 1992. United Nations Framework Convention on Climate Change. May 9, 1992. https://unfccc.int/resource/docs/convkp/conveng.pdf.

United Nations. 1998. Kyoto Protocol to the United Nations Convention on Climate Change. December 11, 1997. https://unfccc.int/resource/docs/convkp/kpeng.pdf.

United Nations. 2009. Draft Decision -/CP.15, proposal by the President, Copenhagen Accord. December 18, 2009. https://unfccc.int/resource/docs/2009/cop15/eng/l07.pdf.

United Nations. 2015. COP21: UN chief hails new climate change agreement as "monumental triumph." *UN News*, December 12, 2015. https://news.un.org/en/story/2015/12/517982.

United Nations. 2016. The Paris agreement: Frequently asked questions. September 12, 2016. https://www.un.org/sustainabledevelopment/blog/2016/09/the-paris-agreement-faqs/.

80   C. HULME

United Nations. n.d. What is the United Nations Framework Convention on Climate Change? https://unfccc.int/process-and-meetings/what-is-the-united-nations-framework-convention-on-climate-change.

United Nations Climate Change. 2015. Press release: Historic Paris Agreement on Climate Change. December 12, 2015. https://unfccc.int/files/press/press_releases_advisories/application/pdf/pr20151112_cop21_final.pdf.

United Nations Climate Change. n.d. What is the Kyoto Protocol? https://unfccc.int/kyoto_protocol.

UN, Sushma. 2018. India is forcing large power consumers to use more renewable energy. *Quartz India*, June 18, 2018. https://qz.com/india/1307648/india-is-forcing-large-power-consumers-to-use-more-renewable-energy.

Vaughan, Adam, and David Adam. 2009. Copenhagen climate deal: Spectacular failure—Or a few important steps? *The Guardian*, December 22, 2009. https://www.theguardian.com/environment/2009/dec/22/copenhagen-climate-deal-expert-view.

Walker, Hayley, and Katja Biedenkopf. 2018. The historical evolution of EU climate leadership and four scenarios for its future. In *EU climate diplomacy: Politics, law and negotiations*, eds. Stephen Minas and Vassilis Ntousas, 33–46. New York: Routledge.

Wehrmann, Benjamin. 2017. German Greens confident pro-climate government coalition possible. *Clean Energy Wire*, October 9, 2017. https://www.cleanenergywire.org/news/german-greens-confident-pro-climate-government-coalition-possible.

Wehrmann, Benjamin. 2020. Government studies find Germany's 2030 climate package fails to reach objective. *Clean Energy Wire*, March 6, 2020. https://www.cleanenergywire.org/news/govt-studies-find-germanys-2030-climate-package-fails-reach-objective.

Weidner, Helmut, and Lutz Mez. 2008. German climate change policy: A success story with some flaws. *The Journal of Environment & Development* 17 (4): 356–378. https://doi.org/10.1177/1070496508325910.

The White House. 1997. Remarks as prepared for delivery for Vice President Al Gore: Kyoto Climate Change Conference. United States National Archives and Records Administration. December 8, 1997. https://clintonwhitehouse2.archives.gov/WH/EOP/OVP/speeches/kyotofin.html.

The White House. 2014. U.S.-China joint announcement on climate change. United States National Archives and Records Administration. November 12, 2014. https://obamawhitehouse.archives.gov/the-press-office/2014/11/11/us-china-joint-announcement-climate-change.

The White House. 2015. U.S. leadership and the historic Paris Agreement to combat climate change. United States National Archives and Records Administration. December 12, 2015. https://obamawhitehouse.archives.gov/the-press-office/2015/12/12/us-leadership-and-historic-paris-agreement-combat-climate-change.

Yeo, Sophie. 2015. Explainer: The "ratchet" mechanism within the Paris climate deal. *Carbon Brief*, December 3, 2015. https://www.carbonbrief.org/Explainer-the-ratchet-mechanism-within-the-paris-climate-deal/.

CHAPTER 3

The Train Has Left the Station: Automotive and Energy-Intensive Industries

INTRODUCTION

During the 2010s, the private sector emerged as an unlikely climate actor, adopting an increasingly climate-active approach and presenting itself as an indispensable leader in an issue area poised to shape the twenty-first century. By the turn of the 2020s, relatively few major corporations seriously challenged the importance of preparing for a climate change-driven global low-carbon transition. Why? This book argues that corporations—specifically, the class of "corporate nations" with the resources and geographic scope of interests to rival the majority of states (Francis 2016)—perceived that their environment was changing in two key ways. First, with climate change gaining international recognition and concern, corporations, recognizing that it was not just one issue among many but one set to shape future trends, increasingly placed their bets on a low-carbon future. Second, while corporations became more convinced that they were headed toward a low-carbon future due to pressures and developments linked to climate change, they became less confident that states would lead in this issue area, providing the type of predictable and effective policy and regulation needed to nurture conditions for corporations' success in such a future. Corporations gradually began behaving in ways that were more compatible with a low-carbon future, acting as if certain

© The Author(s), under exclusive license to Springer Nature Switzerland AG 2023
C. Hulme, *Corporate Climate Action, Transnational Politics, and World Order*, Environmental Politics and Theory, https://doi.org/10.1007/978-3-031-34115-1_3

83

new "rules of the game" existed despite states not providing them and despite lacking confidence that states would do so in the near future.

Strikingly, corporations altered their behavior and arrived at a consensus about climate change and a low-carbon future—and did so specifically in the absence of state leadership—while not perceiving that climate change per se posed increasingly urgent material risks or presented more promising opportunities, including consumer demand for low-carbon, climate-friendly products. Coalescing around certain climate-relevant practices as the new paradigm of behavior necessary to adopt for future success despite individual actors perceiving little sense of urgency, corporations came into an effective concert, "sensing some shift in conditions, sensing each other's intuitions," and beginning to "[shift] direction *en masse*" (Brooks 2020).

This chapter evaluates this overarching pattern of behavior from the perspective of two industry groups—automotive and energy-intensive[1]—which, with fossil fuel-dependent business models, are strong incumbents deeply invested in the high-carbon economy with particularly high barriers to meaningful changes in climate-related behavior. The chapter shows that companies in the energy-intensive group made considerably more progress in climate performance and were earlier in reorienting themselves toward a more climate-active approach than automakers. However, although automakers were weaker climate performers and contributed less to the overall story of the private sector developing into a key climate actor in the 2010s, in both industry groups there was evidence of behavior reflecting the core dynamic that this book investigates: diminishing concern about the urgency of climate-related material risks and opportunities was coupled with increasing levels of climate activity.

In short, this chapter begins to establish the empirical basis for the book's claim that the overarching new pattern of corporate climate action that developed in the 2010s was not grounded in how individual companies perceived the material relevance of climate change per se but instead was a function of a growing shared understanding, or consensus view,

---

[1] The energy-intensive group encompasses six industries: cement, chemical, oil and gas, pharmaceutical, power, and steel. These industries were examined together because while there are seven automakers in the sample set, enabling an industry-level analysis, there are just one to three companies in each of the six energy-intensive industries, making it difficult to draw meaningful conclusions specific to any one industry but possible to consider the significance of their overall behavior.

about the private sector's role in the issue area. As Chapter 1 proposed, the budding consensus—which, in a virtuous cycle, began establishing roots due to early corporate climate activity, and, spurring additional activity, became more deeply entrenched—acted as a "steering mechanism" (Rosenau 1995, 14) leading companies to take up new types and levels of climate activity despite the apparent lack of powerful individual incentives to do so. As this chapter considers, that select companies tethered tightly to the high-carbon economy adopted a certain complement of more climate-active behaviors amid their declining outlook for bold climate regulation and policy underscores how failures of state leadership on critical transnational issues can create conditions for even the unlikeliest of actors to coalesce around a different approach and play an important role in shaping an issue area of high salience in the international security landscape.

PART I: THE AUTOMOTIVE INDUSTRY

The infamous "Dieselgate" scandal began unfolding in September 2015, when Volkswagen admitted to manipulating the software in 11 million cars worldwide so that they would pass laboratory emissions tests while emitting 40 times more nitrous oxide on the road than was legally permitted (Hotten 2015).[2] Dieselgate cost the company over $30 billion in fines and buybacks (Kabel 2019), with part of the late 2015 decline in sales that it registered in Germany, the United Kingdom, and the United States interpreted by some as a consumer backlash (Sharman 2015).[3] Overall, however, consumers hardly imposed a harsh penalty; in fact, Volkswagen posted record sales in 2016 (Cremer 2017). Such a consumer response would have been unsurprising to one sustainability expert, previously at Volkswagen, who, in a 2018 interview for this book, assessed that in Germany consumer demand for green products was a non-issue: "There is none. Consumers don't care" (Telephone conversation with author, November 6, 2018). A Daimler executive shared a similar view

---

[2] The emissions rate of 40 times more nitrous oxide than was legally permitted refers specifically to pollutant standards in the United States, where the "defeat device," or software altering emissions performance during testing, first was discovered.

[3] Volkswagen also had stopped selling models affected by the "defeat device," which accounted for part of the decline in sales.

86   C. HULME

that year: "The current outlook is that we need to be at CO_2 neutral, basically, by 2050. Of course, we can have the portfolio totally turned around by that time. The big question is, are there people who will buy that?" Daimler customers, whether in Germany, the United States, or China, "want to buy more SUVs," she explained. "That is what we see in our sales" (Stuttgart, Germany, October 15, 2018).

Yet, in 2017, Volkswagen forecast that by 2025, "one in every four new vehicles manufactured by our Group around the world will run on all-electric powertrains," and announced plans to electrify the "entire model range" (about 300 models) by 2030 at the latest—an endeavor that would entail over €20 billion in direct investments.[4] That year, Volkswagen partnered with Daimler, BMW, and Ford to launch a joint venture, IONITY, aimed at "the construction and operation of high-performance charging stations for battery electric vehicles in Europe. The plan is to build some 400 fast-charging stations by 2020 in order to support electric mobility on long-haul routes and thereby establish the market" (BMW Group 2018, 149). In a 2018 interview, when asked about the electric vehicle [EV] market in Germany, a Volkswagen executive shared his belief that "we are right now close to a tipping point.... This, I think, is now the time where it totally changes." He explained,

> If you look at the global numbers by the end of 2016, I think in the global market, over history, two million [EVs] were sold. By the end of 2017, it was three million. And we're going to see a massive uptake in the near future. So, according to our plans, we expect to have roughly 25% of sales being [EVs] in 2025, with a steep, steep increase in e-cars on the road. (Telephone conversation with author, November 23, 2018)

Meanwhile, in 2019, in what Tesla CEO Elon Musk characterized as "very meaningful action by the company that invented the internal combustion engine" (Schmidt 2019), Daimler's head of development announced that the company had no plans for developing new internal combustion engines and instead would focus on electrification, electric drives, and battery development (Hebermehl 2019).

---

[4] Information from Volkswagen's 2018 CDP disclosure. Complete access to CDP disclosures available through subscription; contact author for information on all disclosures referenced in this chapter: hulmecharlottej@gmail.com.

By the late 2010s and turn of the 2020s, some of the world's largest automakers were behaving as if a much different future was on the horizon, despite seeming evidence to the contrary. For instance, consistent with the pattern of consumer behavior described by the Daimler executive and former Volkswagen sustainability expert cited above, in 2019, the year of Daimler's announcement, not only did fuel-inefficient sport utility vehicles (SUVs) and off-road vehicles achieve a record-high market share in Germany, its largest single-country market in Europe, but there were only 100,000 EVs registered in the country, falling badly short of Berlin's 2009 target to have one million EVs on the road by 2020 (Franke 2019). Meanwhile, in China, Volkswagen's largest market by one million vehicles, although EVs had gained ground since 2016, growth still was being driven primarily by demand for SUVs, not EVs (Volkswagen 2018, 103).

It was not just German automakers behaving as though a new dominant design, or standard of practice necessary to ensure survival and success in an anticipated future, had arrived. In 2013, Ford had expressed ambivalence about what the future would look like, stating that rather than going all-in on low-emission vehicles, it would pursue an approach called "the power of choice," with a complete technology range of gasoline, diesel, hybrid, plug-in hybrid, and electric propulsion systems. This approach was preferable because "it allows customers to choose the vehicle that best meets their driving needs." Further, Ford explained, "We also believe that traditional gasoline- and diesel-powered vehicles with internal combustion engines will continue to be a major part of the mix for quite some time" (Ford Motor Company n.d., "A portfolio approach"). By 2018, however, Ford had joined the IONITY venture with the Big Three German automakers, created a dedicated EV team to "dramatically accelerate our electric vehicle plans," and announced the planned expansion of its "electrified portfolio to 40 electrified vehicles globally, including 16 full battery electric vehicles" (Ford 2018, "Sustainability" and "Letter from the Executive Chairman").[5] Ford also had "increased planned investments in electrification to over $11 billion by

---

[5] Of particular note concerning Ford's joining IONITY is that the United States remained its largest single-country market by 20 percentage points; in 2016, the United States accounted for 39% of global sales, while China, its second-largest market, accounted for 19%. Ford Motor Company (2017, 4).

2022" to "substantially increase the number of battery electric vehicles we offer around the world" (Ford 2018, 29). In the 2017 annual report, Ford's President and CEO remarked that "we are clearly entering a period of radical disruption" (Ford 2018, "Letter from our President and CEO").

Meanwhile, throughout the decade General Motors (GM) had seemed committed to "business as usual" in terms of its approach to issues concerning climate change and a potential low-carbon future; as this chapter shows, it was one of the weakest performers in the automaker cohort. In its 2017 annual report, however, GM conceded that "the automotive industry will experience significant and continued change in the coming years," and admitted that its own future success would require developing new "products and services that are outside of our historically core business, such as autonomous and electric vehicles" (General Motors 2018, 10). Following President Donald Trump's failed reelection bid in November 2020, GM announced that it no longer would support his administration's legal challenge to California's right to mandate zero-emission vehicles. CEO Mary Barra remarked, "We believe the ambitious electrification goals of the President-elect [Joe Biden], California, and General Motors are aligned, to address climate change by drastically reducing automobile emissions" (CBS News 2020).[6] In early 2021, GM announced that by 2035 it would stop manufacturing all gas and diesel vehicles, a move characterized as "a seismic shift by one of the world's largest automakers that makes billions of dollars today from gas-guzzling pickup trucks and sport utility vehicles" (Boudette and Davenport 2021). After GM's announcement, Ford revealed that it would be "increasing its electric-vehicle investment to $22 billion through 2025, almost double what it had previously pledged to spend." CEO Jim Farley noted, "We're not going to cede the future to anyone." Even prior to its early 2021 announcement, analysts claimed that with its new EV strategy GM was bringing about "one of the most profound strategic turnarounds, not just in the auto industry, but in business" (Stankiewicz 2021). While the outcome of the 2020 presidential election undoubtedly provided a fillip, GM's "profound strategic turnaround" was not simply a function

---

[6] Chrysler and Toyota also had sided with the Trump administration, while Ford, Volkswagen, BMW, and Honda had remained neutral. Notably, General Motors and Chrysler were the weakest climate performers in this chapter, while Volkswagen and BMW were the strongest.

of changing political and regulatory winds in the United States—which can change dramatically from one administration to the next—but was grounded in deeper changes in the landscape. GM, which throughout most of the 2010s was oriented toward the status quo, was behaving as if it had to "catch up" to a new global reality—one not of its own making.

GM was not alone. As this chapter explores, none of the seven incumbent automakers was ahead of the curve in adopting the new dominant design. During most of the 2010s, these strong incumbents did not anticipate how quickly the climate and low-carbon game would change, and failed to appreciate that their old assumptions about the issue area no longer would work going forward. Perhaps nothing so vividly captures their failure as the changing fortunes of Tesla, whose stock had risen by more than 4900% by early 2021 since its initial public offering in 2010. In 2009, Tesla was "on its deathbed" when a $50 million investment by Daimler rescued the EV upstart from the brink of collapse (Thompson 2015); at the time, it would have seemed nearly inconceivable that in 11 years, with a market capitalization of $208 billion, Tesla would surpass Toyota as the world's most valuable automaker (Korosec 2020). It would have been equally difficult to imagine that Tesla would achieve this distinction never having had a profitable year since going public (Kolodny 2020), and having annual sales of 367,500 units compared to Toyota's 10.74 million (Japan Times 2020)—a powerful indication of the market betting on its future profitability, and thus on the low-carbon, EV-centered future on which its business model hinged. During the early to mid-2010s, legacy automakers assumed that such a future was more distant than it actually was.

From the vantage point of the early 2010s, the status quo *had* appeared durable; there was significant market uncertainty about the timing of a potential low-carbon transition, particularly as ramifications of the Great Recession continued to reverberate. Especially unclear was how politicians in key markets planned to bridge the gap between ambitious EV targets and paltry consumer interest. For example, one study found that in 2009, when Berlin announced a target of one million EVs on the road by 2020, there were only 162 EVs among the 3.8 million new cars registered in Germany that year (Lieven et al. 2011, 236). Likewise, a 2012 McKinsey report found that in 2011, there were just 6000 EVs and plug-in hybrid electric vehicles produced in China, "taking the industry just a fraction of the way to the half-million units of production capacity the government had originally expected for 2015." In fact, McKinsey ranked China only

90   C. HULME

fifth globally in terms of EV market maturity, after Japan, the United States, France, and Germany (Krieger et al. 2012). Automakers' failure during the 2010s to appreciate just how quickly the game could change, and ultimately did change, led one Germany-based industry watcher to project in 2019 that, facing the "biggest crisis since the invention of the automobile," no one in the industry "will survive in the form they exist today" (Miller and Campbell 2019).

Automakers' Behavior, 2010–2017

While automakers failed to act as early movers in adjusting their interest sets to reprioritize climate change and a low-carbon future for success and even survival in the future, some began such a reorientation prior to the industry reckoning more seriously with these issues in the late 2010s. For each three-year period spanning 2010–2017, Table 3.1 classifies seven of the world's largest automakers as one of four types: *business as usual* (BAU), *evolutionary*, *innovator*, and *disruptor* (listed from lowest to highest level of climate action). As the appendix describes, each type corresponds to a range of scores. The higher the score, the more robust a company's action and the better its performance across three metrics of climate-related behavior: *product*, capturing the extent to which companies addressed their emissions; *alignment*, conveying the degree to which they made their activities more coherent with a low-carbon future; and *investment*, reflecting the extent to which they allocated resources to support such a future. The industry-specific practices corresponding to these metrics were producing low- and zero-emission vehicles (*product*), applying an internal carbon price (*alignment*), and investing in low-carbon research and development (*investment*). Table 3.1 conveys the degree to which the cohort moved toward a more climate-active approach and the extent to which individual companies increased their cumulative performance across the three metrics. In the last column, company names are in bold if they belonged to higher types in the last period than in the first. The last row shows the total points for all automakers in each period and the percent change between periods, capturing when and to what extent underlying momentum toward increased action gathered in 2010–2017.

By 2015–2017, four automakers (57%) belonged to higher types than in 2010–2012, having made sufficient changes in their climate approach and performance. However, just two of the four that transitioned to

3 THE TRAIN HAS LEFT THE STATION: AUTOMOTIVE ...   91

Table 3.1   Automaker types, 2010–2017

Type (points)	2010–2012 (period 1)	2011–2013 (period 2)	2012–2014 (period 3)	2013–2015 (period 4)	2014–2016 (period 5)	2015–2017 (period 6)
Disruptor (16–20)						
Innovator (13–15)					VW, 13	VW, 15 BMW, 13
Evolutionary (9–12)	BMW, 10 Daimler, 10	BMW, 11 Daimler, 10 VW, 9	BMW, 11 Daimler, 11 VW, 9	BMW, 12 VW, 12 Daimler, 11	BMW, 12 Daimler, 12 Toyota, 9	Daimler, 12 Ford, 10 Toyota, 9
BAU (0–8)	Toyota, 8 VW, 8 Ford, 7 Chrysler, 6 GM, 6	Ford, 7 Toyota, 7 GM, 6 Chrysler, 5	GM, 7 Toyota, 7 Chrysler, 6 Ford, 6	GM, 8 Toyota, 8 Ford, 6 Chrysler, 5	Ford, 8 GM, 8 Chrysler, 7	Chrysler, 7 GM, 7
Total points (% change)	55 (–)	55 (–)	57 (4%)	62 (9%)	69 (11%)	73 (6%) (net:+33%)

Source Author

Note Seven automakers, classified according to three-year performance on *product, alignment*, and *investment*. Companies received points out of 20 based on where they fell on a performance spectrum

a higher type became innovators and none became disruptors, demonstrating a limited level of ambition. Yet, while the company cohort made limited progress in terms of type changes, there were meaningful gains in underlying momentum. For example, while there was little or no change in the cohort's cumulative score in the first two inter-period changes, between periods 3 and 6, there was a 28% increase. Of particular significance is the change (9%) between periods 3 and 4, representing progress achieved prior to either of two events that have been interpreted by some experts as turning points in how automakers worldwide approached the climate change issue area: the Dieselgate scandal, news of which broke in September 2015,[7] and the Paris Climate Conference, which took place in December 2015. Considering momentum at the company level, once automakers transitioned to a higher level of action they never regressed.

---

[7] As Amelang and Wehrmann noted, Dieselgate "started out as a scandal exclusively affecting Germany's largest car company[,] Volkswagen. But since it broke in September 2015, it has morphed into a global issue involving many industry giants" (2020).

92   C. HULME

Identifying New Climate Practices

Table 3.2 displays as a percentage the number of automakers out of seven receiving any points for the three metrics in a given period, capturing the degree to which specific climate-related practices became more widely adopted ("breadth"). To receive points for adopting the industry-specific practice corresponding to each metric, automakers had to meet a certain threshold of action. Table 3.2 also shows the degree to which companies enhanced their commitment to the three practices, conveying the percentage of companies receiving over half the available points for a given metric ("depth").

Considering the breadth of climate activity, automakers demonstrated confidence in a future where low-emissions vehicles would be a key part of their portfolios, consistently addressing their emissions (the product metric) and investing in a low-carbon future (the investment metric). In the early 2010s, a low-carbon future had entered the automakers' field of vision. In period 1, for example, Ford reported that it was "pursuing an aggressive electrified vehicle strategy" (Ford 2011, 20); Volkswagen announced that with fleet trials beginning in 2011, it would "usher in the age of pure e-mobility in the Group in 2013, taking the electric car out of the niche and bringing it to the mass market" (Volkswagen 2011, 200); and BMW launched a separate EV sub-brand (BMW Group 2012, 20). Meanwhile, the 307% increase in participation in the industry-specific

Table 3.2 Breadth and depth of automakers' climate action, 2010–2017

Years (period)	Breadth			Depth		
	Product	Alignment	Investment	Product	Alignment	Investment
2010–2012 (1)	100	14	86	14	100	54
2011–2013 (2)	100	14	86	19	100	39
2012–2014 (3)	100	29	86	24	78	33
2013–2015 (4)	100	43	86	29	53	36
2014–2016 (5)	100	57	86	43	28	45
2015–2017 (6)	100	57	86	57	28	48
Percent change, periods 1–6	0	+307	0	+307	−72	−11

Source Author
Note Breadth captures the percentage of automakers receiving any points for *product, alignment,* and *investment.* Depth captures the percentage receiving over half the available points for performance on these metrics

practice for the alignment metric (using an internal carbon price) captures how automakers became increasingly confident that carbon would carry a cost in the future.

If the data concerning the breadth of climate action captures how automakers perceived from 2010 onward that a low-carbon future was within their field of vision, the data addressing the depth of action shows the shadow of the future shortening, captured by *product*'s 307% gain. In concrete terms, this increase reflects companies placing greater emphasis on EVs in their portfolios. Indeed, early in the decade automakers were long on lofty rhetoric about a low-carbon future but short on action to prepare seriously for such a future. It was not until later in the decade that they put "muscle" behind their rhetoric and began to make strategic decisions supporting root change in their portfolios. In 2015, for example, Volkswagen's low-carbon portfolio gained momentum with a plan to launch more than 20 new plug-in hybrid electric vehicles (PHEVs) and fully battery-powered EVs by 2020 (Volkswagen 2016, 8–9). By 2017, the company announced plans to launch more than 30 different types of EVs "and to sell between two and three million [EVs] by 2025—equivalent to around 20–25% of the Group's expected total unit sales" (Volkswagen 2017, 52). Then, in 2017, with its new "Roadmap E"—"the most far-reaching electrification initiative our industry has ever seen"—Volkswagen became "the first major mobility company to commit to a specific deadline for the full electrification of its fleet," encompassing about 300 models, "across all brands and markets."[8] By 2018, Ford also emphasized EVs to a much greater extent than it had even as recently as 2015 (Ford Motor Company 2018, 29).

In short, companies increasingly were not just making relatively conservative changes to their portfolios (e.g., investing in hybrids), but were moving forward on more ambitious technologies (e.g., producing EVs). While automakers started with low-hanging fruit (e.g., improving the fuel efficiency of conventional vehicles or investing in hybrid technology), by the 2015–2017 period their portfolio strategies were beginning to reflect fundamental change. The major drop in the depth of *alignment* activity—utilizing an internal carbon price—was a function of the fact that more companies became participants in the behavior over time but were not as committed to internal carbon pricing as BMW, which for several periods

---

[8] Information from Volkswagen's 2018 CDP disclosure.

94   C. HULME

both was the only company to report having adopted this practice and consistently took an ambitious approach.[9]

For each industry group that this book explores, certain climate-related practices were treated as more significant than others, depending on the nature of the industry's activities and the major sources of its contribution to greenhouse gas emissions (the appendix provides details about how different practices were treated across different industries). For the automotive industry, the most significant type of behavior was producing low- and zero-emissions vehicles, making *product* the most heavily weighted metric. Thus, Table 3.2 underscores that once automakers "got in the game," however belatedly, they became more committed to the most significant kind of climate-related behavior.

* * *

Examining how automakers behaved during 2010–2017 reveals mixed progress toward a new climate approach. Four of seven (57%) transitioned to higher types; once the company cohort moved forward, it never regressed. Yet, ambitious action was limited; by period 6, only two companies were innovators, while three were evolutionaries and two BAUs. Why did automakers fail to appreciate more fully or respond more quickly to a new dominant design as it was developing around them? The German context powerfully illustrates the changing relationship between corporations and states that is an underlying concern of this book—and that in this industry case study helps to explain why companies failed to more quickly "catch the tide" of the new climate and low-carbon game, and found themselves in a position of scrambling to catch up to a new dominant design that largely had taken shape without them.

Historically, Berlin, while generally behaving in a climate-active fashion, has sought to protect the automotive industry from the most ambitious EU climate-related regulations. As the head of the Federation of German Consumer Organisations put it as the Dieselgate scandal came

---

[9] Some of the newer participants in internal carbon pricing used existing prices of the EU Emissions Trading System or other regional pricing schemes as opposed to setting their own, more ambitious prices. BMW focused on the costs of carbon emissions "in the planning phase of investment decisions" to increase "the incentive to implement emissions reduction activities. Costs of carbon emissions are included in profitability calculations and are reflected in the return on investment." Information from BMW's 2011 CDP disclosure.

to light, "Until now the German auto industry has been handled with kid gloves by the politicians." This was especially true of Volkswagen, which historically enjoyed "particularly strong" political connections (Barkin 2015). While Germany long has prided itself on being a climate leader, at key moments the government has proven unreliable in enforcing tough rules on the automotive industry. As Chapter 2 explored, in 2013, for example, after five years of negotiations had produced agreement among EU Member States about a new round of emissions standards for automobiles, Chancellor Angela Merkel intervened with the EU Council President and succeeded in getting the subject removed from the agenda, delaying the process by one year—and ultimately leading to "watered-down rules" (Thalman and Wettengel 2019).

Berlin's willingness to compromise its climate-active agenda for Germany's most important industry, failing to translate tough rhetoric into action, historically benefitted automakers. By the late 2010s, however, as a low-carbon future seemed increasingly likely and as the climate change issue achieved mounting global recognition and concern, it *also* became clear that such an approach now put automakers at a serious disadvantage.

The conventional wisdom is that by the late 2010s, German automakers believed that Berlin would become tougher in forcing climate-related rules on the industry. A PricewaterhouseCoopers expert articulated this understanding in a 2018 interview, arguing that Dieselgate and the Paris Agreement profoundly altered the regulatory environment for German automakers; he characterized these as two "basic streams" that were "very, very much causing policymakers to step in and force tighter regulation on the industry" (Telephone conversation with author, October 23, 2018). By the late 2010s, automakers undeniably confronted an evolving policy and regulatory environment, not only in Germany but also in other key markets, including China (Loh et al. 2019). But, as the following section explores, the conventional wisdom fails to capture fully how corporations actually interpreted changes in their environment. During the 2010s, automakers reported becoming less concerned with the prospects for climate-related policy and regulation that would entail high levels of material impact—and it was in this context that they began to alter their behavior. Automakers, increasingly wanting predictable, ambitious, and effective rules in the climate issue area, yet lacking confidence that governments, including Berlin, would provide them, belatedly came to appreciate the need to behave as if certain such rules existed nonetheless.

96   C. HULME

Industry-Level Foundations of the Emergent Climate Consensus

Although the automotive industry was "late to the game" in becoming a more serious climate player, some companies did alter their approach meaningfully, particularly in the 2015–2017 period when there was a growing understanding that a low-carbon future would arrive sooner than had been anticipated. The company cohort progressed toward a higher level of climate action, improving its overall performance on the metrics of action (product, alignment, and investment) by 33% in the 2010–2017 timeframe. Strikingly, and parting with the conventional wisdom, automakers altered their behavior, becoming more serious about a low-carbon future, in the context of diminishing concerns about the material impacts of climate change, and, crucially for this book's arguments, specifically amid a declining outlook for robust state climate action. This pattern reflects, at the industry level, the emergent dynamic central to this book: given how companies perceived the material relevance of the climate change issue—most companies did not rank the issue particularly high in their interest sets—a new shared understanding in the private sector about the need for a different strategy would have been hard to anticipate.

Table 3.3 displays results from analyzing annual CDP surveys from 2010 to 2016 tracking whether companies reported salient risks and opportunities tied to climate-related regulation and changing consumer behavior—risks and opportunities were treated as salient depending on the time horizon and degree of certainty that companies reported (see the appendix for details)—and if so, with what anticipated level of material impact.[10] In particular, Table 3.3 reflects whether companies reported to CDP that the two climate-related factors posed high-impact risks or opportunities (with each company defining for itself what high-impact meant). If all automakers in a certain period perceived that climate-related regulation and changing consumer behavior entailed high-impact risks and opportunities, the "perceived high material impact" column would register 100. Table 3.3 separates the data concerning perceptions of climate change overall as a high-impact issue (combining the two factors)

---

[10] The perception data in this chapter excludes 2017 due to changes in the CDP disclosure questions that compromise the comparability of the 2017 responses with those of previous years. Thus, there is perception data only for periods 1 through 5.

from that specific to concerns about high-impact risks and/or opportunities from regulation and from changing consumer behavior, providing a more granular picture of the factors behind changes in how automakers saw the climate change issue.

Within the auto industry, there was a declining perception that climate change overall was a high-impact material concern. The outlook for regulatory action in the climate issue area diminished considerably (27%), while the perception that changing consumer behavior posed a high level of material risk or opportunity declined nearly twice as much (52%). As Chapter 1 considered, one of the key alternative explanations for the new private sector pattern of climate action developing in the 2010s is that companies felt increasing pressure from consumers to alter their behavior. As Table 3.3 underscores, however, this explanation is not supported by the data; during the 2010–2016 timeframe, consumer behavior became significantly less of a concern for automakers as they assessed the climate issue area.

How relevant was climate change perceived to be for those four automakers that transitioned to higher types over time? Table 3.4 captures whether companies that changed types perceived the climate issue as a high-impact material concern. If a company in a given period perceived that climate-related regulation and changing consumer behavior entailed high-impact risks and opportunities, Table 3.4 would reflect a score of

Table 3.3 Perceived high material impact of climate change among automakers, 2010–2016

Years (period)	Perceived high material impact		
	Overall	Regulation	Consumer
2010–2012 (1)	35	41	29
2011–2013 (2)	35	41	29
2012–2014 (3)	31	36	25
2013–2015 (4)	24	32	16
2014–2016 (5)	22	30	14
Percent change, periods 1–5	−37	−27	−52

Source Author

Note Among automakers, the percentage of climate-related risks and opportunities that were perceived to be a high-impact material concern

98   C. HULME

100. Data concerning perceptions of climate change overall as a high-impact issue is separated from that specific to concerns about high-impact risks and opportunities from regulation and from consumer behavior.

Given the industry- and company-level findings about improvements in climate performance, the data in Tables 3.3 and 3.4 suggests a mechanism "steering" automakers toward different practices—the "invisible hand" of a growing corporate consensus about the need for a new approach to the climate issue area amid a leadership lacuna left by states. This mechanism helps to make sense of why the industry became more climate-active when company-level foundations for such behavior seemingly were lacking. For example, in 2015–2017, in the context of the overall outlook for high-impact regulation having declined by 27% between periods 1 and 5, and perceived prospects for major risks or opportunities stemming from changes in consumer behavior having dropped by 52% in the same timeframe, 75% of the cohort's type changes occurred (with BMW becoming an innovator and Ford and Toyota changing from BAUs to evolutionaries).

The data in Table 3.4 demonstrates two cases of especially visible "steering" at work: BMW and Volkswagen. BMW, having never perceived

Table 3.4 Perceived high material impact of climate change for automakers increasing climate performance sufficiently to change types, 2010–2016

Years (period)	Overall				Regulation				Consumer			
	BMW	Ford	TM	VW	BMW	Ford	TM	VW	BMW	Ford	TM	VW
2010–2012 (1)	0	0	58	92	0	0	100	83	0	0	17	100
2011–2013 (2)	0	0	50	75	0	0	100	67	0	0	0	83
2012–2014 (3)	0	0	50	58	0	0	100	50	0	0	0	67
2013–2015 (4)	0	0	50	50	0	0	100	50	0	0	0	50
2014–2016 (5)	0	8	50	58	0	17	100	50	0	0	0	67

Source Author

Note For automakers that increased climate performance sufficiently to change types (i.e., becoming *evolutionaries*, *innovators*, or *disruptors*), the percentage of climate-related risks and opportunities that were perceived to be a high-impact material concern. TM is Toyota Motors climate change to be a high-impact material concern, in terms of regulation or changing consumer behavior, offers a particularly strong example at the company level of a disjunction between perception and action; it was one of just two automakers to become an innovator. Volkswagen offers another clear example of a company seemingly being guided toward certain behavior by a steering mechanism not tied to its individual assessment of the direct material relevance of the climate issue. Over time, its perception of climate change as a high-impact material concern declined by 37%, while it transitioned from a BAU in 2010–2012 to an innovator in 2015–2017.

The most significant changes related to specific climate-related practices were, first, that more automakers came to use an internal carbon price (the indicator practice for the alignment metric) and, second, that they became more deeply committed to including low- and zero-emission vehicles in their portfolios (the indicator practice for the product metric). The fewest number of automakers were using an internal carbon price during the periods (1 and 2) in which they most viewed climate change, in terms of regulation and changing consumer behavior, as likely to have high material impacts. Over time, as climate change became perceived as less of an urgent material concern, more companies came to use an internal carbon price—a particularly striking development, given that internal carbon pricing seeks to mitigate potential material risks from carbon exposure. Likewise, automakers were least committed to emphasizing low- and zero-emission vehicles in their product portfolios during the periods (1 and 2) that the perception that climate change was a high-impact material concern was highest. Over time, as climate change per se became less of a material concern at the individual firm level, automakers became more serious about offering vehicles that were compatible with a low-carbon future.

This counterintuitive inconsistency—where less concern about the material impacts of the climate issue was coupled with instances of broader and deeper climate action—is, this book argues, the signature of an emergent consensus behaving as a steering mechanism, guiding firms to adopt certain behaviors based on a growing shared understanding about the issue area and the private sector's role therein. This was the unexpected context in which automakers accepted by the turn of the 2020s that a new dominant design was on their doorstep, and determined that it was incumbent on them to catch up, having failed to appreciate fully changes in their environment during the 2010s.

Part II: Energy-Intensive Industries

Like some of the world's leading automakers, particularly during the first half of the 2010s, RWE, which is Germany's largest utility and Europe's biggest polluter (Morison and Carr 2018), remained strongly entrenched in the status quo and oriented toward a "business as usual" approach toward the climate change issue area and the question of a low-carbon future. Throughout much of the decade, it registered very little climate-relevant action. In the early 2010s, RWE, reporting that coal accounted for the "lion's share" of its generation capacity at 50% (RWE 2011, 8), announced the goal of "a generation portfolio that is 75% low-carbon or carbon-free by 2025, most of it either renewables- or gas based,"[11] and pledged that by 2020 renewable energy would have at least a 20% share, up from under 8% in 2011 (RWE 2012, 5, 28). Yet, the next year it announced it would invest "much less than we had originally planned" in expanding renewables and that "we cannot maintain our goal for 2020, either" (RWE 2013, 33). In 2012, in fact, coal's share in RWE's generation capacity had increased 26% compared to 2011 (to 63%), while renewable energy's already small share had declined to just 5% (RWE 2013, 53).

However, in 2016, RWE split its renewables-focused subsidiary, Innogy, into a separate entity (which later became a subsidiary of E.ON). The "key idea of this demerger," explained an expert with Innogy who used to work for RWE, "was to separate the conventional parts of the business from the green parts of the business. It was not to separate only the renewables part from the rest, but everything which is not CO_2-emitting: renewables, grid, and retail." Why did RWE make this decision? According to this interviewee, one of the main motivations was "to remain attractive for investors, because there are more and more international investors who say, 'I'm not going to invest in anything which is carbon-rich. I'm not going to invest in coal mines, coal—sometimes even in gas-fired power plants.' So, if you want to remain attractive for these kinds of investors, you have to set up a business which is completely free of carbon." Asked when investors became more reluctant "to invest in anything which is carbon-rich," he observed that "in Europe, a big move was when the Norwegian State Fund [NSF] announced [its divestment from fossil fuels].... It was striking because the NSF [the world's largest

---

[11] Information from RWE's 2011 CDP disclosure.

sovereign wealth fund, worth $1.3 trillion as of 2022] became so rich because of oil and gas." That was "[in 2014 or 2013] and to me, that was a kind of turning point" (Hamburg, Germany, December 6, 2018).

Like RWE, Shell, one of the world's largest oil and gas companies, appeared to remain deeply committed to what had been a highly profitable status quo, particularly in the early 2010s. Insofar as it was concerned with becoming greener, Shell was "focusing on natural gas," announced the CEO in 2011. "About half of the energy we produce comes out of wells in that form already, and we plan to increase that proportion in the coming years. It is, after all, the cleanest fossil fuel" (Royal Dutch Shell 2012, 5).

Yet, in 2016, Shell created a "New Energies" business to "further explore opportunities in alternative transport fuels, such as biofuels and hydrogen," and to "act as an incubator for potentially game-changing technologies of the future" (Royal Dutch Shell 2017, 6). In 2018, Shell observed that, following the World Bank's decision "to stop financing upstream oil and gas projects in 2019," other financial institutions "appear to be considering limiting their exposure to certain fossil fuel projects," potentially adversely impacting "our ability to use financing for future projects" (Royal Dutch Shell 2018, 13). That same year, New Energies agreed to purchase a UK-based residential energy provider, First Utility. By 2019, the rechristened "Shell Energy" had abandoned First Utility's coal- and natural gas-reliant fuel mix and was delivering customers 100% renewable energy (Royal Dutch Shell 2019)[12]; further, it had set its sights on becoming the world's largest power company by 2030, a vision grounded, in the words of its director, Maarten Wetselaar, in the "irreversible choice the world has made to decarbonize, to address climate change, and to go to [a] net-zero energy system." Indeed, noted Wetselaar, Shell's decision to create this new business was partly about "playing a positive role in [the] energy transition" and partly "about survival" (Pyper 2019).

By the mid- to late 2010s, even some of the world's most status quo-oriented companies recognized a new dominant design for the future, determining that a "turning point" had been passed and that the world

---

[12] Green Tech Media underscored that "Shell's offering is certified by Renewable Energy Guarantees of Origin, which ensures that for every unit of electricity Shell Energy customers use, a unit of renewable electricity is put into the grid by renewable generators in the U.K." (Pyper 2019).

102   C. HULME

had made an "irreversible choice" to decarbonize and address climate change, making failure to adopt certain practices no longer a serious option. How did these strong incumbents, deeply committed to and entwined in the high-carbon economy and climate status quo, arrive at this conclusion? Throughout the 2010s, select companies in energy-intensive industries adopted or intensified their commitment to particular kinds of climate-related practices as they became increasingly confident in a low-carbon future, even as states were failing to implement the kind of policy and regulation needed to guide a global low-carbon transition. Whether using an internal carbon price to inform investment decisions or curbing supply chain emissions, select practices increasingly were perceived as the new norm—the standard for any serious actor. Certain companies, acting as early movers, embraced these new practices with marked ambition, nurturing a particular understanding among others about the behaviors necessary to advance their own highest interests in a changing environment. As this part of the chapter explores, over time there was growing momentum toward a new climate consensus, creating a situation, borrowing from Jervis, in which "change in one direction [sets] in motion reinforcing pressures that [produce] further change in the same direction" (1997, 125).

Energy-Intensive Companies' Behavior, 2010–2017

Table 3.5 classifies companies as one of four types: *BAU*, *evolutionary*, *innovator*, or *disruptor*. It establishes the extent to which companies increased their climate performance and the degree to which the cohort overall moved toward a more climate-active approach, as each type corresponds to a range of scores across three metrics of climate action: *product*, *alignment*, and *investment*. As the appendix describes, for the energy-intensive industry group the specific practices corresponding to those metrics were as follows: for *product*, reducing the emissions intensity of their activities (for all industries except power and oil and gas), acquiring/developing renewable energy businesses or addressing methane flaring (for oil and gas companies), and reducing coal's share in their generation portfolios (for power companies); for *alignment*, applying an internal carbon price (for cement, power, and steel companies) and addressing Scope 3 emissions, with a focus on the supply chain (for chemical, oil and gas, and pharmaceutical companies); and for *investment*, allocating resources toward low-carbon research and development. In the last column, companies' names are bolded if they transitioned to higher types between the first and last periods.

Table 3.5 conveys which energy-intensive companies, in altering their climate approach, became part of the process that led to the overarching outcome of interest in this book: a new climate consensus among corporate actors across different industries and headquarter countries. It captures how, by the last period (2015–2017), seven companies (47%) belonged to a higher type than in the first period (2010–2012), having made significant changes in their climate approach and performance. With five of those seven (71%) landing in either the disruptor or innovator camp by the last period, there was a high level of ambition among the type-changers.

Table 3.5 also captures when and to what extent momentum was gathering at the individual and collective levels. The last row shows that there was a 28% increase in companies' collective scores between periods 1 and 6, with three key periods of change: period 2 (2011–2013), period 4 (2013–2015), and period 6 (2015–2017). Considering momentum at the company level, period 6 was especially significant; while three companies (BASF, E.ON, and Heidelberg) maintained their already high performance, four others (Pfizer, Tata Steel, Thyssenkrupp, and Ultratech Cement) increased their performance considerably, transitioning to higher types.

Once momentum was generated toward new kinds of climate behavior, it was sustained; as Table 3.5 underscores, once the company cohort moved forward, it never retreated. Of particular importance is the considerable momentum achieved prior to the December 2015 Paris Conference, widely interpreted as a watershed for the private sector beginning to reckon more seriously with climate change and a low-carbon future (Espinosa 2016). For example, it was in 2014 that Heidelberg became a disruptor, while BASF and E.ON became innovators in 2013 and 2014, respectively. Notably, in 2014, representing another pre-Paris development, E.ON, which was the highest scoring company by 2015–2017, announced that in the future it would be "focusing entirely" on "the building blocks of the new energy world," including renewables and energy networks—and that it was transferring all of its conventional power generation business to a new company, Uniper. In 2016, the deal complete, E.ON described itself as "the first major European energy supplier to orient itself wholly around the new energy world" (E.ON 2017, 5).

Table 3.5 Energy-intensive company types, 2010–2017

Type (points)	2010–2012 (period 1)	2011–2013 (period 2)	2012–2014 (period 3)	2013–2015 (period 4)	2014–2016 (period 5)	2015–2017 (period 6)
Disruptor (16–20)					HEI, 17 E.ON, 16	**E.ON**, 18 **HEI**, 16
Innovator (13–15)		HEI, 13	HEI, 14 JNJ, 13	HEI, 15 BASF, 14 E.ON, 13	BASF, 14	**BASF**, 13 **TATA**, 13 **TYEKF**, 13
Evolutionary (9–12)	HEI, 12 BASF, 11 Bayer, 11 E.ON, 11 JNJ, 10 TATA, 10	BASF, 12 JNJ, 12 E.ON, 11 Bayer, 10 TATA, 10 Pfizer, 9	E.ON, 12 BASF, 11 Dow, 10 Bayer, 9 Pfizer, 9	JNJ, 11 Pfizer, 10 Bayer, 9 Dow, 9 TATA, 9	JNJ, 11 Bayer, 10	Bayer, 10 **Pfizer**, 10 **Ultra**, 10 JNJ, 9
BAU (0–8)	Dow, 7 TYEKF, 7 Chevron, 6 Ultra, 6 Pfizer, 5 RWE, 5 Shell, 5 Exxon, 3 Reliance, 0	Dow, 8 Chevron, 6 Ultra, 6 RWE, 5 Shell, 5 TYEKF, 5 Exxon, 3 Reliance, 0	TATA, 7 Chevron, 6 Ultra, 6 RWE, 5 Shell, 5 TYEKF, 5 Exxon, 3 Reliance, 0	Ultra, 8 TYEKF, 6 Chevron, 5 RWE, 5 Shell, 5 Exxon, 4 Reliance, 0	Pfizer, 8 TATA, 8 TYEKF, 8 Dow, 7 Ultra, 7 Shell, 6 Chevron, 4 Exxon, 4 RWE, 4 Reliance, 1	Dow, 7 Shell, 7 Exxon, 5 Chevron, 4 RWE, 4 Reliance, 0

Type (points)	2010–2012 (period 1)	2011–2013 (period 2)	2012–2014 (period 3)	2013–2015 (period 4)	2014–2016 (period 5)	2015–2017 (period 6)
Total points (% change)	109 (−)	115 (6%)	115 (−)	123 (7%)	125 (2%)	139 (11%) (net:+28%)

Source Author

Note Fifteen energy-intensive companies, classified according to three-year performance on *product*, *alignment*, and *investment*. Companies received points out of 20 based on where they fell on a performance spectrum. HEI is HeidelbergCement; JNJ, Johnson & Johnson; TATA, Tata Steel; TYEKF, Thyssenkrupp; and Ultra, Ultratech Cement

106   C. HULME

Identifying New Climate Practices

In addition to the overall level of climate performance increasing between 2010–2012 and 2015–2017, there is evidence of specific climate-related practices becoming more widespread and of practices reflecting enhanced company commitment over time. Table 3.6 displays as a percentage the number of companies out of 15 receiving any points for each of the three metrics in a certain period ("breadth"), and the degree to which companies enhanced their commitment to these practices, conveying the percentage of companies receiving over half the available points for a given metric ("depth").

Considering the breadth of climate activity, the adoption of certain practices reflected companies' growing confidence in a low-carbon future and in the need for a different approach to the climate issue area; in particular, increasing participation in the alignment and investment metrics indicates that more companies decided to prepare for and invest in a future where carbon would carry a cost for themselves and for their suppliers, and where it would be incumbent to find new methods of producing their goods. The increase in participation in *alignment* is an especially clear indicator of growing confidence in a low-carbon future. As discussed in Chapter 1, internal carbon pricing (one of the industry-specific practices corresponding to the alignment metric in this

Table 3.6   Breadth and depth of energy-intensive companies' climate action, 2010–2017

Years (period)	Breadth			Depth		
	Product	*Alignment*	*Investment*	*Product*	*Alignment*	*Investment*
2010–2012 (1)	69	42	67	57	4	70
2011–2013 (2)	62	49	69	60	13	65
2012–2014 (3)	56	58	73	65	26	61
2013–2015 (4)	44	62	78	71	38	55
2014–2016 (5)	47	69	84	72	40	52
2015–2017 (6)	53	73	84	71	57	52
Percent change, periods 1–6	−23	+74	+25	+25	+1325	−26

Source Author

Note Breadth captures the percentage of energy-intensive companies receiving any points for *product*, *alignment*, and *investment*. Depth captures the percentage receiving over half the available points for performance on these metrics chapter) "helps companies prepare for and hedge against future regulatory changes, and ensures long-term capital investments don't become too costly, or even obsolete, in an environment where greenhouse gas emissions carry a price" (CDP 2017). Meanwhile, addressing supply chain emissions (the other industry-specific practice corresponding to *alignment*), including through engaging thousands or even tens of thousands of suppliers, is one of the more complex and challenging actions that companies can undertake.

Indicating a decline in participation in *product*, Table 3.6 highlights the challenge of making "sticky" progress on advancing one of the practices arguably least amenable to quick change (decreasing the emissions intensity of a company's activities, the practice for the product metric for all industries in this chapter except power and oil and gas), and underscores that even as more companies were becoming confident in a low-carbon future (as evidenced by widening participation in the investment and alignment metrics), for companies in energy-intensive industries this future was not yet perceived to be "on their doorstep" as of 2015–2017. Yet, given that product may act as a lagging indicator, extending the timeframe through 2020 might well show the earlier growth in participation in *alignment* and *investment* translating to increased participation in *product*.[13] In other words, by 2020, a low-carbon future may have seemed closer than it was in 2017—partly due to decisions that companies made and actions they undertook during the early and mid-2010s.

If the data on breadth of climate action demonstrates confidence in a low-carbon future becoming more widespread—two of three practices became more widely adopted over time—the data on depth of action shows confidence in such a future intensifying, captured most clearly by the dramatic gain in *alignment*. Specifically, it captures how companies that engaged at all with their suppliers on addressing supply chain emissions engaged more intensely over time.[14] In addition, although fewer companies lowered the emissions intensity of their activities (the specific

---

[13] The logic is that if, for example, a cement company decided to more closely align its activities with a low-carbon future by using a higher percentage of lower-carbon materials in its cement, this decision would appear in later data about the carbon intensity of its cement (the product metric).

[14] The gains in depth of action in terms of the alignment metric reflect progress among those companies for whom the indicator behavior was addressing supply chain emissions (chemical, oil and gas, and pharmaceutical companies); a comparable deepening did not occur among those for whom the indicator behavior was using an internal carbon price

108   C. HULME

practice for the product metric), those that did made more progress. Notably, with the product metric reaching 71% "deep" participation in period 4 (the same as in period 6), all progress occurred prior to the Paris Conference.

While Table 3.6 conveys insights about how committed companies were to specific practices, it does not capture whether they were participating in-depth in the most significant practices, or the metrics that were weighted most heavily for their industries (which differed depending on an industry's activities and the key culprit behind its emissions; see the appendix for details). Over time, the percentage of companies receiving over half the available points on the most heavily weighted metric for their respective industries increased 55%, from 33% in period 1 to 51% in period 6.[15] In other words, energy-intensive companies did not just dabble at the margins (for example, increasing low-carbon R&D expenditures, a relatively low-cost action and thus one of comparatively less significance, while registering no progress on addressing the emissions intensity of their activities); rather, they increasingly moved forward on aspects of their activities that posed particularly complex challenges (for example, addressing supply chain emissions).

* * *

Examining how energy-intensive companies behaved during six three-year periods spanning 2010–2017 to assess change over time in their climate approach, this part of the chapter identified which of the 15 companies became part of the process that contributed to the formation and progressive entrenchment of a new corporate climate consensus.

(cement, power, and steel companies). An illustrative example of deepening commitment to addressing supply chain emissions comes from Johnson & Johnson. In 2012, the company launched its "expanded Responsibility Standards for Suppliers, supported by assessment tools, protocols and implementation guidance, to assist our suppliers in complying with the standards." By 2017, it had enrolled suppliers covering 51% of its spending in its Sustainability Procurement Program; the target for 2020 was to enroll suppliers covering 80% of its spending. Johnson & Johnson (2012, 7); and Johnson & Johnson's 2018 CDP disclosure.

[15] For companies in industries with two metrics carrying the same weight, a company had to score 51% on only one of those metrics to be counted as receiving over half of the available points on the most heavily weighted metric. For periods 1–6, the percent of companies meeting the 51% threshold for deep participation on the most heavily weighted metric was 33, 40, 42, 49, 47, and 51, respectively.

3 THE TRAIN HAS LEFT THE STATION: AUTOMOTIVE ... 109

Climate action gained momentum early on and was sustained; the company cohort never retreated once it achieved a higher level of climate activity. Nearly half of the companies altered their approach in a decisive fashion, belonging to a higher type in the last period than in the first. More companies became confident in the low-carbon future, with participation in two climate-related practices broadening, while companies' conviction about this future intensified, with the depth of participation in two practices increasing. Importantly, companies were not simply deepening their commitment to relatively low-cost behaviors, but were realizing increasingly meaningful results on more challenging actions that had the potential to help lock in their commitments to lower-carbon behavior.

Industry-Level Foundations of the Emergent Climate Consensus

Companies in energy-intensive industries perceived climate change as less of a high-impact material concern over time—in particular, their outlook for robust regulatory action declined—and it was in this context that they shaped and gradually aligned themselves with a new shared understanding about the need for a different climate approach. Their behavior foreshadowed at the industry level the emergent quality of the overall pattern of corporate climate action that this book investigates, with individual firms' perceptions of the material relevance of climate change not corresponding to the private sector's shift to a new approach to the climate change issue.

Table 3.7 presents results from analyzing annual CDP surveys tracking whether corporations perceived high-impact material risks and/or opportunities tied to climate-related regulation, changing consumer behavior, and, in the case of oil and gas companies, physical impacts.[16] If all companies in a given period perceived high-impact climate-related risks and opportunities in these categories, the "perceived high material impact" column would register 100. Table 3.7 separates data concerning perceptions of climate change overall as a high-impact issue from that specific to concerns about regulation and consumer behavior, providing a more

---

[16] Oil and gas companies belong to one of a relatively short list of industries set to be significantly impacted by climate change in terms of its physical implications. Other examples include wineries and insurers (Duva 2014).

110   C. HULME

detailed picture of the factors driving change in how companies perceived the issue.[17]

Table 3.7 captures that the overall diminishing perception that climate change was a highly salient material issue was driven by companies becoming considerably less concerned about prospects for states enacting high-impact climate-related regulation (i.e., measures that would impose serious financial costs or offer major financial opportunities). Meanwhile, Table 3.7 underscores that the consumer-based alternative explanation for changes in companies' behavior finds little support, as consumer behavior remained a marginal concern.

Considered alongside the steady, positive momentum toward a higher overall level of climate action, data on companies' perceptions of the material impacts of climate change demonstrates at the industry level how the developing pattern of climate action was not driven by how individual firms perceived the relevance of climate change, but instead is more accurately understood as a function of the emergent steering mechanism of consensus acting as an "invisible hand" in the issue area. Borrowing from Rosenau, this steering mechanism functioned as a channel "through

Table 3.7 Perceived high material impact of climate change among energy-intensive companies, 2010–2016

Years (period)	*Perceived high material impact*		
	Overall	*Regulation*	*Consumer*
2010–2012 (1)	23	39	11
2011–2013 (2)	22	35	12
2012–2014 (3)	20	31	13
2013–2015 (4)	18	26	13
2014–2016 (5)	19	29	14
Percent change, periods 1–5	−17	−26	+27

Source Author

Note Among energy-intensive companies, the percentage of climate-related risks and opportunities that were perceived to be a high-impact material concern

[17] The strength of perception for physical impacts is not considered separately, as this included only three oil and gas companies. Note, however, that none of those three perceived any high-impact risks or opportunities from physical impacts at any time during the 2010–2016 timeframe.

which 'commands' flow in the form of... policies pursued" (1995, 14); companies pursued new climate policies not in response to powerful individual incentives but rather in response to the "command" of a growing consensus.

Indeed, the data shows, strikingly, that individual perceptions of climate change's material impact and relevance were strongest during the only period—2010–2012—when there were *no* companies undertaking ambitious action (i.e., all 15 companies behaved as BAUs or evolutionaries). When company-level perceptions that climate change was a serious concern were at their zenith (which, at just 23%, was still low), the overall level of climate action was at its nadir.

Further, in examining the patterns of changing breadth and depth of certain climate practices, the previous section found that the most significant changes pertained to practices falling under the umbrella of the alignment metric. Adoption of the indicator practice for this metric (or the "breadth" of action) increased by 74%, while the percentage of companies that were making deep commitments to the practice (or the "depth" of action) increased over 14-fold. This indicates that companies were participating least in, and were least deeply committed to, the crucial climate action of *alignment* during the period (2010–2012) when they most viewed climate change as having high-impact material effects. As climate change was perceived as less of a serious material concern over time, more companies participated in *alignment*, and they also became more deeply committed to it. This counterintuitive finding, where less concern about climate change as a major material concern for individual firms was coupled with more convergence around a certain set of climate practices, and broader and deeper alignment with a low-carbon future, points to the disjunction between individual traits and an overall outcome that is the signature of emergence. The cohort of energy-intensive companies altered its behavior not as a result of how individual members perceived the impact of the issue but rather due to a growing shared understanding of the need to self-regulate its climate-related behavior amid a perceived abdication of state leadership and action.

* * *

Drawing on Granovetter's threshold model, Chapter 1 considered how, depending on the thresholds for action of a given group of actors at a certain point, a collective outcome can be achieved despite it not

112   C. HULME

being of very high importance for many actors, or not ranked very high in their interest sets, in which case the outcome is emergent—a second-order effect coming about through actors' interactions as opposed to their individual attributes. Table 3.8 captures the extent to which companies changing types at any point viewed the climate issue as a high-impact material concern.[18] It demonstrates, in short, which companies' behavior reflected the logic of emergence, illustrating a core dynamic of the threshold model: companies altering their behavior and contributing to a different private sector climate approach despite the climate issue not ranking particularly high in their individual interest sets (i.e., registering as a pressing material risk or a promising opportunity). If a company in a given period perceived that climate-related regulation and changing consumer behavior entailed high-impact risks and opportunities, Table 3.8 would register 100. Table 3.9 separates data concerning how companies assessed the material impact of regulation and of changing consumer behavior. The perception data concerning regulation is displayed in the top half of Table 3.9 and the consumer-related perception data in the bottom half.

Considered alongside the steady momentum toward a higher overall level of climate action, Tables 3.8 and 3.9 capture that four companies—HeidelbergCement, E.ON, Johnson & Johnson, and Pfizer—did not perceive climate change as a high-impact material concern during the periods when they most improved their performance (periods 5, 5, 3, and 2, respectively), as well as in the periods immediately prior to the change periods. For a fifth company, Ultratech Cement, climate change barely registered as a high-impact material concern during the period of change (period 5), and it was even less concerning then (at 8%) than it had been in the period immediately prior (at 17%).[19]

Three cases—Heidelberg, E.ON, and, to a lesser extent, Johnson & Johnson—are especially useful in illustrating the logic of emergence. These are actors whose behavior most evidently cannot be accounted for

---

[18] Table 3.8 includes the seven companies that belonged to a higher type in period 6 compared to period 1, as well as two companies that made type-changes that were not "sticky": Johnson & Johnson began and ended as an evolutionary, though it changed to an innovator in period 3, while Dow began and ended as a BAU, though it changed to an evolutionary in periods 3 and 4.

[19] Considering period 5 (2014–2016), Ultratech Cement had a 25% perception strength in 2014 and then a score of 0 in 2015 and 2016, seeing *no* high-impact risks and/or opportunities.

Table 3.8 Perceived high material impact of climate change for energy-intensive companies increasing climate performance sufficiently to change types, 2010–2016

Years (period)	Perceived high material impact: overall								
	Pfizer	JNJ	HEI	E.ON	Ultra	Dow	TATA	BASF	TYEKF
2010–2012 (1)	0	0	33	50	25	25	13	50	67
2011–2013 (2)	0	0	33	33	25	25	8	50	58
2012–2014 (3)	0	0	17	17	25	25	25	50	50
2013–2015 (4)	0	0	0	0	17	25	33	50	50
2014–2016 (5)	0	0	0	0	8	25	50	58	67

Source Author

Note For energy-intensive companies that increased climate performance sufficiently to change types (i.e., becoming *evolutionaries*, *innovators*, or *disruptors*), the percentage of climate-related risks and opportunities that were perceived to be a high-impact material concern. Ultratech Cement did not participate in CDP during the 2010 or 2011 response cycles, so period 1 data reflects perceptions from 2012 only and period 2 data reflects perceptions from 2012 and 2013 only. Tata Steel did not participate in CDP during the 2010 response cycle, so period 1 data reflects perceptions from 2011 and 2012 only. HEI is HeidelbergCement; JNJ, Johnson & Johnson; TATA, Tata Steel; TYEKF, Thyssenkrupp; and Ultra, Ultratech Cement

by company-level assessments of a material need for action, but rather is better understood in the context of their participation in a broader process unfolding in the private sector ecosystem, namely, the shaping and strengthening of an emergent climate consensus.

First, as Tables 3.8 and 3.9 capture, Heidelberg reported a moderate level of concern with high-impact material costs and benefits linked to climate change in only two periods, 1 and 2; by periods 4 and 5, it perceived neither regulation nor changing consumer behavior to entail any high-impact material costs or opportunities. Meanwhile, as Table 3.5 indicates, it transitioned from evolutionary to innovator in period 2 (2011–2013) and to disruptor in period 5 (2014–2016). Its move into the disruptor camp, representing the most ambitious climate approach (where it would remain in 2015–2017), coincided with a span of time (2013–2016) when the company expected no high-impact ramifications either from climate action by states or from changing consumer practices.

Second, considering E.ON, in period 1, climate change was a serious material issue for the company, which anticipated high-impact material consequences from regulation in particular, as Table 3.9 captures. In periods 2 and 3, high-impact consequences were only a moderate

114   C. HULME

Table 3.9   Perceived high material impact of regulation and changing consumer behavior for energy-intensive companies increasing climate performance sufficiently to change types, 2010–2016

Years (period)	Perceived high material impact: regulation & consumer behavior								
	Pfizer	JNJ	HEI	E.ON	Ultra	Dow	TATA	BASF	TYEKF
2010–2012 (1)	0	0	67	100	50	50	0	50	100
2011–2013 (2)	0	0	67	67	50	50	0	50	67
2012–2014 (3)	0	0	33	33	50	50	17	50	50
2013–2015 (4)	0	0	0	0	33	50	33	50	50
2014–2016 (5)	0	0	0	0	17	50	50	67	83
2010–2012 (1)	0	0	0	0	0	0	25	50	33
2011–2013 (2)	0	0	0	0	0	0	17	50	50
2012–2014 (3)	0	0	0	0	0	0	33	50	50
2013–2015 (4)	0	0	0	0	0	0	33	50	50
2014–2016 (5)	0	0	0	0	0	0	50	50	50

Source Author

Note For energy-intensive companies that increased climate performance sufficiently to change types (i.e., becoming *evolutionaries*, *innovators*, or *disruptors*), the percentage of regulatory (top half of the table) and consumer-related (bottom half of table) risks and opportunities that were perceived to be a high-impact material concern. HEI is HeidelbergCement; JNJ, Johnson & Johnson; TATA, Tata Steel; TYEKF, Thyssenkrupp; and Ultra, Ultratech Cement

concern; by periods 4 and 5, there were no concerns about high-impact risks or opportunities tied to climate change. As Table 3.5 shows, E.ON became an innovator in 2013–2015, and in 2014–2016 joined Heidelberg as a disruptor. Its two instances of transitioning to a higher type coincided with the timeframe (2013–2016) when it expected no high-impact effects either from climate action by states or from changing consumer practices.

Finally, the inconsistency between Johnson & Johnson's perception of the climate issue and its actions offers another illustrative example of the logic of emergence at the company level, although less pronounced than that of Heidelberg and E.ON, given that it began and ended as an evolutionary, as Table 3.5 shows. Johnson & Johnson adopted practices that seemingly indicated that climate change was becoming more relevant from a material perspective, despite never reporting perceiving any high-impact climate-related regulation or changes in consumer behavior on the horizon, as Table 3.8 indicates. For example, by 2016, it had adopted science-based emissions reduction targets, or targets aligning with the 2°C scenario outlined in the Paris Climate Agreement—an exceptional kind of climate action that by 2018 had been adopted by only 103 companies worldwide (Science Based Targets 2018).

Exploring the industry and company levels demonstrates an inconsistency in how the energy-intensive industry cohort overall moved toward a different climate approach and how companies individually perceived the material importance of the issue, reflecting the logic of emergence. Likewise, there was a disjunction between the behavior of those companies that specifically shaped or were steered by the growing climate consensus, or that contributed to the process ultimately producing a new corporate pattern of response to the climate issue area (i.e., the type-changers), and their perceptions of its material relevance. Companies' diminishing outlook for bold state action on the climate issue (in the form of high-impact policy and regulation) declined considerably throughout the 2010s, an especially crucial development supporting this book's argument about the key factor accounting for corporate actors' coalescence around a new climate approach. Meanwhile, a prominent alternative explanation gained no purchase; at the start of the decade, changing consumer behavior was a minimal concern for energy-intensive companies, becoming only marginally more relevant over time.

* * *

A cohort of 15 of the world's largest energy-intensive and thus most "climate-critical" companies, spanning various industries and headquarter countries, moved toward a different climate approach throughout the 2010–2017 timeframe—and did so specifically in the context of declining outlooks for bold climate action by states. Over time, momentum gathered; once the cohort moved forward toward a different climate approach it never retreated, with companies increasingly adopting practices suggestive of a new paradigm of behavior. Even some of the most staunchly "BAU" actors acknowledged by the late 2010s that there was a new dominant design on the horizon; as a Berlin-based climate and energy expert put it in 2018, reflecting on how major energy actors in Germany "fought the energy transition over years," it took these companies "quite some time to realize that in the end, they have also entered the game" (Berlin, November 13, 2018).

116   C. HULME

Conclusion

This chapter demonstrated that half (11 of 22) of automakers and energy-intensive companies belonged to a higher type in 2017 than in 2010. With seven of those eleven (64%) landing in the disruptor or innovator camp, overall there was a high level of ambition among those companies that improved their climate performance sufficiently to change types. However, considering differences between the industry groups, the automotive industry was much less ambitious overall than the energy-intensive industry group. Just two of four automakers (50%) that transitioned to a higher type over time became innovators and none became disruptors, demonstrating a limited degree of ambition. Meanwhile, three of the seven energy-intensive companies that changed types (or 43%) became innovators, while two (29%) became disruptors, demonstrating the highest level of activity and ambition. In addition, energy-intensive companies progressed toward a higher level of climate action earlier than automakers.

During the 2010s, even some corporations most strongly invested in the high-carbon economy acknowledged a new dominant design—perceiving, in the words of a Stiftung 2 Grad expert, that "the train of transforming the economy has left the station and is not going to return" (Berlin, November 13, 2018). But, as this chapter demonstrated, the train "left the station" in a very particular context. Select companies increasingly placed their bets on a low-carbon future and altered their climate-related behavior despite having scant confidence either in the near-term outlook for states providing "rules of the game" (i.e., effective regulation and policy paving the way toward a low-carbon future) or in prospects for states playing this role even in the long term (in their CDP disclosures, companies defined for themselves what "long term" entailed; frequently it was 10 years). As Chapter 2 explored, states assumed that their behavior during the 2010s, particularly from the mid-2010s onward, sent a clear signal to the private sector: finally, they were addressing climate change and nurturing a low-carbon future in a serious and concerted manner. For example, in a context like post-Dieselgate Germany, the government had a certain image of itself, which many observers shared, as stepping in and forcing tighter regulation on industry, thus getting climate laggards moving in the right direction.

Yet, corporations frequently did not share this positive image; policy and regulatory developments during the 2010s, including after apparent

3 THE TRAIN HAS LEFT THE STATION: AUTOMOTIVE ... 117

watersheds like Dieselgate and the Paris Conference, did not spur companies to see states in a new light in terms of their commitment to robust climate action. In fact, as this chapter examined, given how many companies throughout the 2010s became considerably less confident in prospects for high-impact state action, those developments simply deepened corporations' long-held sense that states lacked answers about how to achieve shared mitigation objectives and spur a global low-carbon transition. Amid this perceived abdication of state leadership, select powerful corporations adopted new practices, embraced the idea that failing to get on board with addressing climate change and advancing a low-carbon future no longer was a serious option, and, as Chapter 7 explores, helped cast a new international reality to which states increasingly had to align themselves.

References

Amelang, Sören, and Benjamin Wehrmann. 2020. "Dieselgate"–a timeline of the car emissions fraud scandal in Germany. *Clean Energy Wire*, May 25, 2020. https://www.cleanenergywire.org/factsheets/dieselgate-timeline-car-emissions-fraud-scandal-germany.

Barkin, Noah. 2015. VW scandal exposes cozy ties between industry and Berlin. *Reuters*, September 26, 2015. https://www.reuters.com/article/us-volkswagen-emissions-germany-politics-idUSKCN0RQ0BU20150926.

BMW Group. 2012. Annual report 2011. March 8, 2012. https://www.bmwgroup.com/content/dam/grpw/websites/bmwgroup_com/ir/downloads/en/2011/2011-BMW-Group-Annual-Report.pdf.

BMW Group. 2018. Annual report 2017. March 8, 2018. https://www.press.bmwgroup.com/global/article/detail/T0279390EN/bmw-group-annual-report-2017?language%3Den.

Boudette, Neal, and Coral Davenport. 2021. G.M. will sell only zero-emission vehicles by 2035. *The New York Times*, January 28, 2021. https://www.nytimes.com/2021/01/28/business/gm-zero-emission-vehicles.html.

Brooks, David. 2020. Biden's rise gives the establishment one last chance. *The New York Times*, March 5, 2020. https://www.nytimes.com/2020/03/05/opinion/joe-biden-2020.html.

CBS News. 2020. GM drops out of air pollution lawsuit against California, says it's all in on electric cars. November 23, 2020. https://www.cbsnews.com/news/gm-drops-out-of-lawsuit-against-california-says-its-all-in-on-electric-cars/.

118   C. HULME

CDP. 2017. More than eight-fold leap over four years in global companies pricing carbon into business plans. October 12, 2017. https://www.cdp. net/en/articles/media/more-than-eight-fold-leap-over-four-years-in-global-companies-pricing-carbon-into-business-plans.

Cremer, Andreas. 2017. VW manages record 2016 sales despite Dieselgate crisis. *Reuters*, January 10, 2017. https://www.reuters.com/article/us-volkswagen-vehicleregistrations-idUSKBN14U1G0.

Duva, Nicholas. 2014. 7 industries at greatest risk from climate change. CNBC. October 22, 2014. https://www.cnbc.com/2014/10/22/7-industries-at-gre atest-risk-from-climate-change.html.

E.ON. 2017. Sustainability report 2016. March 15, 2017. https://www.eon. com/en/about-us/sustainability/sustainability-report.html.

Espinosa, Patricia. 2016. Paris Agreement enters into force – Celebration and reality check. United Nations Climate Change. November 4, 2016. https://unfccc.int/news/paris-agreement-enters-into-force-celebr ation-and-reality-check.

Ford Motor Company. 2011. 2010 Annual report. March 10, 2011. https:/ /www.annualreports.com/HostedData/AnnualReportArchive/f/NYSE_F_ 2010.pdf.

Ford Motor Company. 2017. 2016 Annual report. February 9, 2017. https:/ /www.annualreports.com/HostedData/AnnualReportArchive/f/NYSE_F_ 2016.pdf.

Ford Motor Company. 2018. 2017 Annual report. March 15, 2018. https:/ /www.annualreports.com/HostedData/AnnualReportArchive/f/NYSE_F_ 2017.pdf.

Ford Motor Company. n.d. Sustainability 2011/12. http://ophelia.sdsu.edu: 8080/ford/09-03-2012/doc/sr11.pdf.

Francis, David. 2016. The top 25 corporate nations. *Foreign Policy*, March 15, 2016. https://foreignpolicy.com/2016/03/15/these-25-companies-are-more-powerful-than-many-countries-multinational-corporate-wealth-power/.

Franke, Andreas. 2019. A million German EV charge points needed by 2030: Merkel. S&P Global. November 4, 2019. https://www.spglobal.com/com modityinsights/en/market-insights/latest-news/electric-power/110419-a-million-german-ev-charge-points-needed-by-2030-merkel.

General Motors. 2018. 2017 Annual report. February 6, 2018. https://www. annualreports.com/HostedData/AnnualReportArchive/g/NYSE_GM_2017. pdf.

Hebermehl, Gregor. 2019. Volle konzentration auf elektroantrieb. *Auto Motor Sport*, September 17, 2019. https://www.auto-motor-und-sport.de/tech-zuk unft/daimler-stoppt-verbrennungsmotoren-entwicklung-2019/.

Hotten, Russell. 2015. Volkswagen: The scandal explained. *BBC News*, December 10, 2015. https://www.bbc.com/news/business-34324772.

Japan Times. 2020. Toyota second in 2019 car sales, overtaking Nissan-Renault. January 30, 2020. https://www.japantimes.co.jp/news/2020/01/30/business/corporate-business/toyota-second-in-2019-car-sales/.

Jervis, Robert. 1997. *System effects: complexity in political and social life.* Princeton, NJ: Princeton University Press.

Johnson & Johnson. 2012. 2012 Citizenship & sustainability report. https://www.responsibilityreports.com/HostedData/ResponsibilityReportArchive/j/NYSE_JNJ_2012.pdf.

Kabel, Greg. 2019. Volkswagen's Dieselgate costs top $33.6 billion. *WardsAuto,* May 2, 2019. https://www.wardsauto.com/industry/volkswagen-s-dieselgate-costs-top-336-billion.

Kolodny, Lora. 2020. Tesla stock is up more than 4,000% since its debut 10 years ago. CNBC. June 29, 2020. https://www.cnbc.com/2020/06/29/tesla-stock-up-4125percent-since-ipo-ten-years-ago.html.

Korosec, Kirsten. 2020. Tesla blows past Toyota to become most valuable automaker in the world. *Tech Crunch,* July 1, 2020. https://techcrunch.com/2020/07/01/tesla-blows-past-toyota-to-become-most-valuable-automaker-in-the-world/.

Krieger, Axel, Phillip Radtke, and Larry Wang. 2012. Recharging China's electric-vehicle aspirations. McKinsey & Company. July 2012. https://www.mckinsey.com/industries/automotive-and-assembly/our-insights/recharging-chinas-electric-vehicle-aspirations.

Lieven, Theo, Silke Muehlmeier, Sven Henkel, and Johan Waller. 2011. Who will buy electric cars? An empirical study in Germany. *Transportation Research* 16 (3): 236–243. https://doi.org/10.1016/j.trd.2010.12.001.

Loh, Brian, Abhijit Mahindroo, and Nick Santhanam. 2019. Snapshots of the global mobility revolution. *McKinsey Quarterly,* March 13, 2019. https://www.mckinsey.com/industries/automotive-and-assembly/our-insights/snapshots-of-the-global-mobility-revolution.

Miller, Joe, and Peter Campbell. 2019. German car industry faces "day of reckoning." *The Financial Times,* December 1, 2019. https://www.ft.com/content/5c304e72-120a-11ea-a7e6-62bf4f9e548a.

Morison, Rachel, and Mathew Carr. 2018. How EU's biggest polluter escaped a tripling of carbon price. Bloomberg. August 14, 2018. https://www.bloomberg.com/news/articles/2018-08-14/how-europe-s-biggest-polluter-escaped-a-tripling-of-carbon-price.

Pyper, Julia. 2019. Shell New Energies director on investing in clean energy: "It's about survival." Green Tech Media. April 1, 2019. https://www.greentechmedia.com/articles/read/shell-new-energies-director-on-investing-in-clean-energy.

Rosenau, James. 1995. Governance in the twenty-first century. *Global Governance* 1 (1): 13–43. https://doi.org/10.1057/9780230245310_2.

120   C. HULME

Royal Dutch Shell. 2012. 2011 Annual report. https://reports.shell.com/ann
ual-report/2011/servicepages/downloads/files/entire_shell_20f_11.pdf.
Royal Dutch Shell. 2017. 2016 Annual report. https://reports.shell.com/ann
ual-report/2016/servicepages/download-centre.php.
Royal Dutch Shell. 2018. 2017 Annual report. https://reports.shell.com/ann
ual-report/2017/servicepages/download-centre.php.
Royal Dutch Shell. 2019. First utility becomes Shell Energy Retail Ltd and
switches customers to 100% renewable electricity. March 25, 2019. https:/
/www.shell.com/energy-and-innovation/new-energies/new-energies-media-
releases/first-utility-becomes-shell-energy-retail-ltd.html#:~:text=Shell%20t
oday%20rebranded%20First%20Utility%20as%20Shell%20Energy%2A,discou
nts%20at%20Shell%20service%20stations%20across%20Great%20Britain.
RWE. 2011. Our responsibility. Report 2010. March 31, 2011. https://
www.responsibilityreports.com/HostedData/ResponsibilityReportArchive/r/
OTC_RWNEF_2010.pdf.
RWE. 2012. Our responsibility. March 28, 2012. https://news.rwe.com/
-/media/RWE/documents/09-verantwortung-nachhaltigkeit/cr-berichte/
EN/en-bericht-2011.pdf.
RWE. 2013. 2012 Annual report. March 5, 2013. https://www.rwe.com/-/
media/archive/ir-archiv/25-en/2013/RWE-Annual-Report-2012.pdf.
Schmidt, Bridie. 2019. Daimler calls time on fossil fuel cars, draws praise from
Musk. *The Driven,* September 20, 2019. https://thedriven.io/2019/09/20/
musk-congratulates-daimler-shift-electric-vehicles/.
Science Based Targets. 2018. Over 100 global corporations using science-
based targets to align strategies with Paris Agreement. April 17,
2018. https://sciencebasedtargets.org/news/over-100-global-corporations-
using-science-based-targets-to-align-strategies-with-paris-agreement.
Sharman, Andy. 2015. Volkswagen hit by consumer backlash after emissions
scandal. *The Financial Times,* December 4, 2015. https://www.ft.com/con
tent/9ac95faa-9a79-11e5-be4f-0abd1978acaa.
Stankiewicz, Kevin. 2021. Ford CEO confident in electric-vehicle strategy,
says automaker won't "cede the future to anyone." CNBC. February
5, 2021. https://www.cnbc.com/2021/02/05/ford-wont-cede-the-future-
to-anyone-on-electric-vehicles-ceo-farley.html.
Thalman, Ellen, and Julian Wettengel. 2019. The story of "Climate Chancellor"
Angela Merkel. *Clean Energy Wire,* September 23, 2019. https://www.cleane
nergywire.org/factsheets/making-climate-chancellor-angela-merkel.
Thompson, Cadie. 2015. The Christmas miracle that saved Tesla. *Business
Insider,* December 14, 2015. https://www.businessinsider.com/elon-musk-
shares-the-miracle-that-saved-tesla-2015-12.

3   THE TRAIN HAS LEFT THE STATION: AUTOMOTIVE ...   121

Volkswagen. 2011. Annual report 2010. March 10, 2011. https://www.volksw
agenag.com/presence/investorrelation/publications/annual-reports/2011/
volkswagen/GB_2010_e.pdf.
Volkswagen. 2016. Annual report 2015. April 28, 2016. https://annualreport
2015.volkswagenag.com/servicepages/downloads/files/entire_vw_ar15.pdf.
Volkswagen. 2017. Annual report 2016. March 14, 2017. https://annualreport
2016.volkswagenag.com/servicepages/downloads/files/entire_vw_ar16.pdf.
Volkswagen. 2018. Annual report 2017. March 13, 2018. https://www.volksw
agenag.com/presence/investorrelation/publications/annual-reports/2018/
volkswagen/en/Y_2017_e.pdf.

CHAPTER 4

Climate Influencers: Technology

INTRODUCTION

In early 2019, Amazon and NGO partner Global Optimism founded The Climate Pledge, a coalition of global businesses committing to net-zero emissions by 2040; within two years, the coalition included 100 signatories across 25 industries and 16 countries. In 2020, Amazon brought its total renewable energy investment for the year to 35 projects and over 4 gigawatts (gw) of capacity (for the sake of comparison, in 2014, India unveiled its much acclaimed national goal of 100 gw of solar power by 2022), marking the largest-ever "corporate investment in renewable energy in a single year" (Berthiaume 2020). By the end of 2020, Amazon was on track to achieve 100% renewable energy usage by 2025, five years ahead of its original target. Meanwhile, in 2020, Microsoft announced a plan "to shift to renewable energy for its buildings and data centers by 2025, become 'carbon negative' by 2030," and, in an unprecedented commitment, "remove its historical carbon emissions from the atmosphere by 2050." Especially notable about its ambitious plan, *Forbes* observed, was that, until recently, "Microsoft was considered somewhat of a climate laggard among the high-tech giants." In fact, *Forbes* concluded, Microsoft and Amazon's "dueling" announcements suggested that the "competition among the two Seattle-based tech giants seems to

© The Author(s), under exclusive license to Springer Nature   123
Switzerland AG 2023
C. Hulme, *Corporate Climate Action, Transnational Politics,*
and World Order, Environmental Politics and Theory,
https://doi.org/10.1007/978-3-031-34115-1_4

be headed in an unexpected direction: climate leadership" (Dolsak and Prakash 2020).

In fact, by the early 2020s, it no longer *was* a very unexpected direction; by that point other industry titans were behaving as leaders in the climate change issue area—it was incumbent on laggards to catch up—and there was a growing consensus about the kind of climate-related behavior that any serious company should adopt. What was unexpected, however, as this chapter explores, was that the industry became increasingly climate active in the context of individual companies not perceiving that climate change was becoming a more urgent material issue. In seizing the mantle of climate leadership and bringing to bear their immense resources and capabilities to influence the renewable energy landscape, technology companies were responding to a certain condition in their environment: states' abdication of leadership on a transnational issue set to shape future global trends.

In the information technology (IT) sector, corporations are especially relevant to climate change mitigation given their large and growing energy usage; in fact, data centers alone use 200 terawatt hours of energy annually, greater than that used by Iran (Jones 2018), and IT giants are poised to rank in the 2020s "among the largest users of electrical power on the planet" (Microsoft 2017, 42). But perhaps even more significant is that tech companies have the potential to influence climate-related developments outside of their industry. As Vandenbergh and Gilligan noted in 2017, the southeastern states of the United States

> would be the sixth largest emitter if they were a country, and these states are not known as leaders in climate policy ... Although these states are not pursuing carbon emissions reductions, Google, Facebook, and other companies are pushing utilities in the region to provide renewable energy for new facilities such as data centers and are extending their influence by encouraging other electricity buyers to do the same. (Vandenbergh and Gilligan 2017)

In 2015, one observer pointed out that over "the past two years, Microsoft has contracted for 285 [megawatts] of renewable power from two off-site wind energy projects. These two wind farms—capable of generating enough electricity to power 125,000 U.S. homes—could not have been built without the long-term off-take agreement provided by Microsoft" (Abbott 2015). In 2018, the Rocky Mountain Institute's

Business Renewable Center tracker reported that "around 2.4 gw of new U.S. wind and solar generation are directly attributable to Google's power purchase agreements" (Marcacci 2018).

Big tech companies pioneered corporate clean power purchasing and have continued to dominate the landscape. In fact, a 2020 study found that while global corporations combined "have purchased enough clean energy in the past 12 years to eclipse the entire energy capacity of countries such as Vietnam or Poland," tech companies alone bought almost 25% of all renewable energy sold to corporations in 2019 (Ambrose 2020). Meanwhile, the International Energy Agency (IEA) reports that there is "evidence that prospective [renewable energy] investments from big tech companies have influenced policy decisions in a pro-renewables direction, for example, by leading to moves to improve network access." The opportunity to enter into a renewable energy power purchase agreement with a major tech company can alter the calculus of other actors in the landscape, as "a long-term contract with any of them provides strong investment security and enables project financing at attractive conditions" (Varro and Kamiya 2021).

Of the 34 companies whose behavior this book explores, none so clearly demonstrate the immense resources, reach, and potential influence of "corporate nations" as the companies that this chapter considers (Francis 2016). Indeed, by 2021, the "concentration of financial value in the top three tech firms" was "twice as high as what Standard Oil, AT&T, and US Steel represented at the time of the Rockefellers and Carnegies" (Varro and Kamiya 2021). From Apple, whose market capitalization hit $3 trillion in 2022—higher than the GDPs of all but four countries (Nahar 2022)—and that has an "active installed base" of 1.65 billion devices and 620 million subscribers on its platform (Nellis 2021), to Google, whose search engine processes two trillion searches annually and that has seven products with over one billion monthly users (Sullivan 2016; Balakrishnan 2017), these companies enjoy not just exceptional economic power and political clout but also sheer ubiquity in society.

* * *

This chapter explores the conditions under which select technology companies developed into key climate players during the 2010s. These companies became more confident that the world was headed toward a low-carbon future, less confident that states were providing, or in the

126   C. HULME

near future would provide, adequate "rules of the game" in the form of robust policy to pave the way to that future, and more ambitious in marshaling their own resources and exerting their influence to shape the climate change issue area. By the turn of the 2020s, these companies had arrived at a consensus that they had an indispensable role to play in leading the world toward a low-carbon future, and that failing to be out front and engaged on climate issues no longer was an option.

The first part of this chapter explores the behavior of five leading technology companies, including Apple, Google, and Microsoft, three "Big Tech" players in the United States; Infosys, India's second-largest IT company by revenue; and South Korea-based Samsung, the world's second-largest IT company by revenue and largest smartphone manufacturer by market share (Oberlo, n.d.). Amazon and Meta (formerly Facebook) are excluded due to inadequate data. During the 2010s, Amazon especially was notorious for its lack of transparency on climate-related issues; a 2017 Greenpeace report characterized it as "one of the least transparent companies in the world in terms of its environmental performance," noting that its refusal to report its greenhouse gas footprint was a "failure that is drawing the attention of its investors" (Cook and Jardim 2017, 13). In 2019, a journalist for *Wired*, highlighting that Amazon had released data on its global carbon footprint for the first time, observed that it had "made a habit of keeping information about its carbon footprint out of public view" (Oberhaus 2019). Meta, while registering considerable progress in key areas like clean power purchasing—between 2013 and 2020, the company signed contracts for more than three gw of new renewable energy (Facebook 2018)—released its first sustainability report in 2020 (Meta 2020), eight years after its initial public offering, and during the 2010s, like Amazon, did not disclose climate performance data to CDP. That by the turn of the 2020s, these companies perceived that failing to adopt particular practices, including meeting a certain level of transparency in reporting on climate issues, no longer was tenable points to the development of a new "dominant design," or shared understanding among actors about the sort of behavior necessary to prepare for and succeed in an anticipated future.

Part I of this chapter underscores how the company cohort made significant progress on its climate performance in 2010–2017; one company, Apple, became exceptionally climate active, becoming a "disruptor" by 2015–2017, while two others, Google and Infosys, became "innovators." Part II examines whether their behavior demonstrates a disjunction between the traits of individual companies, in terms of their perceptions of the material relevance of climate change, and the overall pattern of broadening and deepening climate action, indicative of a growing corporate consensus about the issue. It shows that there is evidence in this industry case study of the signature logic of emergence; companies improved their climate performance and came into the fold of corporate climate actors amid declining perceptions that climate-related factors entailed major material risks or opportunities. Their behavior captures this book's main argument: during the 2010s, the private sector, appreciating that the "story" of the climate issue area and the low-carbon future would be written by somebody, and perceiving states effectively to have opted out of being the lead authors in the writing process, seized the chance to shape the issue area in advantageous ways, becoming a de facto leader. For technology companies, there were relatively low barriers to adopting new behaviors and assuming a leadership mantle; in contrast to strong incumbents in industries such as automotive, cement, and oil and gas, they are weak incumbents, only loosely tethered to the high-carbon economy.

Part I: Climate Action, 2010–2017

Examining how companies behaved in 2010–2017 demonstrates that four out of five made significant changes in their climate approaches, while the cohort realized a 62% increase in overall performance. Certain practices became more widespread and companies became more deeply committed to them, providing support for a new paradigm of behavior taking shape.

Technology Companies' Behavior, 2010–2017

Table 4.1 captures change in companies' performance on three metrics of climate action: product, alignment, and investment. As the appendix describes, the industry-specific practices for the metrics were as follows: addressing the emissions intensity of their activities (*product*); addressing Scope 3 emissions, with a focus on the supply chain (*alignment*)[1]; and

---

[1] In contrast to hardware-focused companies, whose degree of alignment with a low-carbon future depends heavily on the decisions of hundreds or even thousands of suppliers, software-focused companies, relying on fewer suppliers, have a higher degree of influence over the degree to which their overall activities align with a low-carbon future. For

128   C. HULME

investing in renewable energy (*investment*). The stronger a company's performance on these practices, the higher its score, listed after its name. Presenting the cohort's cumulative score in each period, the last row highlights inter-period change and captures gains in underlying momentum. For each three-year period spanning the 2010–2017 timeframe, companies were classified as one of four types, each corresponding to a range of scores: *business as usual* (BAU), *evolutionary*, *innovator*, and *disruptor*. In the last column, companies' names are in bold to underscore their transition to higher types between periods 1 and 6.

Table 4.1 conveys that four companies (80%) achieved a greater level of climate activity, transitioning to higher types by 2015–2017. With three of those four landing in the disruptor or innovator camp by the last period, there was a high level of ambition among the type-changing companies. Beyond the positive overall change in direction, Table 4.1 also shows when and to what extent momentum was gathering. Between periods 1 and 6, there was a 62% increase in companies' cumulative score. The 27% inter-period gain in period 2 is of particular significance as it occurred well before the December 2015 Paris Conference, widely interpreted as a watershed for private sector climate action. Further, considering the three US-based companies—Apple, Google, and Microsoft, which count the United States as their most important market (Wallach 2020)—the gains realized or sustained in period 6 also are significant as this period encompasses the beginning of the Trump presidency, which heralded a clear change in the climate-related political winds in the United States.

Considering momentum at the company level, Table 4.1 shows that three of the four companies that transitioned to a higher type never regressed, making "sticky" progress toward more robust action; once momentum toward an enhanced climate approach was achieved, it was sustained. Importantly, while Google regressed to the evolutionary camp in periods 4 and 5, it ultimately landed among the innovators. Had the timeframe of interest been extended to 2019, there likely would have been further evidence of sticky progress at the company level. Indeed, technology companies subsequently doubled-down on commitments that were nascent in the timeframe captured by Table 4.1. For example, in 2019, Google set a record for the largest-ever corporate renewables procurement deal in an agreement that increased its procurement by

---

software-focused companies, therefore, a secondary indicator practice for *alignment*—internal carbon pricing—also was considered.

Table 4.1 Technology company types, 2010–2017

Type (points)	2010–2012 *(period 1)*	2011–2013 *(period 2)*	2012–2014 *(period 3)*	2013–2015 *(period 4)*	2014–2016 *(period 5)*	2015–2017 *(period 6)*
Disruptor *(16–20)*				Apple, 16	Apple, 17	**Apple**, 17
Innovator *(13–15)*		Google, 13	Google, 13			**Google**, 13 **Infosys**, 13
Evolutionary *(9–12)*	Google, 11	Infosys, 11 Apple, 9	Apple, 12 Infosys, 11	Infosys, 11 Google, 10	Infosys, 12 Google, 11	**Microsoft, 9**
BAU *(0–8)*	Infosys, 8 Apple, 7 Microsoft, 6 Samsung, 5	Microsoft, 7 Samsung, 7	Microsoft, 7 Samsung, 7	Samsung, 8 Microsoft, 7	Microsoft, 8 Samsung, 7	Samsung, 8
Total points (% change)	**37** (–)	**47** (27%)	**50** (6%)	**52** (4%)	**55** (6%)	**60** (9%) *(net:+62%)*

Source Author

Note Five technology companies, classified according to three-year performance on *product*, *alignment*, and *investment*. Companies received points out of **20** based on where they fell on a performance spectrum

130   C. HULME

40% (Golden 2019); likewise, in 2019, Microsoft increased its renewable energy portfolio by 60% compared to 2018 (Oberhaus 2019).

Identifying New Climate Practices

Given that the company cohort improved its climate performance by 62%, there is good preliminary evidence for a new paradigm of climate-relevant behavior. Table 4.2 displays as a percentage the number of companies receiving any points for each of the three metrics in a certain period ("breadth"), as well as the degree to which companies enhanced their commitment to the three metrics, showing the percentage of companies receiving over half the available points for a given metric ("depth").

Table 4.2 conveys that technology companies increasingly addressed Scope 3 emissions, particularly supply chain emissions (the practice for the alignment metric), which represent the major culprit in the carbon footprint of companies primarily focused on hardware (e.g., Apple, Microsoft, and Samsung),[2] while also constituting a key source (though overall

Table 4.2 Breadth and depth of technology companies' climate action, 2010–2017

Years (period)	Breadth			Depth		
	Product	Alignment	Investment	Product	Alignment	Investment
2010–2012 (1)	93	33	60	86	0	44
2011–2013 (2)	100	40	73	80	0	64
2012–2014 (3)	87	47	87	85	13	54
2013–2015 (4)	73	60	93	91	22	50
2014–2016 (5)	53	67	100	100	30	47
2015–2017 (6)	53	73	100	88	36	60
Percent change, periods 1–6	−43	+121	+67	+2	n/a (36 pts.)	+36

Source Author
Note Breadth captures the percentage of technology companies receiving any points for *product*, *alignment*, and *investment*. Depth captures the percentage receiving over half the available points for performance on these metrics. As *alignment* participation for "depth" began at 0, calculating a percent change is not possible; thus, the point increase is shown

[2] For example, as Dolsak and Prakash (2020) note, 75% of Microsoft's emissions are "Scope 3" emissions, which includes suppliers and end-users.

a smaller share) of emissions for companies whose main focus is software (e.g., Google and Infosys). The decline in participation in *product*, meanwhile, indicates that fewer companies were reducing the emissions intensity of their operations, which for companies that focus on hardware represent the relatively small percentage of emissions tied to their own activities (e.g., powering corporate facilities), but for companies that focus on software constitute a greater share of their total emissions.

Capturing the sustained momentum on the alignment and investment metrics, Table 4.2 points to the stickiness, or lock-in potential, of the relevant practices, including working with suppliers to address supply chain emissions (an especially vital component of Scope 3 emissions) and entering into commercial partnerships to procure renewable energy. The lock-in potential of the latter behavior is of particular interest, as some of the technology companies that in 2010–2017 rose to rank among the world's largest purchasers of green power (e.g., Apple, Google, and Microsoft) have not merely sustained but significantly increased their green power purchasing ambition since 2017.

Meanwhile, the significant increase in deep participation in *alignment* captures how companies that were doing anything to address Scope 3 emissions did progressively more over time, becoming increasingly ambitious in how they sought to address what for hardware-focused companies constitute the source of the vast majority of their total emissions. Apple offers an illustrative example. In 2015, reporting that the carbon footprint of its supply chain represented 72% of its total emissions, the company announced that it aimed to see "the same progress in our suppliers' use of clean energy that we've seen in our own" (Apple 2015, 8). By 2016, Apple was "working with suppliers to install more than 4 gigawatts of new clean energy worldwide, including 2 gigawatts in China by 2020." This effort, Apple projected, "will avoid over 30 million metric tons of carbon pollution, equivalent to taking over 6 million cars off the road for one year" (Apple 2016, 6). By 2017, Greenpeace reported that Apple had "made impressive progress" since 2014 on helping its "entire global supply chain" move toward 100% renewable energy use, having secured "commitments from 14 suppliers to power their operations with enough renewable energy needed to manufacture Apple devices or components" (Cook and Jardim 2017, 1).

Table 4.2 also captures that, with a 36% increase in deep participation in the investment metric, companies that produced or procured renewable energy became more ambitious in terms of the variants of the behavior they adopted. At one end of the ambition continuum is the purchasing of renewable energy certificates (RECs), which are "tradable instruments that represent the clean energy attributes of renewable energy and give the owner the legal right to claim renewable energy use from a specific source." By purchasing RECs, businesses can maintain their existing power contracts and do not need to change their energy mix; in fact, a company can claim to be powered by 100% renewable energy when it is merely purchasing sufficient RECs to match its conventional energy usage. In many cases, companies purchase a particular type called "unbundled RECs," which means that their purchase does not enable new renewable energy projects to be built that otherwise would not have been built, a principle called "additionality" (Urban Grid 2019).

In contrast, at the high end of the ambition continuum, companies can enter into long-term power purchase agreements with renewable energy producers, which "are much stronger in terms of additionality than the purchase of unbundled RECs. The long-term contract to buy a project's renewable energy is a critical factor in enabling the financing and construction of a new renewable energy project" (Urban Grid 2019). A particularly strong arrangement entails a company entering into a power purchase agreement with a supplier in sufficiently close proximity to the company's facilities so that the company itself can use the energy it purchases.

Table 4.2 captures that those companies that reported using renewable energy increasingly were actually doing so, as opposed to buying unbundled RECs or otherwise offsetting emissions from their conventional power usage. In addition, companies that started small in terms of renewables purchasing or procurement became increasingly ambitious in their efforts to effect larger-scale, extra-industry change. Google was a trailblazer in this domain; already by 2013, it reported having committed "over $1 billion to renewable energy project investments, signed agreements to procure over 260 megawatts (MW) of wind power near our data centers, and installed 1.7 MW of solar at our corporate headquarters," indicating that Google had invested in projects that were influencing its own power supply (Google 2013, 1). By 2016, Google reported,

> We're also looking beyond our business to drive wide-scale adoption of renewable energy. We're supporting new energy purchasing models that others can follow, such as our pioneering commitment to long-term contracts to buy renewable energy directly from developers ... and our

4 CLIMATE INFLUENCERS: TECHNOLOGY   133

support of renewable energy purchasing programs with utilities. We're also helping to green the power grid through … our \$2.5 billion in equity investment commitments for renewable energy projects. (Google 2016b, 26)

By 2017, Google had signed 20 power purchase agreements to purchase 2.6 gw of renewable energy "that is new to the grid"—meeting the standard of additionality—"generating emissions savings that are equivalent to taking more than 1.2 million cars off the road" (Google 2017, 26). By contrast, as of 2016, Microsoft, which during the decade lagged behind Google and Apple in its level of climate ambition, still relied on purchasing green power via unbundled RECs (and thus its purchases did not enable new renewable energy projects to be built, failing to align with the additionality principle). As *Bloomberg New Energy Finance* noted, this approach "sets Microsoft apart, as most corporate buyers of renewable energy have turned away from purchasing unbundled RECs" (2016, 1).

While Table 4.2 captures how committed companies were to specific practices, it does not capture whether they were deeply committed to those practices that were weighted most heavily, which depended on whether a company's primary focus was hardware or software, a key factor influencing the main culprit of its carbon footprint (see the appendix for details). Over time, the percentage of companies receiving over half the available points on the most heavily weighted metric for their sector increased from 33% in period 1 to 60% in period 6.[3] This indicates that companies were making progress on actions that were least amenable to short-term change (for software-focused companies, addressing the emissions intensity of their operations—the product metric), or that posed especially complex challenges (for hardware-focused companies, addressing Scope 3 emissions, particularly supply chain emissions—the alignment metric).

* * *

Examining how companies behaved from 2010 through 2017 shows that the cohort progressed toward a higher level of climate activity (and achieved momentum early on), with 80% of companies altering their

---

[3] From period 1 to period 6, the percentage of companies meeting the 51% threshold for deep participation on the most heavily weighted metric was 33, 40, 47, 47, 53, and 60, respectively.

134 C. HULME

approach in a significant fashion, transitioning to a higher type over time. It also found evidence of coalescence in the patterns of participation in specific practices; participation in two practices widened and participation in all three practices deepened. Of particular significance was that companies' behavior had the potential to influence developments outside their industry; in applying the additionality standard to their procurement of renewable energy, for example, companies like Apple and Google drove renewables projects that otherwise would not have been built. Renewable energy procurement had the potential to transform the landscape in another sense; entering into a long-term power purchase agreement has a high potential to nurture lock-in, or a situation of immediate durability, as companies cannot easily reverse their behavior in the short term and this, in turn, can lead to a dynamic of self-reinforcement, or perceived rising reversal costs over time.[4] Climate practices with a high potential for lock-in and self-reinforcement are indispensable for entrenching a certain set of behaviors as the new dominant design, or de facto standard of behavior with which corporations must align themselves to prepare for an anticipated future.

PART II: THE LOGIC OF EMERGENCE

This part of the chapter explores how technology companies—which became increasingly climate active during the 2010s and, in select cases, among the leading corporate climate actors overall—perceived the material importance of the climate issue. In this industry case, there is strong support that the development of interest in this book—a new corporate climate consensus—was emergent, marked by an inconsistency between the attributes of individual actors and the cohort's behavior. In fact, technology companies did not just fail to perceive climate change as a high-impact material concern—their outlook for robust state action declined over time, while perceived prospects for climate-related changes in consumer behavior remained consistently low.

Table 4.3 presents data from annual CDP disclosures from 2010 to 2016 tracking whether companies perceived high-impact material risks and/or opportunities tied to climate-related regulation and changing consumer behavior; it separates the data concerning perceptions of climate

---

[4] On lock-in and self-reinforcement, see Levin et al. (2012).

change overall as a high-impact issue (combining the two factors) from that specific to perceptions concerning regulation and changing consumer behavior.[5] If all companies in a given period perceived that climate change presented risks and opportunities entailing a high level of impact, the "perceived high material impact" column would register 100.

Table 4.3 conveys that not only was climate change never widely perceived to be a high-impact material concern (with perception strength peaking at 28% in period 1), but that perceptions of its significance moved in the "wrong" direction; put differently, the 21% decline would be unexpected given the degree to which tech companies altered their approach to the climate change issue. As Table 4.3 highlights, this development occurred in the context of declining outlooks for state action (through policy and regulation presenting major material opportunities and/or risks). Meanwhile, for the tech industry the consumer-based alternative explanation for changes in corporate behavior finds no traction; there was no net change in perceived prospects for climate-related changing consumer behavior, which remained a limited concern at just 20%.

There is strong evidence for the logic of emergence underpinning technology companies' behavior. As Table 4.3 shows, companies most

Table 4.3 Perceived high material impact of climate change among technology companies, 2010–2016

Years (period)	Perceived high material impact		
	Overall	Regulation	Consumer
2010–2012 (1)	28	36	20
2011–2013 (2)	25	35	15
2012–2014 (3)	23	33	18
2013–2015 (4)	23	27	20
2014–2016 (5)	22	23	20
Percent change, periods 1–5	−21	−36	0

Source Author
Note Among technology companies, the percentage of climate-related risks and opportunities that were perceived to be a high-impact material concern

---

[5] The perception data in this chapter excludes 2017 due to changes in the CDP disclosure questions that compromise the comparability of the 2017 responses with those of previous years. Thus, there is perception data only for periods 1 through 5.

136   C. HULME

perceived climate change overall as a serious material concern in period 1; from period 2 onward, it steadily declined in importance. In Part I, Table 4.2 showed that the breadth and depth of companies' participation in both the alignment and investment metrics increased significantly over time. In short, companies were participating neither extensively nor intensively in *alignment* (addressing Scope 3 emissions) and *investment* (investing in renewable energy) when they most saw climate change as a significant material concern. Over time, as the issue became less of a material concern, participation in both kinds of action became broader and deeper. This counterintuitive finding points to the disjunction between individual companies' perceptions about the climate issue area, on the one hand, and the coalescence around a set of behaviors reflecting a shared understanding about the need to respond to the issue, on the other, that is the signature of emergence.

How relevant was climate change perceived to be specifically by those four companies that changed types over time? Table 4.4 captures whether companies that belonged to a higher type in the last period than in the first perceived the climate change issue as a high-impact material concern, separating data addressing their overall perception from that concerning regulation and changing consumer behavior.

Table 4.4 captures an inconsistency between how companies perceived the material importance of climate change and how they behaved; all four cases provide support for this book's argument that an emergent climate consensus behaved as a "steering mechanism" (Rosenau 1995, 14), leading companies to adopt certain behaviors while seemingly lacking strong material incentives to do so. Beginning with the strongest example of a company whose behavior reflected this logic, Apple was the most active climate performer—the only technology company to become a disruptor (and as Chapter 6 discusses, one of the few disruptors among all 34 companies that this book examines). Table 4.4 conveys that for Apple, climate change never was a high-impact material concern; there were no perceived prospects either for robust state action (in the form of regulation offering major opportunities or presenting serious risks) or for changes in consumer practices driven by climate concerns. Considering its exceptionally strong climate performance alongside a perception strength of "zero," Apple's case demonstrates the largest possible inconsistency between action and perception.

The case of Google also captures an actor whose behavior was not grounded in company-level perceptions of climate-related material

Table 4.4 Perceived high material impact of climate change for technology companies increasing climate performance sufficiently to change types, 2010–2016

Years (period)	Overall				Regulation				Consumer			
	AAPL	*GOOG*	*MSFT*	*INFY*	*AAPL*	*GOOG*	*MSFT*	*INFY*	*AAPL*	*GOOG*	*MSFT*	*INFY*
2010–2012 (1)	–	0	0	25	–	0	0	50	–	0	0	0
2011–2013 (2)	0	0	0	33	0	0	0	50	0	0	0	17
2012–2014 (3)	0	0	0	42	0	0	0	50	0	0	0	33
2013–2015 (4)	0	0	0	42	0	0	0	33	0	0	0	50
2014–2016 (5)	0	0	0	33	0	0	0	17	0	0	0	50

Source Author

Note For technology companies that increased climate performance sufficiently to change types (i.e., becoming *evolutionaries*, *innovators*, or *disruptors*), the percentage of climate-related risks and opportunities that were perceived to be a high-impact material concern. AAPL is Apple; GOOG, Google; MSFT, Microsoft; and INFY, Infosys. Apple does not have a perception score for period 1 given that it did not participate in CDP disclosure during the reporting cycles covering 2010–2012 (it began participating in 2013)

138   C. HULME

impacts, but rather in the broader development of corporations coming to recognize the need for a different approach to an increasingly important issue area marked by inadequate governance by states. Like Apple, Google perceived no high-impact material risks or opportunities related to climate change. Also like Apple, Google was a strong climate actor; it was the first to become an innovator in 2011–2013. But whereas Apple increased its performance by 143% between periods 1 and 6, Google only improved by 18%, as Table 4.1 captures.

Microsoft offers another example of the logic of emergence at the company level, but to a lesser degree than Apple or Google. Like those two companies, it never perceived climate change to be of high material importance. But whereas Apple and Google were among the strongest climate performers overall, Microsoft only landed in the evolutionary camp; there was a relatively smaller disjunction between its perception and action. Finally, Infosys' type change in period 5, from evolutionary to innovator, signifying its move toward a more climate-active approach, coincided with a 21% decline in strength of perception compared to period 4—a clear example of the inconsistency between action and perception that is the signature of emergence.

In sum, there was a marked inconsistency in how this company cohort moved toward a more climate-active approach and how companies individually perceived the material importance of climate change. There was a stark disjunction between how the most climate-active technology companies (Apple and Google) perceived the issue's direct business relevance and how they behaved; these companies became among the leading private sector climate actors overall in the context of perceiving *no* prospects for robust, high-impact state action on the issue and *no* outlook for significant changes in consumer practices tied to growing climate concerns.

* * *

A closer look at technology companies' trajectories toward not just a higher level of climate action but toward climate leadership captures how, more markedly than other industries that this book considers, the technology industry demonstrated a certain sensibility about the leadership role that it could—and should—play in addressing climate change and supporting a global low-carbon transition. Technology companies framed their behavior partly in terms of their potential to influence climate-related developments in other industries—and in certain cases, contrasted their own leadership with the inadequate action of governments.

For example, considering those companies that transitioned to higher types in 2010–2017, Google reported seeking to ensure that its activities in the renewable energy space were "scalable" and had "the highest possible impact on the industry. When possible, our efforts should directly address problems that limit the growth of renewable energy" (Google 2013, 1). The company highlighted its influence in the global landscape; in 2016, it reported signing "renewable energy contracts in five countries across three continents. These contracts have driven the construction of renewable energy projects around the world and will generate more than $3.5 billion in capital investment by renewable energy project developers." Beyond "continuing to aggressively move forward with renewable energy technologies like wind and solar, we will work to achieve the much more challenging long-term goal of powering our operations on a region-specific, 24-7 basis with clean, zero-carbon energy." This "more ambitious goal," Google explained, was a "key next step necessary to drive clean energy from being an important but limited element of the global electricity supply portfolio today to a resource that fully and completely powers both our operations and the entire electric grid of the future" (Google 2016a, 1).

Like Google, Apple underscored its global reach and influence as a key player in the climate arena, highlighting in 2018 that 100% of its operations around the world, spanning 43 countries, "now [run] on clean power. In the process, we've paved the way for other companies and organizations to purchase renewable energy and transition their own operations to greener power." Apple implicitly contrasted its proactive approach to the climate issue with that of the federal government in the United States; for example, it reported, "After the U.S. withdrew from the Paris [Climate Agreement], Apple responded by issuing a $1 billion green bond for environmental projects, bringing our total to $2.5 billion" (Apple 2018, 3, 7).

Like Apple, Infosys not only defined itself as being out front on the climate issue but also showed how its approach contrasted with behind-the-curve policymakers. In 2011, the Executive Co-Chair of the Board wrote, "The time has come for us to take leadership of the movement" to reduce corporate carbon footprints; he highlighted that the "challenges

140 C. HULME

before us are gigantic and require a close partnership between governments and the private sector." That year, the head of green initiatives framed the company's approach toward climate action in these terms: "Trailblazing businesses don't wait for government regulations to act" (Infosys 2012, 4, 32). Infosys echoed Google in underscoring its efforts to shape the global landscape. In 2012, it reported that it was the first Indian IT company "to take up the carbon neutrality goal and we strongly hope that this will make carbon accounting and carbon footprint reduction more acceptable and popular among industries not just in the developing world but across the globe" (Infosys 2013, 10).

Samsung was unique in the company cohort in terms of never changing types and remaining a BAU throughout the 2010–2017 timeframe. Notably, however, during much of the decade it followed a very similar path as Microsoft in terms of level of climate activity and commitment. For instance, from period 1 (2010–2012) through period 5 (2014–2016), both were BAU companies. They both focused primarily on increasing the energy efficiency of their products—relatively low-hanging fruit compared to pioneering efforts by Apple and Google in domains like corporate clean power purchasing and reducing global supply chain emissions. But in 2015–2017, when Microsoft began pivoting toward a higher level of ambition, Samsung remained a BAU. In fact, a 2017 Greenpeace report noted that Samsung lagged "far behind other brands in tackling its corporate contribution to climate change." The company had failed to set a renewable energy or greenhouse gas mitigation target for its "expanding supply chain" (Cook and Jardim 2017, 12). Indeed, Greenpeace argued, Samsung, which has the "largest smartphone market share globally and is one of the main suppliers of key components to other major tech brands, with 38 production sites and more than 2,000 suppliers across the world" (Greenpeace 2018), was holding back the entire IT sector "by failing to tackle its climate change responsibility by committing to 100% renewable energy for its operations." Indeed, by 2017, only 1% of the company's energy use came from renewable energy (Cook and Jardim 2017, 4).

Their similarities throughout much of the decade notwithstanding, a key difference between Microsoft and Samsung concerned their attitude toward, and expectations for, robust climate action by governments. Microsoft grounded its climate approach in terms of how governments had fallen short in the climate policy arena. In fact, while ramping up its climate action in 2015–2017, Microsoft never mentioned the Paris Agreement in its annual or corporate citizenship reports; whatever meaning states accorded to the commitments they made at the Paris Conference, apparently from Microsoft's perspective they did not warrant mention in its key strategic documents. In contrast, in its 2016 sustainability report Samsung reflected, "Through the work of [the] United Nations Framework Convention on Climate Change (UNFCCC), Paris COP21 in December 2015 and the World Economic Forum in Davos in January 2016[,] the global economy is unanimously recognizing that climate change is a significant threat to the global economy. Governments have committed to accelerate the shift to a low-carbon economy model" (Samsung Electronics 2016, 144).

Samsung's CDP disclosures confirm that the company viewed the climate change issue as a matter for governments to address, and, more precisely, as one that they *would* address; in contrast to the other tech titans, during the 2010–2016 timeframe Samsung reported perceiving high-impact risks and opportunities from climate-related policy and regulation. In this context of strong expectations for robust state climate action, it behaved as a climate laggard, eschewing proactive efforts to align itself with a low-carbon future. This pattern of behavior—where high expectations for state action corresponded with low levels of action on Samsung's part—suggests that Samsung decided that it would wait and see what "rules of the game" states developed before taking action. To the extent that Samsung began to "get in the game" by the late 2010s—in 2018, for instance, it became the first Asian electronics manufacturing company to "commit to 100% renewable energy in the United States, Europe, and China by 2020," a "major commitment," according to Greenpeace, with the potential to have "an enormous impact in reducing the company's massive global manufacturing footprint" (Greenpeace 2018)—it may have done so on the basis of its expectation that its old strategy no longer would work going forward.

The most significant cost to Samsung of its "wait and see" approach was forgoing the opportunity to be an early mover in shaping the climate change arena. Indeed, peers like Microsoft ultimately became influencers in that arena specifically in the context of "factoring out" governments as the indispensable and decisive climate players (as discussed, during the 2010s, Microsoft never expected states to undertake high-impact climate action). As one journalist observed following Microsoft's path-breaking 2020 pledge to go carbon negative as opposed to merely carbon neutral, the company "is setting new standards, especially in the rigor and transparency it is applying to the effort, and it is deliberately attempting

142   C. HULME

to bring other companies, both suppliers and competitors, along with it into a world of shared metrics and data" (Roberts 2020). In short, Samsung embodied the old world, where companies relied on, expected, and waited for states to provide the rules of the climate game. Microsoft, meanwhile, came to align itself with the new world, where it was precisely those companies that recognized that states would not provide bold leadership that identified the necessity of shaping the rules themselves.

CONCLUSION

Examining the behavior of five leading technology companies, this chapter found that in 2010–2017, the cohort significantly increased its level of climate action, with select companies becoming global leaders in such key climate practices as procuring renewable energy in alignment with the additionality principle. Of the 34 companies that this book explores, with few exceptions none have played so influential a role as technology companies in shaping a corporate consensus about climate change and the role of the private sector in establishing rules for a low-carbon future. Companies like Apple and Google were influential early movers in the issue area, while companies such as Microsoft relatively recently started "getting in the game" more seriously.

Other major players also have shaped and been shaped by the new consensus about the technology industry's role as a climate change and low-carbon leader. For example, according to an analysis published by Harvard Business School, Hewlett Packard became an unlikely climate leader; in 2016, for instance, it "set new aggressive emissions reduction goals by establishing a first of its kind supply-chain-specific greenhouse gas reduction goal of 15% by 2025 (compared to 2015 levels) via science-based emissions targets at each supplier." Why did Hewlett Packard behave this way? The company "is keenly focused on getting out ahead of climate change policy so it can avoid energy cost spikes caused by last-minute desperate regulatory measures" (Harvard Business School Digital Initiative 2017). CDP disclosures confirm that during the 2010–2016 timeframe, Hewlett Packard never perceived any high-impact material costs or opportunities from climate-related regulation—in the short, medium, or long term. Like its industry peers, it became increasingly confident in a low-carbon future (and more confident that at some point states would have no choice but to act, and indeed would be forced to impose "desperate" measures on account of being so late to the game) and began to alter its behavior accordingly, acting as if certain "rules of the game" existed despite states not providing them, and despite a stark lack of confidence that they would provide them in the near future.

As weak incumbents with relatively loose ties to the high-carbon economy—or with a limited degree of embeddedness in the status quo compared to companies in energy-intensive industries—as well as ubiquitous reach, major technology firms are uniquely well-positioned to shape and influence the climate change issue area. During the 2010s, they took advantage of that position, in some cases becoming climate active to such an extent that they were treated as the "yardstick" against which other global actors—including the most powerful states—should be compared. For example, in 2019, during "Climate Week" held on the margins of the opening of a new session of the United Nations General Assembly, the president of the EDF + Business initiative of the Environmental Defense Fund highlighted that whereas the Trump administration had "cede[d] global leadership on climate by formally withdrawing from the Paris Agreement," Microsoft had "upped its renewable portfolio to more than 1900 [megawatts]—enough to power 1.5 million U.S. homes," while Google had "announced the largest-ever renewable energy procurement deal," making its "total clean energy portfolio large enough to power Uruguay" (Murray 2019). This chapter foregrounds one of the key unintended consequences of states relinquishing their traditional role as lead authors of the global response to transnational issues impacting the international security environment: other actors can come to the fore and in short order make states that have absented themselves from leadership increasingly peripheral to the global "conversation."

REFERENCES

Abbott, Stephen. 2015. Inside Microsoft's wind energy strategy. GreenBiz. August 18, 2015. https://www.greenbiz.com/article/inside-microsofts-wind-energy-strategy.

Ambrose, Jillian. 2020. Tech giants power record surge in renewable energy sales. *The Guardian*, January 28, 2020. https://www.theguardian.com/env ironment/2020/jan/28/google-tech-giants-spark-record-rise-in-sales-of-ren ewable-energy.

144 C. HULME

Apple. 2015. Environmental responsibility report: 2015 progress report, covering fiscal year 2014. May 2015. https://www.apple.com/environment/pdf/Apple_Environmental_Responsibility_Report_2015.pdf.

Apple. 2016. Environmental progress report: 2016 progress report, covering fiscal year 2015. September 2016. https://www.apple.com/environment/pdf/Apple_Environmental_Responsibility_Report_2016.pdf.

Apple. 2018. Environmental responsibility report: 2018 progress report, covering fiscal year 2017. April 2018. https://www.apple.com/environment/pdf/Apple_Environmental_Responsibility_Report_2018.pdf.

Balakrishnan, Anita. 2017. Here's how billions of people use Google products, in one chart. CNBC. May 18, 2017. https://www.cnbc.com/2017/05/18/google-user-numbers-youtube-android-drive-photos.html.

Berthiaume, Dan. 2020. Amazon launching 26 renewable energy projects. Chain Store Age. December 9, 2020. https://chainstoreage.com/amazon-launching-26-renewable-energy-projects.

Bloomberg New Energy Finance. 2016. Corporate renewable energy procurement monthly. December 2016. https://assets.bbhub.io/professional/sites/24/2016/12/Corporate_Renewable_Energy_Procurement_Monthly_December_BNEF.pdf.

Cook, Gary, and Elizabeth Jardim. 2017. Greenpeace guide to greener electronics – 2017 company report card. Greenpeace. October 17, 2017. https://www.greenpeace.org/usa/wp-content/uploads/2017/10/Guide-to-Greener-Electronics-2017.pdf.

Dolsak, Nives, and Aseem Prakash. 2020. The climate leadership race: Microsoft's climate moonshot and Amazon's climate pledge. *Forbes*, January 17, 2020. https://www.forbes.com/sites/prakashdolsak/2020/01/17/the-climate-leadership-race-microsofts-climate-moonshot-and-amazons-climate-pledge/?sh=3b6539256298.

Facebook. 2018. On our way to lower emissions and 100% renewable energy. August 28, 2018. https://about.fb.com/news/2018/08/renewable-energy/.

Francis, David. 2016. The top 25 corporate nations. *Foreign Policy,* March 15, 2016. https://foreignpolicy.com/2016/03/15/these-25-companies-are-more-powerful-than-many-countries-multinational-corporate-wealth-power/.

Golden, Sarah. 2019. Google's jaw-dropping renewable procurement proclamation. GreenBiz. September 19, 2019. https://www.greenbiz.com/article/googles-jaw-dropping-renewable-procurement-proclamation.

Google. 2013. Expanding renewable energy options for companies through utility-offered "renewable energy tariffs." April 19, 2013. https://static.googleusercontent.com/media/www.google.com/en//green/pdf/renewable-energy-options.pdf.

4 CLIMATE INFLUENCERS: TECHNOLOGY   145

Google. 2016a. Achieving our 100% renewable energy purchasing goal and going beyond. December 2016. https://static.googleusercontent.com/media/www.google.com/en//green/pdf/achieving-100-renewable-energy-purchasing-goal.pdf.

Google. 2016b. Environmental report. November 1, 2016. https://www.gstatic.com/gumdrop/sustainability/environmental-report-2016b.pdf.

Google. 2017. Environmental report: 2017 progress update. October 2017. https://www.gstatic.com/gumdrop/sustainability/google-2017-environme ntal-report.pdf.

Greenpeace. 2018. Breaking: Samsung commits to 100% renewable energy after global protests: Greenpeace response. June 13, 2018. https://www.greenp eace.org/usa/news/breaking-samsung-commits-100-renewable-energy-glo bal-protests-greenpeace-response/.

Harvard Business School Digital Initiative. 2017. Hewlett Packard Enterprise—an unexpected leader in the fight against climate change. November 15, 2017. https://d3.harvard.edu/platform-rctom/submission/hewlett-packard-enterprise-an-unexpected-leader-in-the-fight-against-climate-change/.

Infosys. 2012. Sustainability report 2011–2012. https://www.infosys.com/sustai nability/documents/infosys-sustainability-report-2011-12.pdf.

Infosys. 2013. Relevance through innovation: sustainability report 2012–2013. https://www.infosys.com/sustainability/documents/infosys-sustainab ility-report-2012-13.pdf.

Jones, Nicola. 2018. How to stop data centres from gobbling up the world's electricity. *Nature*, September 13, 2018. https://www.nature.com/articles/d41586-018-06610-y.

Levin, Kelly, Benjamin Cashore, Steven Bernstein, and Graeme Auld. 2012. Overcoming the tragedy of super-wicked problems. *Policy Sciences* 45: 123–152. https://doi.org/10.1007/s11077-012-9151-0.

Marcacci, Silvio. 2018. The world's biggest corporations are charging toward 100% renewable energy. Google and Apple are leading the way. *Energy Central*, April 25, 2018. https://energycentral.com/c/ec/worlds-biggest-corporations-are-charging-toward-100-renewable-energy-google-and.

Meta. 2020. A closer look at Facebook's commitment to sustainability. July 8, 2020. https://about.fb.com/news/2020/07/sustainability-report/.

Microsoft. 2017. Microsoft 2016 corporate social responsibility. https://www.microsoft.com/en-us/CMSFiles/Microsoft_2016_Corporate_Social_Respon sibility.pdf%3Fversion%3D889768cf-2300-6a48-33e1-5fca73a1836e%26Coll ectionId%3Ddf8dab12-dbf6-441f-a2db-5996225f2c6a.

Murray, Tom. 2019. The businesses that are—and are not—leading on climate change. *Forbes*, November 8, 2019. https://www.forbes.com/sites/edfene rgyexchange/2019/11/08/the-businesses-that-are--and-are-not--leading-on-climate-change/?sh=342ee2f47aa1.

146   C. HULME

Nahar, Pawan. 2022. Apple's m-cap at $3 trillion less than just four nations' GDP. *The Economic Times*, January 4, 2022. https://economictimes.indiat imes.com/markets/stocks/news/apple-m-cap-at-3-trillion-only-four-nations-worth-more-than-the-iphone-maker/articleshow/88685135.cms.

Nellis, Stephen. 2021. Apple posts record profit as iPhone sales surge in China. *The Economic Times*, January 28, 2021. https://economictimes.indiatimes.com/tech/tech-bytes/apple-posts-record-profit-as-iphone-sales-surge-in-china/articleshow/80490035.cms.

Oberhaus, Daniel. Amazon, Google, Microsoft: Here's who has the greenest cloud. *Wired*, December 10, 2019. https://www.wired.com/story/amazon-google-microsoft-green-clouds-and-hyperscale-data-centers/.

Oberlo. n.d. Smartphone market share worldwide. https://www.oberlo.com/sta tistics/smartphone-market-share.

Roberts, David. 2020. Microsoft's astonishing climate change goals, explained. Vox. July 30, 2020. https://www.vox.com/energy-and-environment/2020/7/30/21336777/microsoft-climate-change-goals-negative-emissions-techno logies.

Rosenau, James. 1995. Governance in the twenty-first century. *Global Governance* 1 (1): 13–43. https://doi.org/10.1057/9780230245310_2.

Samsung Electronics. 2016. Samsung sustainability report 2016. June 30, 2016. https://images.samsung.com/is/content/samsung/assets/global/our-val ues/resource/about-us-sustainability-report-and-policy-sustainability-report-2016-en.pdf.

Sullivan, Danny. 2016. Google now handles at least 2 trillion searches per year. Search Engine Land. May 24, 2016. https://searchengineland.com/google-now-handles-2-999-trillion-searches-per-year-250247.

Urban Grid. 2019. What is a REC and how do they work? June 25, 2019. https://www.urbangridsolar.com/what-is-a-rec-how-do-they-work/.

Vandenbergh, Michael, and Jonathan Gilligan. 2017. Why private "actors" are taking center stage on climate change. GreenBiz. December 9, 2017. https://www.greenbiz.com/article/why-private-actors-are-taking-cen ter-stage-climate-change.

Varro, Laszlo, and George Kamiya. 2021. 5 ways Big Tech could have big impacts on clean energy transitions. International Energy Agency. March 25, 2021. https://www.iea.org/commentaries/5-ways-big-tech-could-have-big-impacts-on-clean-energy-transitions.

Wallach, Omri. 2020. How Big Tech makes their billions. *Visual Capitalist*, July 6, 2020. https://www.visualcapitalist.com/how-big-tech-makes-their-bil lions-2020/.

CHAPTER 5

"The Earth Is Shifting Beneath Their Feet": Finance

INTRODUCTION

In January 2020, in his annual letter to company executives, BlackRock CEO Larry Fink wrote that climate change "has become a defining factor in companies' long-term prospects" and that the "evidence on climate risk is compelling investors to reassess core assumptions about modern finance" (Fink 2020). In the letter, an annual event for Wall Street that has been described as "a bellwether for the financial services industry" and as having "the influence to change the conversations inside boardrooms around the globe" (Kaplan 2020; Sorkin 2020), Fink announced, "I believe we are on the edge of a fundamental reshaping of finance," and set forth that BlackRock, the world's largest asset manager, would undertake initiatives like exiting investments "that present a high sustainability-related risk, such as thermal coal producers" (Fink 2020). That month, BlackRock also joined Climate Action 100+, an "investment

---

The phrase, "The earth is shifting beneath their feet," is borrowed from Bloomberg and Pope, who noted, "While some fossil fuel companies cling to their market share, more investors and CEOs recognize that the earth is shifting beneath their feet" (2017, 199).

© The Author(s), under exclusive license to Springer Nature 147
Switzerland AG 2023
C. Hulme, *Corporate Climate Action, Transnational Politics, and World Order*, Environmental Politics and Theory,
https://doi.org/10.1007/978-3-031-34115-1_5

pact" comprising investors managing $41 trillion of assets, which "pressures the companies responsible for two-thirds of annual global industrial emissions to show how they will reduce carbon dioxide emissions," and that treats climate change as "a systemic risk—one which investors cannot diversify away from" (Herz 2020). Prior to 2020, BlackRock was notorious for undermining this particular organization's efforts by voting against shareholder resolutions that it brought forth, which were aimed at holding fossil fuel companies to account on climate issues (Greenfield and Jolly 2020).

What was the significance of Fink's letter? For some, it represented "a seismic shift in the way mainstream finance is starting to think about climate change and investing" and marked a "major turning point" for BlackRock, a climate laggard (Kaplan 2020; Ceres 2020). But for others, while the letter did represent "a significant change from just a year ago [2019] when Fink's annual letter didn't even mention climate change," its import ultimately would depend on whether BlackRock altered such behavior as using its "enormous financial leverage to support fossil fuel CEOs and spike climate-critical shareholder resolutions" (Brune 2020).

In the context of this book, Fink's letter was significant for articulating the essence of the corporate consensus on climate change that had developed during the 2010s. But the letter was significant in another respect. In articulating the new consensus, Fink spoke less as a leader of one industry among many that would be affected by impending challenges to the high-carbon status quo, and more as a representative of the status quo itself. BlackRock was not simply a company with deep ties to the old fossil fuel-centered dominant design, or standard of behavior seen as necessary to adopt in order to succeed—it effectively *embodied* the old dominant design. Chapters 3 and 4 examined the extent to which both strong incumbents, tightly tethered to the high-carbon status quo (such as automakers and companies in energy-intensive industries), and weak incumbents, with relatively loose bonds to the status quo (such as technology companies), began loosening their ties to the old dominant design and adopting behaviors compatible with the new. This chapter examines the behavior of six companies that are not heavily invested only in a certain piece of the high-carbon economy—they are linchpins of that economy.

The chapter is divided into three parts. The first presents a snapshot of the landscape in the late 2010s and early 2020s, presenting initial evidence that the status quo approach to climate change was under increasing pressure in the finance industry. The second part examines the behavior of six of the world's most powerful players in insurance and banking (AIG, Allianz, Bank of America, Citigroup, Deutsche Bank, and JPMorgan), evaluating the extent to which the cohort moved toward a new climate approach in 2010–2017. All six companies behaved as "business as usual" companies, or BAUs, in 2010–2012, and all but one (Allianz) remained BAUs as of 2015–2017. Yet, all six improved their performance, and select companies adopted practices that appeared to be canaries in the coal mine for where the industry was heading. In 2020, when Fink published the letter that sent "shockwaves" through the business world (Vermillion 2020), select leviathans of global finance, still deeply entwined in the status quo, had begun to behave as if there were new, fundamental cracks in the old dominant design.

Finally, the third part of this chapter examines whether there is evidence of the pattern of emergent action in the finance industry. The six companies never perceived climate change as being of high material concern—in fact, as the decade unfolded, its perceived importance decreased—yet all made improvements in their performance. The case points to the disjunction between perception and action that is the essence of an emergent pattern; given the scant material relevance these finance heavyweights accorded climate change, even the modest gains in performance they realized would have been unexpected. This part of the chapter underscores how these companies, despite often fierce resistance, ultimately became part of the process that shaped a new corporate consensus about the need to prepare for a low-carbon future on account of climate-related developments. By 2020, the finance industry found itself standing, in Fink's words, "on the edge of a fundamental reshaping" due to climate change (2020)—despite that, from the individual perspective of six key players, material impacts tied to climate change had not provided decisive "pushes" or "pulls" toward that edge during the 2010s.

Part I: The Old Dominant Design Comes Under Pressure

In a 2015 speech to Lloyd's of London in which he warned that "once climate change becomes a defining issue for financial stability, it may already be too late," Governor of the Bank of England Mark Carney observed that since the 1980s, "the number of registered weather-related loss events has tripled," and that inflation-adjusted "insurance losses from these events have increased from an annual average of around $10bn in the 1980s to around $50bn over the past decade" (Carney 2015). Four years later, in 2019, when Carney issued another clarion call warning of climate change's potentially "catastrophic impact" (Herz 2020), Munich Re, the world's largest reinsurer, reported that 2017–2018 "was the worst two-year period for natural catastrophes on record, with insured losses of $225 [billion]" (Jenkins 2019).

Yet, despite increasingly dire warnings about climate-related economic losses,[1] during the 2010s major finance firms appeared to be doubling-down on, not abandoning their commitment to, the high-carbon economy. A 2019 study released by BankTrack and partner non-governmental organizations (NGOs) reported that 33 "major global banks poured $1.9 trillion into fossil fuels since the Paris Agreement was adopted" (Kirsch et al. 2019, 3); by 2020, BankTrack noted that 35 global banks had "funneled USD $2.7 trillion into fossil fuels" since Paris (Kirsch et al. 2020, 3).

However, by the late 2010s and turn of the 2020s, amid their ongoing investments in the high-carbon economy and apparent conviction about the durability of the old dominant design, some major banks and insurers were behaving as if there were fissures emerging in their long-held approach to the climate change issue. As of July 2019, for example, Chubb became the first US insurance company to begin phasing out underwriting and investing in coal-based companies, a development that such NGOs as Insure Our Future and the Sierra Club hailed, respectively, as a "gamechanger" and as a signal that "coal is becoming uninsurable worldwide" (Volcovici and Nair 2019; GreenBiz 2019). While Chubb was the first US insurer to establish a coal underwriting exclusion policy, by 2019, seventeen insurers worldwide representing 46% of the reinsurance market and 9.5% of the primary insurance market had announced such policies, with European companies like Zurich and Swiss Re in the vanguard. By December 2019, 35 insurers had "divested coal from roughly $8.9 trillion of investments—over one-third (37%) of the industry's global assets." Just one year prior, in 2018, only 19 insurance companies had taken action on divestment; as of 2017, only 15 companies had done so. In short, between 2017 and 2019, there was a 133%

---

[1] For example, in 2018, the Intergovernmental Panel on Climate Change estimated global economic damage related to climate change would be between $54 and $69 trillion by 2100 (Lafakis et al. 2019, 2).

increase in the number of insurers that had divested from coal (Insure Our Future 2019).

The trend away from unrestricted support for coal extended beyond insurers; as a February 2019 report by the Institute for Energy Economics and Financial Analysis noted, "Today, over 100 globally significant financial institutions have divested from thermal coal, including 40% of the top 40 global banks and 20 globally significant insurers. Momentum is building" (Buckley 2019, 1). In February 2020, one month after Fink wrote his letter to CEOs, even JPMorgan, which provides nearly 30% more financing for fossil fuel projects than any other bank worldwide, announced a prohibition on direct financing for all new coal-fired power plants (previous restrictions were limited to new plants in developed countries) and on "direct finance for new oil and gas development in the Arctic." The announcement came "less than a week after the leak of a report written by two JPMorgan economists warning of 'catastrophic consequences' if emissions are not slashed over the next 30 years" (Rainforest Action Network 2020).

While there is an urgent need to make coal uninsurable and to eliminate financing for coal-based businesses given coal's outsized contribution to climate change (Kollewe 2019), also crucial is mobilizing capital to finance the low-carbon transition. According to a 2019 International Energy Agency estimate, "a low-carbon transition could require $3.5 trillion in energy investment every year for decades—twice the current rate" (as cited in Carney 2019, 12). By the turn of the 2020s, heavyweights of global finance still were making insufficient low-carbon investments—but the quality and quantity of their investments differed appreciably in comparison to much of the 2010s. For example, in 2012, three years after the World Bank issued the first green bond (a type of bond designated for renewable energy and other low-carbon projects), "green bond issuance amounted only to $2.6 billion" (Segal 2020); by 2019, this figure exceeded $200 billion (Chestney 2019). Major banks that initially had underwritten other businesses' and institutions' green bonds began issuing such bonds of their own by the late 2010s; in other words, banks themselves were providing financing for low-carbon ventures, thus putting their own assets on the line, as opposed simply to securing financing for others.

Three of this chapter's four case-study banks followed a strikingly similar pattern of behavior in this respect, becoming active in green bond underwriting around 2013 but not in green bond issuance until 2020;

152 C. HULME

the exception was Bank of America, the second-largest US bank, which in 2013 issued one of the first corporate green bonds (Boulle 2014). For example, JPMorgan underwrote $1.1 billion and $2.2 billion in green bonds in 2013 and 2014, respectively, and "more than $4 billion in green and sustainability themed bonds" in 2015, but it was only in 2020 that the largest US bank completed its "inaugural green bond issuance of $1 billion" (JPMorgan Chase & Co. 2020). Likewise, in 2013, Citigroup, the third-largest US bank, underwrote its "first green bond for the International Finance Corporation"; in 2014, it underwrote "the auto industry's first asset-based green bond issuance"; and in 2015, it "helped clients to raise nearly $8 billion in green bonds." But it was only in 2020 that Citigroup issued its "first USD-denominated benchmark green bond" of $1.5 billion (Citigroup 2020). Finally, from 2013 onward Deutsche Bank was active in green bonds. In 2014, for example, it helped Unilever issue "the first ever sterling green bond" (Deutsche Bank 2015, 73); in 2015, it became "bookrunner for the first green bond to come out of China" (Deutsche Bank 2016, 59); and in 2017, it supported the issuance of €10 billion in green bonds (Deutsche Bank 2018, 24). But it was not until 2020 that Germany's largest bank issued its first green bond, a €500 million issue (Deutsche Bank, n.d., 3).

What is the significance of these developments? By the late 2010s, the old dominant design, while still intact in the finance industry, was coming under growing strain; for example, it no longer was tenable to insure and invest in coal unconditionally, and financing a low-carbon future (specifically by investing one's own assets) increasingly was treated as a growing part of financial actors' dealings. When Fink remarked in early 2020 that climate risk was "compelling investors to reassess core assumptions about modern finance" and announced that the industry was on the cusp of a paradigm shift, he was acknowledging that, however broadly and deeply it presently was entwined in the high-carbon economy, his industry's grip on the old dominant design *was* weakening, and *had* to weaken. As was observed on CNBC in January 2020, the month Fink published his letter, "Fossil fuels are done. We're starting to see divestment the world over.... You can tell the world's turned on them, and it's actually ... happening very quickly.... It's going to be a parade [of divestiture by funds] that says look, 'These are tobacco, and we're not going to own them'" (Pound 2020).

Part II: Climate Action, 2010–2017

Examining how the six finance companies behaved over time demonstrates that just one (Allianz) altered its climate approach sufficiently to transition away from a "business as usual" approach. However, companies' behavior indicated a slow-dawning recognition in the industry that old assumptions about the climate change issue would face mounting challenges going forward.

Finance Companies' Behavior, 2010–2017

As the appendix describes, companies were classified as one of four types: *BAU*, *evolutionary*, *innovator*, and *disruptor* (listed in order from lowest to highest level of climate action). Each type corresponds to a range of scores; the higher the score, the better a company's performance across three metrics of climate-related action: product, alignment, and investment. The industry-specific practices for the metrics were as follows: for *product*, expanding investment in renewable energy and underwriting or issuing green bonds (for banks) and acknowledging climate-related risks or integrating climate-related standards into underwriting policies, with a focus on coal exclusion (for insurers); for *alignment*, reducing financing for extreme oil projects (for banks), and divesting from proprietary investments in coal-based businesses (for insurers); and for *investment*, reducing financing for coal (for banks), and investing in renewable energy projects (for insurers). Classifying companies by type in each of six three-year periods spanning 2010–2017, Table 5.1 captures change over time in companies' climate performance. The last row shows companies' cumulative score in each period to highlight inter-period change and capture potential gains in underlying momentum. Allianz' name is in bold to underscore that it transitioned to a higher type between periods 1 and 6.

As Table 5.1 shows, only Allianz changed types, transitioning from BAU to evolutionary in 2015–2017. Notably, finance is the sole case-study industry in which no company became even an innovator by 2015–2017. As discussed, the finance industry's low climate performance in large part is a function of its degree of embeddedness in the old dominant design; whereas most of the other companies in the book's sample set are invested in a particular part of the high-carbon economy, the six companies in this chapter are entwined in virtually every facet of it.

Table 5.1   Finance company types, 2010–2017

Type (points)	*2010–2012* (*period 1*)	*2011–2013* (*period 2*)	*2012–2014* (*period 3*)	*2013–2015* (*period 4*)	*2014–2016* (*period 5*)	*2015– 2017* (*period 6*)
Disruptor (16–20)						
Innovator (13–15)						
Evolutionary (9–12)						**Allianz**, 9
BAU (0–8)	Citigroup, 6 Allianz, 5 BAC, 5 JPMorgan, 4 AIG, 3 Deutsche, 2	Citigroup, 6 JPMorgan, 6 Allianz, 5 BAC, 5 AIG, 4 Deutsche, 3	Citigroup, 7 JPMorgan, 7 BAC, 6 AIG, 5 Allianz, 5 Deutsche, 3	Citigroup, 7 JPMorgan, 7 Allianz, 6 BAC, 6 AIG, 5 Deutsche, 4	Allianz, 7 Citigroup, 7 JPMorgan, 7 BAC, 6 AIG, 5 Deutsche, 5	BAC, 7 Citigroup, 7 Deutsche, 6 JPMorgan, 6 AIG, 5
Total points (% change)	**25** (–)	**29** (16%)	**33** (14%)	**35** (6%)	**37** (6%)	**40** (8%) (*net:+60%*)

Source Author

Note Six finance companies, classified according to three-year performance on *product*, *alignment*, and *investment*. Companies received points out of 20 based on where they fell on a performance spectrum. BAC is Bank of America and Deutsche, Deutsche Bank

Despite the lack of significant change in terms of transitioning to higher types, however, the last row of Table 5.1 captures that underlying momentum did gather; between periods 1 and 6, there was a 60% increase in companies' cumulative scores. Considering company-level momentum, meanwhile, Allianz and Deutsche Bank registered the most progress, making 80% and 200% gains, respectively, over time. The remaining four (all the US companies) made less progress, improving by 67% (AIG), 50% (JPMorgan), 40% (Bank of America), and 17% (Citigroup). While overall momentum increased most in 2011–2013 (period 2) and 2012–2014 (period 3), capturing changes occurring in the pre-Paris Conference context, it was in 2015–2017 (period 6) that Allianz became the only company to transition to a higher type. As the next section addresses, this transition was a function of its announcement that, in light of "the two-degree target [enshrined in the Paris Agreement] and aware of the economic risks involved," Allianz would "stop financing coal-based business models," including through investment of proprietary assets.[2]

Identifying New Climate Practices

Despite the lack of type changes, meaningful change in behavior occurred; particularly telling is that the 60% increase in performance within the cohort was driven by across-the-board improvements, not just by gains registered only by select companies. Presenting results from analyzing how many companies received any points for each of the three metrics in each year, Table 5.2 captures how widespread each type of climate practice was ("breadth") and how deeply committed companies were to different practices ("depth").

While Table 5.2 indicates that breadth of participation in *alignment* increased significantly, in fact there was a low level of participation in the practices for this metric: restricting either proprietary investments in coal-based businesses (for insurers) or financing for extreme oil projects (for banks). Data shows that only one company, Citigroup, participated in every year from 2010 through 2017; it was only in 2015 that Allianz joined as a fellow participant. Table 5.2 also shows that from period

---

[2] Information from Allianz's 2015 CDP disclosure. Complete access to CDP disclosures available through subscription; contact author for information on all disclosures referenced in this chapter: hulmecharlottej@gmail.com.

156   C. HULME

Table 5.2   Breadth and depth of finance companies' climate action, 2010–2017

Years (period)	Breadth			Depth		
	Product	Alignment	Investment	Product	Alignment	Investment
2010–2012 (1)	83	22	89	44	0	28
2011–2013 (2)	89	17	100	56	0	33
2012–2014 (3)	94	17	100	61	0	33
2013–2015 (4)	94	22	100	67	6	33
2014–2016 (5)	89	28	100	67	11	33
2015–2017 (6)	89	33	100	67	17	33
Percent change, periods 1–6	+7	+50	+12	+52	n/a (17 pts.)	+18

Source Author

Note Breadth captures the percentage of finance companies receiving a score for *product, alignment,* and *investment*. Depth captures the percentage receiving over half the available points for performance on these metrics. As *alignment* participation for "depth" began at 0, calculating a percent change is impossible; thus, the point increase is shown

2 onward, all companies participated in the indicator practices for the investment metric: investing in renewable energy projects (for insurers) and restricting financing for coal (for banks). Likewise, companies consistently participated in the practices for the product metric: acknowledging climate-related risks or integrating climate-related standards into underwriting policies, with a focus on coal exclusion (for insurers), and expanding investment in renewable energy and underwriting or issuing green bonds (for banks).

But there was variation in how deeply committed companies were to these practices. For example, Table 5.2 conveys that the product metric saw a significant increase in deep participation; however, this change pertained only to banks, as neither of the insurers, Allianz and AIG, met the 51% threshold for deep participation on the relevant practice: addressing climate-related risks or integrating climate-related standards into their underwriting policies, with a focus on coal exclusion. By 2013, all four banks had reached the 51% threshold for deep action on the relevant behavior: expanding investment in renewable energy and underwriting or issuing green bonds. The three US banks were the first to invest deeply in this action (Bank of America and Citigroup met the 51% threshold from 2010 on, while JPMorgan did so beginning in 2011); the one German bank, Deutsche Bank, reached the 51% threshold in 2013.

5 "THE EARTH IS SHIFTING BENEATH THEIR FEET": FINANCE   157

Illustrative data highlights the significant gains in the amount of green capital that banks were mobilizing, underpinning the increase in their deep participation in *product*. For example, in 2015, JPMorgan was the underwriter for over $4 billion in "green and other social and sustainability-themed bonds"[3]; by 2016, this figure was over $5 billion,[4] and by 2017, it was $13.5 billion (JPMorgan Chase & Co. 2018, 25). Similarly, in 2013, when it became active in green bond underwriting, Deutsche Bank highlighted its role as "one of two other lead managers for one of the first Green Bonds, supporting the European Investment Bank in raising CHF350 million [roughly 390 million USD] for renewable energy and energy efficiency projects" (Deutsche Bank 2014, 41). By 2017, Germany's largest bank reported having "supported clients to issue more [than] about €10 billion in green bonds. Many of these transactions were of high strategic importance to the issuers, and moreover helped to advance and develop the green bond market itself" (Deutsche Bank 2018, 24).

While Table 5.2 indicates that the alignment metric registered an increase in depth of participation, this reflects the behavior of just one company, Allianz. Of the two insurers included in the sample, only Allianz developed a policy for investment of proprietary assets in coal, the indicator behavior for *alignment* (for insurers). Although it was not until 2015 that Allianz unveiled such a policy, when it did so it was relatively ambitious, clearing the 51% threshold for deep action. The company announced that it would "no longer invest proprietary assets in companies that derive more than 30% of revenue from coal mining, or generate over 30% of energy from burning coal. Equities amounting to €225 million have been divested by March 2016 while bonds amounting to €3.9 billion will be expiring."[5] As a 2017 study noted, in addition to Allianz being among the first insurers to divest from coal, its 30% threshold for mining companies and utilities signified "a more comprehensive definition of coal companies than AXA, Zurich and other peers" that also had issued divestment policies (Harrell and Bosshard 2017, 16).

Meanwhile, Citigroup, the only other participant in *alignment*, did not meet the 51% threshold for deep participation on the relevant practice for

---

[3] Information from JPMorgan's 2016 CDP disclosure.

[4] Information from JPMorgan's 2017 CDP disclosure.

[5] Information from Allianz's 2016 CDP disclosure.

158   C. HULME

banks: restricting financing for extreme oil projects. It had committed to phasing out financing for these kinds of projects but had not yet actually prohibited such financing (Collins et al., n.d., 30).

Finally, considering the increase in depth of participation on the investment metric, the data shows that from 2011 on, the two insurers reached the 51% threshold for the relevant practice—both Allianz and AIG were active in shepherding renewable energy projects as investors themselves and/or by de-risking projects to pave the way for others' investments—but that none of the banks ever met the 51% threshold for committing to restricting financing for coal. There were several key instances of progress, however, capturing how certain banks increasingly appreciated that existing approaches to coal financing were untenable. For example, in 2016 and 2017, Deutsche Bank improved its performance on reducing financing for both coal mining and coal power (the latter of which often was a particular sticking point).[6] In 2016, Deutsche Bank explained that the company "and its subsidiaries will not grant new financing for greenfield thermal coal mining and new coal-fired power plant construction. Moreover, the Bank will gradually reduce its existing exposure to the thermal coal mining sector." It underscored that it would "not be expanding our coal financing business, even if market opportunities present themselves. But we want to be even more ambitious and scale back our activities in this sector by up to 20% by 2020" (Deutsche Bank 2017, 4). This was a potentially significant step for a company that from 2013 through 2015 was identified by BankTrack as the world's number one financier of coal mining projects, and that in 2013 appeared to plant its flag on the issue, stipulating that "we do not generally avoid doing business with the coal industry" (Deutsche Bank 2014, 33). Meeting the threshold for deep action, however, would have required that Deutsche Bank already be excluding financing for all coal projects.

While any gains in deep participation in the metrics of climate action were positive, a key question was whether companies were becoming more deeply committed to the most important type of action, or the most heavily weighted metric for their industry; for insurance companies

---

[6] For its 2013–2015 performance, Deutsche Bank received a BankTrack grade of C− and D+, respectively, for coal mining and coal power financing (Collins et al., n.d., 7). By the next cycle of BankTrack reporting, covering 2016–2018, its scores on both were C+, representing a slight improvement on coal mining and a letter grade improvement on coal power financing (Kirsch et al., 2019, 15).

5 "THE EARTH IS SHIFTING BENEATH THEIR FEET": FINANCE   159

this was *product* (i.e., acknowledging climate-related risks or integrating climate-related standards into their underwriting policies, with a focus on coal exclusion), while for banks it was *investment* (i.e., restricting financing for coal). Uniquely among the industry groups this book examines, none of the companies in this chapter's industry group received over half the available points on the most significant type of action in any year from 2010 through 2017, further underscoring just how far "behind the curve" finance companies were in altering their climate behavior and stepping up as key players in the issue area.

For example, even Allianz, which was climate active compared to AIG, failed to enact sufficiently strict coal exclusion criteria to be classified as a deep participant in that practice. While it had no coal exclusion policy through 2016, in 2017 it announced that "in Property and Casualty Insurance, with effect as of May 2018, we will no longer provide insurance to single coal-fired power plants or coal mines, that are operational or planned."[7] This was a potentially significant development; given that "coal projects cannot be financed, built or operated without insurance," insurers are especially well-positioned to undercut the future of coal (Kollewe 2019). But meeting the threshold for deep action would have required Allianz to be actively reducing insurance coverage for all coal projects and companies with coal operations.

Meanwhile, AIG, one of the largest insurers in the United States, had no policy even for partially excluding coal underwriting. By 2017, in fact, its stance toward climate-related underwriting barely had evolved since 2010.[8] Throughout the decade, AIG consistently acknowledged that "climate change potentially poses a serious financial threat to society as a whole, with implications for the insurance industry."[9] But such recognition did not lead to changes in its approach to coal, which is the "single biggest contributor to climate change" (Kollewe 2019), and, compared to

---

[7] This policy did not exclude companies "that generate electricity from multiple sources, such as coal, other fossil fuels or renewable energies," which would "continue to be insured, and individually reviewed on the basis of defined ESG criteria. However, our stated goal is to completely phase out coal risks ... in the insurance business by 2040 latest." Information from Allianz's 2018 CDP disclosure.

[8] In its 2010 annual report, AIG set forth that "while it is not possible to precisely quantify the impact of a policyholder's operations on climate change, underwriters routinely evaluate the potential effects on greenhouse gas emissions when considering policy renewals" (American International Group 2011, 153).

[9] AIG used this language in all annual reports from 2013 to 2017.

160   C. HULME

other fossil fuels, low-hanging fruit for companies seeking to start somewhere on incorporating fossil fuel standards. AIG's 2017 annual report recycled the language that it had been using since 2013 to discuss climate risks in broad terms, with no mention of coal (American International Group 2018, 18).

Likewise, none of the four banks reached the threshold for deep participation in restricting financing for coal, the indicator behavior for the investment metric (the most heavily weighted metric for banks). Notably, banks typically imposed relatively strong restrictions on coal mining compared to coal power. For example, for their performance in 2013–2015, BankTrack and partner NGOs awarded Bank of America, Citigroup, and JPMorgan grades of B− for coal mining, indicating progress toward phasing out financing for this part of the fossil fuel economy. But during the same period, they received grades of D, D+, and C, respectively, for financing coal power, capturing how coal power was the major hindrance to better performance on coal-related activities. While the banks' low scores for participation in *investment* largely hinged on their poor performance on financing for coal power, three out of the four banks improved in this area over time.[10] Deutsche Bank realized the most significant gains in its performance on coal power financing, advancing a full letter grade, from D+ to C+, according to BankTrack's methodology, signifying that it had gone from just setting "a minimum efficiency or technology threshold for new power plant financing" to actually excluding certain coal power projects from financing.[11]

* * *

Examining how finance companies behaved from 2010 through 2017 reveals limited evidence of a new paradigm of behavior or perceived new dominant design. The cohort overall included only one company, Allianz, that took the kind of decisive steps toward a more climate-active approach necessary to transition to a higher type. Yet, all companies realized gains, and companies' cumulative 60% increase in performance between

[10] For example, over time, on coal power financing Bank of America moved from a BankTrack grade of D to C−, while Citigroup moved from D+ to C−, indicating that both banks had introduced some prohibitions on financing for coal power projects where previously there were none (Collins et al., n.d., 6; Kirsch et al. 2019, 15).

[11] Deutsche Bank received a D+ on coal power financing for the 2013–2015 period and a C+ for the 2016–2018 period (Collins et al., n.d., 7; Kirsch et al. 2019, 15).

5 "THE EARTH IS SHIFTING BENEATH THEIR FEET": FINANCE   161

2010 and 2017 reflected such developments as one of the world's largest insurers (Allianz) adopting a coal divestment policy; Germany's largest bank (Deutsche Bank) prohibiting expansion of its coal financing business, regardless of potential "market opportunities"; and the second-largest US bank (Bank of America) leading the expansion of the nascent green bond market as one of the first corporate issuers of a green bond and as "the number one underwriter of green bond issuances."[12]

Companies consistently participated in two types of climate-relevant behavior (linked to the product and investment metrics). One metric (product) saw meaningful change in terms of how deeply invested companies were in the relevant practices.[13] But the pattern of behavior indicated that companies ultimately were not departing meaningfully from "business as usual." Banks were not phasing out all financing for coal-based businesses and insurers were not eliminating coverage for coal projects—actions that would have signified serious blows to the old dominant design.

Part III: Patterns of Emergent Action

This part of the chapter shows that the six finance companies never perceived climate change as being of high material importance—and its perceived importance declined over time. Given that all companies realized improvements in climate performance, even if only Allianz altered its approach sufficiently to transition to a higher type, this industry case study demonstrates a clear pattern of emergent action.[14]

Table 5.3 displays results from annual CDP surveys from 2010 to 2016 tracking whether companies perceived risks and opportunities in three categories: climate-related regulation, changing consumer behavior, and physical impacts—and if so, on what time horizon, with what degree

---

[12] Information from Bank of America's 2016 CDP disclosure.

[13] All three metrics registered increases in terms of companies' depth of participation. However, the increase in *alignment* in fact captures change in just one company's behavior, while the modest increase in *investment* occurred exclusively between periods 1 and 2.

[14] As discussed throughout this book, the essential marker of emergence is a misalignment between perceptions of climate change as a material concern and changes in climate-related action. The disjunction, as opposed to the absolute level of climate action, is key.

162 C. HULME

Table 5.3 Perceived high material impact of climate change among finance companies, 2010–2016

Years (period)	Perceived high material impact			
	Overall	Regulation	Consumer	Physical
2010–2012 (1)	18	22	3	28
2011–2013 (2)	18	20	8	28
2012–2014 (3)	14	11	8	22
2013–2015 (4)	11	6	11	17
2014–2016 (5)	6	0	5	11
Percent change, periods 1–5	−67	−100	+67	−61

Source Author
Note In the finance industry, the percentage of climate-related risks and opportunities that were perceived to be a high-impact material concern

of certainty, and with what anticipated level of material impact.[15] If all companies in a given period perceived that climate change entailed high-impact risks and opportunities, the "perceived high material impact" column would register 100.

Table 5.3 shows not only that climate change never was perceived to be of high material importance, but also that perceptions of its importance moved in the opposite direction of what would have been expected given where the industry landed at the end of the 2010s—a place where, in BlackRock CEO Larry Fink's words, it saw the need to reassess its "core assumptions" on account of climate change (Fink 2020). This overall development occurred in the context of vanishing outlooks for bold state climate action and a declining sense of serious material impacts tied to the physical effects of climate change. Meanwhile, Table 5.3 demonstrates negligible concern with the impact of climate-driven changes in consumer behavior, which registered at just 5% by period 5.

Considering how each company perceived climate-related risks and opportunities addresses the extent to which there is evidence of the pattern of emergent action at the company level. While just one company (Allianz) altered its climate approach to a sufficient degree to transition to

[15] The perception data in this chapter excludes 2017 due to changes in the CDP disclosure questions that compromise the comparability of the 2017 responses with those of previous years. Thus, there is perception data only for periods 1 through 5.

5 "THE EARTH IS SHIFTING BENEATH THEIR FEET": FINANCE   163

a higher type, all companies made modest improvements in their performance; meanwhile, select companies made notable changes to certain aspects of their approaches (e.g., Deutsche Bank's progress on restricting financing for coal power). Examining the data on how individual companies perceived the material impacts of climate change underscores how such progress in performance, however limited, occurred in the context of very low and/or declining perceptions that climate change presented high-impact costs or benefits.[16] Table 5.4 presents data on how companies individually assessed the material impacts of climate-related regulation (displayed in the top third), changing consumer behavior (middle third), and physical impacts (bottom third).

Table 5.4 captures the disjunction between companies' changing behavior and their declining or static perceptions of the material significance of the climate change issue. Consider Deutsche Bank. As Table 5.1 in Part II captured, although Germany's largest bank did not improve its climate performance enough to transition to a higher type, it made the most underlying progress of any company, improving its score by 200% between period 1 (2010–2012) and period 6 (2015–2017). This improvement largely was a function of establishing a policy for coal financing; in 2016, to recall, Deutsche Bank announced it would not expand coal financing, regardless of potential business opportunities (Deutsche Bank 2017, 4). Notably, this decision was made during period 5, when, as Table 5.4 captures, it reported no high-impact climate risks or opportunities—a stark change from the first part of the decade when the bank perceived that both climate-related regulation and physical effects were serious material concerns. Instituting a coal financing policy during the period that concern about climate change's material impacts was at its nadir is exactly the type of disjunction that is the signature of emergent action.

Table 5.4 points to another case of the pattern of emergent action: Allianz, which in 2015–2017 became the only financial company to change types, transitioning from BAU to evolutionary. Allianz never altered its estimation of the financial implications of climate change. Yet, its performance improved, initially in 2015 due to its announcement that it would "stop financing coal-based business models" and divest

---

[16] Because only one company, Allianz, changed types over time, the approach to this part differs from the previous empirical chapters, which examined company-level perception data only for those companies that changed types.

164   C. HULME

Table 5.4   Perceived high material impact of regulation, changing consumer behavior, and physical impacts for individual finance companies, 2010–2016

Years (period)	Perceived high material impact: regulation, consumer, physical					
	AIG	Allianz	BAC	Citi	Deutsche	JPM
2010–2012 (1)	0	0	0	33	100	0
2011–2013 (2)	0	0	0	17	100	0
2012–2014 (3)	0	0	0	0	67	0
2013–2015 (4)	0	0	0	0	33	0
2014–2016 (5)	0	0	0	0	0	0
2010–2012 (1)	0	0	0	17	0	0
2011–2013 (2)	0	0	0	33	17	0
2012–2014 (3)	0	0	0	33	17	0
2013–2015 (4)	0	0	0	50	17	0
2014–2016 (5)	0	0	0	33	0	0
2010–2012 (1)	0	50	0	17	100	0
2011–2013 (2)	0	50	17	17	83	0
2012–2014 (3)	0	50	33	0	50	0
2013–2015 (4)	0	50	33	0	17	0
2014–2016 (5)	0	50	17	0	0	0

Source Author

Note For individual finance companies, the percentage of risks and opportunities related to climate-related regulation (top third of the table), consumer behavior (middle third of the table), and physical impacts (bottom third of the table) that were perceived to be a high-impact material concern. BAC is Bank of America; Citi, Citigroup; Deutsche, Deutsche Bank; and JPM, JPMorgan

"from equity stakes in coal-based business models in early 2016" (Allianz 2016, 9). Then, in 2017, its performance improved further following its announcement about excluding underwriting for all operational or planned single coal-fired power plants or coal mines, leading to its transition to an evolutionary. When a company changes its approach to the climate change issue despite no change in its perception of its material importance, this suggests another factor motivating its behavior. This book argues that for a company like Allianz, that factor was the recognition that states could not be counted on to play their expected role in addressing an issue of transnational importance set to shape future global trends.

Indeed, throughout the 2010s, in corporate reports Allianz repeatedly raised the issue of disappointing outcomes at international climate meetings and of the need for the private sector to take an active role in the climate change arena as a partner to governments. In 2010, for instance, the company noted, "In view of the disappointing outcome of the Copenhagen Climate Change Conference in 2009, private companies will have to take a more active role in tackling climate change" (Allianz 2010, 23). In 2014, noting that in Germany, its headquarter country, "it is disappointing that CO_2 emissions from electricity generation have increased over the past two years," Allianz pointed out that "the advantages of partnerships between the public sector and investors like Allianz are obvious" (Allianz 2014, 5).

Allianz appeared to be spurred to heightened climate action in the context of the Paris Conference; for example, in 2015, consistent with its commitments as a member of the Portfolio Decarbonization Coalition, which it joined during the Paris negotiations, it unveiled a coal-divestment strategy, and by 2017 had "significantly expanded" its climate strategy, "sharpened the criteria for exclusion of proprietary investments in coal-based business models," and committed to align its "proprietary investment portfolio of approximately 700bn EUR with the Paris Agreement."[17] But did Allianz interpret Paris as a promising departure from previously disappointing international climate efforts, or rather as confirmation that given states' limitations the private sector needed to step up to shape the "rules of the game" for a low-carbon future? The data suggests the latter, as Allianz became appreciably more climate-active post-Paris,[18] while its outlook for prospects for state climate action saw no change.[19]

$$* \quad * \quad *$$

[17] Information from Allianz's 2018 CDP disclosure.

[18] According to a Berlin-based energy sector expert, post-Paris, Allianz, in the context of its desire to phase out its holding of coal power assets, became one of a select few finance players exerting meaningful pressure on German power companies (Berlin, November 14, 2018).

[19] From period 1 (2010–2012) through period 5 (2014–2016), Allianz saw no high-impact material risks or opportunities from regulation or changing consumer behavior; it always saw high-impact risks tied to physical impacts of climate change.

In the finance industry, there is evidence of the pattern of emergent action at the industry and company levels. First, the six-company cohort registered an overall 60% increase in climate performance amid a stark (67%) decline in the perception that climate change was a high-impact material concern. Second, there were two clear examples of the pattern of emergent action at the company level. Allianz improved its climate performance by 80%, becoming an evolutionary, despite unchanging assessments of the material importance of the climate change issue; meanwhile, Deutsche Bank improved its performance by 200% despite perceiving in 2015–2017 no high-impact risks or opportunities from climate-related regulation, changing consumer behavior, or physical effects.

In terms of this book's overall argument about the variable or condition accounting for the private sector's new pattern of behavior and approach toward climate change, an especially key finding is that finance companies' outlook for bold state action on the issue vanished, with expectations for high-impact policy and regulation dropping to zero in 2015–2017. What this suggests is that while states might have assumed that their behavior during the 2010s conveyed a certain signal about their commitment to a low-carbon future—indeed, post-Paris Conference states were confident that they had given markets the signal they needed to scale up low-carbon investments (United Nations 2015)—some of the most powerful players in global finance did not receive the signal as intended. Contrary to states' assumptions, throughout the 2010s they did not perceive that states had become more committed to nurturing the conditions that would define a low-carbon transition.

CONCLUSION

Examining the behavior of six of the world's largest companies in the finance industry, this chapter found that in 2010–2017, the cohort, while not undertaking dramatic steps forward or becoming leaders in the climate change issue area, improved its performance and adopted practices that reflected certain shared understandings about the kind of behavior needed to succeed in a changing global environment. By the turn of the 2020s something *had* changed, even for longtime climate laggards of global finance. In April 2021, for example, just over a year after Larry Fink published his famous letter, 160 finance firms, representing over $70 trillion in assets under management, formed the Glasgow Financial

Alliance for Net Zero (GFANZ), whose members "must use science-based guidelines to reach net zero emissions, cover all emissions scopes ... and commit to transparent reporting and accounting in line with the UN Race to Zero criteria" (United Nations Climate Change 2021), which sets standards for "initiatives of businesses, investors, cities, regions and universities for robust and credible net zero commitments" (Climate Champions 2021b). Among the 43 GFANZ founding banks were Bank of America, Citigroup, and Deutsche Bank; meanwhile, Allianz was one of seven participating insurers (United Nations Environment Programme, n.d.; Climate Champions 2021a).

Of the 34 companies that this book examines, arguably none are so important as the six in this chapter in terms of the role they ultimately must play in a global low-carbon transition. Finance companies are entwined in every facet of the high-carbon economy; once the linchpins of that economy change course, the entire game will change, as carbon-intensive sectors cannot survive without their support. Indeed, in a 2018 interview, when asked about when and why a low-carbon future became perceived as a foregone conclusion in Europe, a Berlin-based energy sector expert pointed out that companies have started to "[see] in the marketplace these developments, and then they are asked by the investors, 'Where do you see yourself [in the long term]?'" (Berlin, November 14, 2018). Similarly, discussing the factors behind the success of renewable energy in India, a veteran of the conventional power sector and current CEO of a renewables company noted that "a lot of funds have decided that most of [their capital] will be for green power, but not for conventional power" (Telephone conversation with author, September 26, 2018). As this chapter demonstrated, during an unlikely decade, in the wake of the collapse of the global economy, some of the companies that *embody* the old dominant design began to question where they saw themselves in the long term. Following the pattern of unexpected behavior that this book explores, in less than a decade even some of the actors most deeply invested in the high-carbon status quo began to behave as though "business as usual" was less durable than previously they had assumed.

168 C. HULME

References

Allianz. 2010. Allianz sustainable development report 2010. July 1, 2010. https://www.allianz.com/content/dam/onemarketing/azcom/Allianz_com/responsibility/documents/allianz_sd_report_2010.pdf.

Allianz. 2014. From alternative energy to zero emissions. February 21, 2014. https://www.allianz.com/content/dam/onemarketing/azcom/Allianz_com/responsibility/documents/2013_Allianz_Climate_Booklet_EN.pdf.

Allianz. 2016. Sustainability report 2015. May 2, 2016. https://www.allianz.com/content/dam/onemarketing/azcom/Allianz_com/sustainability/images/media-2016/Allianz-Sustainability-Report-2015.pdf.

American International Group. 2011. Annual report 2010. February 24, 2011. https://www.aig.com/content/dam/aig/america-canada/us/documents/investor-relations/2010-annual-report.pdf.

American International Group. 2018. Annual report 2017. February 16, 2018. https://www.aig.com/content/dam/aig/america-canada/us/documents/investor-relations/2018/aig_2017_annual_report.pdf.

Bloomberg, Michael, and Carl Pope. 2017. *Climate of hope*. New York: St. Martin's Press.

Boulle, Bridget. 2014. 2013 Overview: The dawn of an age of green bonds? Climate Bonds Initiative. February 6, 2014. https://www.climatebonds.net/2014/02/2013-overview-dawn-age-green-bonds.

Brune, Michael. 2020. What one of BlackRock's biggest climate critics thinks about Larry Fink's letter. CNBC. January 15, 2020. https://www.cnbc.com/2020/01/15/one-of-blackrocks-biggest-critics-on-larry-finks-climate-letter.html.

Buckley, Tim. 2019. Over 100 global financial institutions are exiting coal, with more to come. Institute for Energy Economics and Financial Analysis. February 27, 2019. https://ieefa.org/wp-content/uploads/2019/02/IEEFA-Report_100-and-counting_Coal-Exit_Feb-2019.pdf.

Carney, Mark. 2015. Breaking the tragedy of the horizon: Climate change and financial stability. September 29, 2015. https://www.bankofengland.co.uk/-/media/boe/files/speech/2015/breaking-the-tragedy-of-the-horizon-climate-change-and-financial-stability.pdf?la=en&hash=7C67E785651862457D99511147C7424FF5EA0C1A.

Carney, Mark. 2019. Fifty shades of green. International Monetary Fund. December 6, 2019. https://www.elibrary.imf.org/view/journals/022/0056/004/article-A005-en.xml.

Ceres. 2020. BlackRock CEO letter on sustainable investing is a game changer for the global investor and corporate community. *3BL CSR Wire*, January 21, 2020. https://www.csrwire.com/press_releases/43398-blackrock-ceo-letter-on-sustainable-investing-is-a-game-changer-for-the-global-investor-and-corporate-community.

5 "THE EARTH IS SHIFTING BENEATH THEIR FEET": FINANCE   169

Chestney, Nina. 2019. Green bond issuance surpasses $200 bln so far this year. *Reuters*, October 23, 2019. https://www.reuters.com/article/us-greenb onds-issuance/green-bond-issuance-surpasses-200-bln-so-far-this-year-idU SKBN1X21L1.

Citigroup. 2020. Citi announces inaugural USD-denominated benchmark green bond issuance. May 11, 2020. https://www.citigroup.com/global/news/ press-release/2020/citi-announces-inaugural-usd-denominated-benchmark-green-bond-issuance.

Climate Champions. 2021a. GFANZ: Net zero financial alliance launches. United Nations Climate Change. April 21, 2021. https://climatechampions.unfccc. int/net-zero-financial-alliance-launches/.

Climate Champions. 2021b. The Race to Zero strengthens and clarifies criteria. United Nations Climate Change. April 29, 2021. https://climatechampions. unfccc.int/the-race-to-zero-strengthens-and-clarifies-campaign-criteria/.

Collins, Ben, Jason Disterhoft, Alison Kirsch, Yann Louvel, Greg Aitken, Johanna deGraffenreif, Rebekah Hinojosa, et al. n.d. Shorting the climate: Fossil fuel finance report card 2016. Rainforest Action Network, Sierra Club, BankTrack, and Oil Change International. https://priceofoil.org/content/ uploads/2016/06/Shorting_the_Climate_2016.pdf.

Deutsche Bank. 2014. Corporate responsibility report 2013. March 2014. https://www.db.com/files/documents/csr/reports/deutsche-bank-cr-rep ort-2013.PDF.

Deutsche Bank. 2015. Annual review 2014. March 20, 2015. https://investor-relations.db.com/files/documents/annual-reports/Deutsche_Bank_Annual_ Report_2014_entire.pdf?language_id=1.

Deutsche Bank. 2016. Corporate responsibility report 2015. March 10, 2016. https://www.db.com/files/documents/csr/reports/deutsche-bank-cr-report-2015.pdf.

Deutsche Bank. 2017. Corporate responsibility report 2016. March 20, 2017. https://cr-report.db.com/2016/en/servicepages/downloads/files/dbc r2016_entire.pdf.

Deutsche Bank. 2018. Non-financial report 2017. March 12, 2018. https:// investor-relations.db.com/files/documents/annual-reports/Deutsche_Bank_ Non-Financial_Report_2017.pdf?language_id=1.

Deutsche Bank. n.d. Green financing instruments report 2020. https://inv estor-relations.db.com/files/documents/green-financing/DB_Green_Financ ing_Instruments_Report_2020.pdf?language_id=1.

Fink, Larry. 2020. A fundamental reshaping of finance. BlackRock. January 14, 2020. https://www.blackrock.com/americas-offshore/en/larry-fink-ceo-letter.

GreenBiz. 2019. Chubb is first big U.S. insurer that won't underwrite new coal plants. July 3, 2019. https://www.greenbiz.com/article/chubb-first-big-us-insurer-wont-underwrite-new-coal-plants.

170   C. HULME

Greenfield, Patrick, and Jasper Jolly. 2020. BlackRock joins pressure group taking on biggest polluters. *The Guardian*, January 9, 2020. https://www.theguardian.com/environment/2020/jan/09/blackrock-joins-pressure-group-taking-on-biggest-polluters.

Harrell, Casey, and Peter Bosshard. 2017. Insuring coal no more: An insurance scorecard on coal and climate change. Unfriend Coal. November 2017. https://unfriendcoal.com/wp-content/uploads/2017/11/UnfriendCoal-Insurance-Scorecard.pdf.

Herz, Jonathan. 2020. The financial sector is waking up to climate change. Environmental and Energy Study Institute. February 11, 2020. https://www.eesi.org/articles/view/the-financial-sector-is-waking-up-to-climate-change.

Insure Our Future. 2019. Insurers withdrawing cover from coal projects double in 2019. December 2, 2019. https://global.insure-our-future.com/2019scorecardnews/.

Jenkins, Patrick. 2019. Why climate change is the new 9/11 for insurance companies. *The Financial Times*, September 12, 2019. https://www.ft.com/content/63c80228-cfee-11e9-99a4-b5ded7a7fe3f.

JPMorgan Chase & Co. 2018. Environmental social and governance report 2017. https://www.jpmorganchase.com/content/dam/jpmc/jpmorgan-chase-and-co/documents/jpmc-cr-esg-report-2017.pdf.

JPMorgan Chase & Co. 2020. JPMorgan Chase issues $1 billion inaugural green bonds. September 16, 2020. https://www.jpmorganchase.com/ir/news/2020/inaugural-green-bonds-091620.

Kaplan, Rob. 2020. What Larry Fink got right (and wrong) in his 2020 investor letter. *Forbes*, January 24, 2020. https://www.forbes.com/sites/robkaplan/2020/01/24/what-larry-fink-got-right-and-wrong-in-his-2020-investor-letter/?sh=295756ae2055.

Kirsch, Alison, Jason Opeña Disterhoft, Grant Marr, Greig Aitken, Claire Hamlett, Yann Louvel, Lise Masson, et al. 2019. Banking on climate change—Fossil fuel finance report card 2019. March 20, 2019. Rainforest Action Network, BankTrack, Sierra Club, Oil Change International, Indigenous Environmental Network, and Honor the Earth. https://www.banktrack.org/download/banking_on_climate_change_2019_fossil_fuel_finance_report_card/banking_on_climate_change_2019.pdf.

Kirsch, Alison, Jason Opeña Disterhoft, Grant Marr, Paddy McCully, Ayse Gürsöz, Greig Aitken, Claire Hamlett, et al. 2020. Banking on climate change—Fossil fuel finance report card 2020. March 18, 2020. Rainforest Action Network, BankTrack, Indigenous Environmental Network, Oil Change International, Reclaim Finance, and Sierra Club. https://www.bankingonclimatechaos.org/wp-content/uploads/2021/10/Banking_on_Climate_Change__2020_vF.pdf.

5 "THE EARTH IS SHIFTING BENEATH THEIR FEET": FINANCE 171

Kollewe, Julia. 2019. Coal power becoming "uninsurable" as firms refuse cover. *The Guardian*, December 2, 2019. https://www.theguardian.com/enviro nment/2019/dec/02/coal-power-becoming-uninsurable-as-firms-refuse-cover.

Lafakis, Chris, Laura Ratz, Emily Fazio, and Maria Cosma. 2019. The economic implications of climate change. Moody's Analytics. June 2019. https://www.moodysanalytics.com/-/media/article/2019/economic-implications-of-climate-change.pdf.

Pound, Jesse. 2020. Cramer sees oil stocks in the "death knell phase," says they are the new tobacco. CNBC. January 31, 2020. https://www.cnbc.com/2020/01/31/cramer-sees-oil-stocks-in-the-death-knell-phase-says-new-tob acco.html.

Rainforest Action Network. 2020. JPMorgan Chase coal and Arctic policy a step forward but fails to match its responsibility as the world's #1 fossil fuel bank. February 24, 2020. https://www.ran.org/press-releases/jpmorgan-chase-ran-policy-response/.

Segal, Troy. 2020. Green bond. *Investopedia*, March 9, 2020. Updated September 21, 2022. https://www.investopedia.com/terms/g/green-bon d.asp.

Sorkin, Andrew Ross. 2020. BlackRock C.E.O. Larry Fink: Climate crisis will reshape finance. *The New York Times*, February 24, 2020. https://www.nyt imes.com/2020/01/14/business/dealbook/larry-fink-blackrock-climate-cha nge.html.

United Nations. 2015. COP21: UN chief hails new climate change agreement as "monumental triumph." *UN News*, December 12, 2015. https://news.un. org/en/story/2015/12/517982.

United Nations Climate Change. 2021. New financial alliance for net zero emissions launches. April 21, 2021. https://unfccc.int/news/new-financial-alliance-for-net-zero-emissions-launches.

United Nations Environment Programme. n.d. Net-zero banking alliance. https://www.unepi.org/net-zero-banking/.

Vermillion, James. 2020. The climate shockwave that rocked Wall Street. *Medium*, August 19, 2020. https://medium.com/swlh/the-climate-sho ckwave-that-rocked-wall-street-how-one-letter-will-change-the-world-19242a ce7245.

Volcovici, Valerie, and Shanti Nair. 2019. U.S. insurer Chubb pulls back from coal. *Reuters*, July 1, 2019. https://www.reuters.com/article/us-chubb-ltd-ch-coal-policy/u-s-insurer-chubb-pulls-back-from-coal-idUSKCN1TW3I2.

CHAPTER 6

The Emergent Corporate Climate Consensus

INTRODUCTION

Few companies so clearly demonstrate the resources, reach, and potential influence of the club of "corporate nations" (Francis 2016) as Walmart, the world's largest private employer with an annual revenue of half a trillion dollars, a supply chain spanning 100 countries, and 265 million weekly customers (Stimage 2018). Among corporations, arguably, it has an unsurpassed capability to influence the global conversation on an issue; as Green has observed, "When Walmart decides on a new set of practices, the world has to listen" (2013, 1). Few actors rival Walmart in terms of level of climate activity and ambition. In 2005, the world's largest retailer outlined three major goals of "zero waste, 100 percent renewable energy sourcing, and sustainable sourcing of its products." In 2009, it pioneered a "sustainability index" aimed at encouraging 100,000 suppliers worldwide to reduce emissions (Green 2013, 1). In the 2010s, Walmart doubled down on its climate commitment, becoming progressively more ambitious in cutting supply chain emissions, the most significant contributor to its emissions by a large margin. For example, in 2010, it committed to eliminating 20 million metric tons of supply chain emissions (Walmart 2010, 11); in 2014, it piloted a program for suppliers which, if implemented by 1000 factories, was projected to "reduce coal consumption by an estimated 230,000 tons" (Walmart 2014, 106); and

© The Author(s), under exclusive license to Springer Nature   173
Switzerland AG 2023
C. Hulme, *Corporate Climate Action, Transnational Politics, and World Order*, Environmental Politics and Theory,
https://doi.org/10.1007/978-3-031-34115-1_6

174   C. HULME

in 2017, it launched "Project Gigaton," whose goal of eliminating one billion tons of supply chain emissions between 2015 and 2030, "roughly the same reduction that would be achieved by a government regulation that required the U.S. iron and steel industry to cut its emissions to zero" (Vandenbergh and Gilligan 2017), represented a 50-fold increase from its 2010 target (Stevens 2019).

Walmart likewise became a leading corporate purchaser of renewable energy during the 2010s. As Chapter 4 explored, companies can claim to be using 100% renewable energy when in fact they simply are purchasing enough "renewable energy credits" to offset their conventional power usage; a more ambitious approach is entering into a long-term clean power purchase agreement, especially when the supplier is in sufficiently close proximity that a company can use the clean power it purchases. In 2010, Walmart entered into such a power purchase agreement with Duke Energy wind farm in Notrees, Texas, supplying "up to 15 percent of the energy needs in 350 of [its] Texas locations" (Walmart 2011, 11). Between 2010 and 2013, it increased its global procurement of renewables by 600%, eliminating the need for two fossil fuel power plants (Walmart 2013). By 2015, Walmart was "ranked as the leading commercial solar energy user and the largest on-site renewable energy user" in the United States and had more than two billion kilowatt hours of renewable energy contracted annually, more than double its total in 2012 (Walmart 2016, 60, 63). Corporate clean power purchasing is an especially significant practice for a behemoth like Walmart, which potentially can influence developments beyond its own operations. As Walmart observed in 2014, "We hope our commitment to renewables will encourage innovation and new market entries into the sector" (2014, 5). By the mid-2010s, Walmart understood its role in the climate change issue area as one of a trailblazer; in 2016, for example, it noted that the sections in the Paris Agreement "relating to non-state actors affirm what we have already been doing" (2016, 62).

Walmart's consistent, increasingly ambitious climate activity did not reflect an underlying perception of material risks and opportunities tied to climate change, but rather captured the logic of emergence that this book has explored. During the 2010s, its cumulative performance on the three metrics of climate action (product, alignment, and investment) increased by 21%; meanwhile, it became considerably less concerned with the possibility of high-impact risks or opportunities tied to climate change (in particular, its outlook for policy and regulatory action declined 66%).

While perceiving limited material incentives to broaden its response to the climate change issue or deepen its commitment to climate action, Walmart nonetheless adopted more ambitious practices. Given the threat that "climate change poses in general" and the perceived lack of state leadership on the issue, the company sought to "lead by example on this issue and send the right signals to all our stakeholders. In many cases, leading through intentional action is a powerful proof of concept for the business community" (Walmart 2016, 62). During the 2010s, other companies looked specifically to its climate leadership; in 2012, for instance, the head of research and development for Infosys (India's second-largest IT company) credited Walmart for building a global network to "green" its supply chain, "spurring innovation in areas such as materials, processes, supply chains and engineering" (Infosys 2012, 42).

Walmart extended its pioneering role in corporate climate action during a decade when it perceived a lessening likelihood that states would provide "rules of the game" for a low-carbon future. This pattern of behavior, marked by a counterintuitive mismatch between Walmart's perception of the material incentives for heightened climate action, on the one hand, and its activity, on the other, captures the logic of the emergent corporate climate consensus whose development this book has traced.

$$* \quad * \quad *$$

Evaluating the composite findings of the empirical chapters, this chapter highlights one of the key overarching insights of this book: corporations that individually do not appear inclined to alter their approach vis-à-vis a transnational issue can come to move in a remarkably cohesive direction amid states' failure to provide adequate leadership—even, in certain cases, becoming leaders themselves. As climate change attracted growing international recognition and concern, corporations became increasingly convinced that the world was headed toward a low-carbon future. Yet, they became less confident that states would provide the rules required to pave the way toward such a future in the form of policy and regulation. In this situation of increased certainty about the future but decreased confidence in prospects for state action, companies had two options. The first was to adopt a "wait and see" approach, continuing with "business as usual" and counting on states to act eventually

176   C. HULME

to provide the policy and regulatory conditions necessary for corporations to navigate toward, and succeed in, a low-carbon future. The second option was to begin to behave as if certain "rules of the game" already existed despite states not providing them and companies lacking confidence that they would do so in the foreseeable future. In the cohort of 34 companies whose behavior this book has examined, 82% (28 companies) chose the second option, making demonstrable changes in their climate policies or intensifying previous commitments—with 50% (17 companies) transitioning to higher "types" over time (i.e., becoming *evolutionaries*, *innovators*, or *disruptors*), even becoming global leaders on select practices. A particular complement of climate-related practices became more widespread and more deeply entrenched among companies. By the late 2010s, debates about whether corporations needed to take seriously the matter of climate change and a potential low-carbon future, which had flourished as recently as the late 2000s, were on the wane.

The empirical chapters argued that the development of a corporate climate consensus was emergent, a collective outcome that was achieved despite most companies not ranking climate change highly in their interest sets, and despite most companies' assessment of the material importance of climate change not only not increasing, but actually declining significantly. As Chapter 1 considered, Granovetter's threshold model sheds important light on this process. As dispersed and uncoordinated actors gather new information in their environment, they may or may not reprioritize a particular interest within their interest set—and even if they do, it still might not be ranked particularly high. Chapters 3–5 examined how most companies that altered their climate approach did not perceive the issue to be of high material importance. In terms of the threshold model, they did not have an especially low threshold for joining the activity in question (adopting new climate-related practices)—yet, they joined nonetheless. By watching early movers take action or perceiving that others were on the brink of acting, and by increasingly sensing that failing to join in certain practices might disadvantage them in the future, select companies with relatively high thresholds for action altered their approach, contributing to the collective outcome of the new corporate climate consensus.

* * *

Part I of this chapter presents composite findings about how the case-study corporations, representing four major industry groups and spanning three main headquarter countries, performed in the 2010s on three metrics of climate action. Part II considers the conditions under which select companies, to varying degrees, eschewed the "wait and see" approach, adopting new practices increasingly recognized as "rules of the game" for a low-carbon future amid diminishing confidence that states would provide them. Demonstrating that climate action broadened and deepened amid a significant decline in companies' outlook for high-impact climate-related regulation and little change in their limited concern with climate-driven changes in consumer behavior, Part II captures the explanatory power of this book's argument about the emergent nature of the corporate climate consensus.

Finally, Part III of this chapter examines hypotheses about industry- and country-level factors affecting the likelihood that actors will increase their level of climate activity absent strong individual incentives to do so. In all four case-study industry groups, there was an inconsistency between how individual companies perceived the material importance of climate change and how they behaved, demonstrating the logic of emergence at the industry level. Part III finds that this logic was most evident in technology and finance—although the former paired emergent activity with a high level of ambition, while the latter demonstrated a very low level of ambition. Further, within all but the automotive industry, US-based companies accounted for most of the climate activity that was misaligned with individual-level perceptions about the extent to which climate change posed pressing material risks or offered significant material opportunities; meanwhile, such activity increased most appreciably among Germany-based companies. Part III discusses what these findings suggest about conditions that may make it more likely that corporations will not simply recognize the need for a new approach to certain transnational issues like climate change but will seize the initiative, taking on a new role vis-à-vis these challenges.

Part III also considers the argument, introduced in Chapter 2, that while states throughout the 2010s perceived that their behavior sent a clear message—namely, that they had become more serious about addressing climate change and spurring a low-carbon transition—corporations may not have shared that perception. In failing to appreciate that their favorable self-image was not necessarily shared by others, states inadvertently opened the door to other players carving out new roles in the

178   C. HULME

climate issue area. But there also was a broader failure of imagination at work. States, having historically been the dominant actor in responding to global risks that for centuries have been primarily military in nature, inadequately considered the changing dynamics of a landscape increasingly defined by unconventional challenges that by their nature cannot be addressed by states alone. They tended to assume that others would continue to see even the most unconventional and complex of global risks as ultimately the purview of states, particularly the most powerful. Yet, during the 2010s, there was a change in the center of gravity in the climate change issue area; by the turn of the 2020s, non-state climate actors, including the kind of corporate giants at the heart of this book, played an increasingly prominent role relative to states.

Part I: The Development of a Corporate Climate Consensus

Corporate Behavior, 2010–2017

Classifying companies by type in six three-year periods spanning 2010–2017, Table 6.1 presents change in how companies performed on three metrics of climate action: *product* (capturing the extent to which companies addressed their emissions); *alignment* (gauging the degree to which they made their activities more coherent with a low-carbon future); and *investment* (assessing the extent to which they allocated resources to support a low-carbon future). As the empirical chapters presented, companies were classified by type (*business as usual [BAU], evolutionary, innovator*, or *disruptor*) based on scores for performance on industry-specific climate practices corresponding to each metric. The last column indicates parenthetically the cumulative percent change between periods 1 and 6 in each company's score; company names are in bold if they belonged to higher types in the final period than in the first. The last row displays the percent change between periods, capturing when and to what extent underlying momentum toward increased climate action gathered from 2010 through 2017.

As Table 6.1 captures, performance increased over time; in addition, once the company cohort's level of activity increased, it never regressed. By 2015–2017, 82% of companies had realized positive changes in performance, with 50% moving decisively toward a more climate-active approach, transitioning to higher types. With 65% of the type-changers

Table 6.1 Company types, 2010–2017

Type	2010–2012 (period 1)	2011–2013 (period 2)	2012–2014 (period 3)	2013–2015 (period 4)	2014–2016 (period 5)	2015–2017 (period 6)
Disruptor				Apple	Apple Heidelberg E.ON	**E.ON** (+64) **Apple** (+143) **Walmart** (+21) **Heidelberg** (+33)
Innovator	Walmart	Walmart Google Heidelberg	Walmart Heidelberg Google JNJ	Heidelberg Walmart BASF E.ON	Walmart BASF VW	VW (+88) **BASF** (+18) **BMW** (+30) **Google** (+18) **Infosys** (+63) **Tata Steel** (+30) **TYEKF** (+86)
Evolutionary	Heidelberg BASF Bayer E.ON Google BMW Daimler JNJ Tata Steel	BASF JNJ BMW E.ON Infosys Bayer Daimler Tata Steel Apple Pfizer VW	Apple E.ON BASF BMW Daimler Infosys Dow Bayer Pfizer VW	BMW VW Daimler Infosys JNJ Google Pfizer Bayer Dow Tata Steel	BMW Daimler Infosys Google JNJ Bayer Toyota	Daimler (+20) Bayer (−9) **Ford** (+43) **Pfizer** (+100) **Ultratech** (+67) **Allianz** (+80) JNJ (−10) **Microsoft** (+50) Toyota (+13)

(continued)

Table 6.1   (continued)

Type	2010–2012 (period 1)	2011–2013 (period 2)	2012–2014 (period 3)	2013–2015 (period 4)	2014–2016 (period 5)	2015–2017 (period 6)
BAU	Infosys	Dow	Citigroup	GM	Ford	Samsung (+60)
	Toyota	Ford	GM	Samsung	GM	BAC (+40)
	VW	Microsoft	JPMorgan	Toyota	Microsoft	Chrysler (+17)
	Apple	Samsung	Microsoft	Ultratech	Pfizer	Citigroup (+17)
	Dow	Toyota	Samsung	Citigroup	Tata Steel	Dow (−)
	Ford	Chevron	Tata Steel	JPMorgan	TYEKF	GM (+17)
	TYEKF	Citigroup	Toyota	Microsoft	Allianz	Shell (+40)
	Chevron	GM	BAC	Allianz	Chrysler	Deutsche (+200)
	Chrysler	JPMorgan	Chevron	BAC	Citigroup	JPMorgan (+50)
	Citigroup	Ultratech	Chrysler	Ford	Dow	AIG (+67)
	GM	Allianz	Ford	TYEKF	JPMorgan	Exxon (+67)
	Microsoft	BAC	Ultratech	AIG	Samsung	Chevron (−33)
	Ultratech	Chrysler	AIG	Chevron	Ultratech	RWE (−20)
	Allianz	RWE	Allianz	Chrysler	BAC	Reliance (−)
	BAC	Shell	RWE	RWE	Shell	
	Pfizer	TYEKF	Shell	Shell	AIG	
	RWE	AIG	TYEKF	Deutsche	Deutsche	
	Samsung	Deutsche	Exxon	Exxon	Chevron	
	Shell	Exxon	Deutsche	Reliance	Exxon	
	JPMorgan	Reliance	Reliance		RWE	
	AIG				Reliance	
	Exxon					
	Deutsche					
	Reliance					
% change	(−)	+9%	+3%	+6%	+5%	+9% (net: +37%)

Source Author

Note Thirty-four companies, classified according to three-year performance on metrics capturing the extent to which they addressed their emissions (***product***), made current activities more coherent with a low-carbon future (***alignment***), and allocated resources to support a low-carbon future (***investment***). Within each column, companies are listed in descending order of score, with companies receiving the same score listed in alphabetical order. BAC is Bank of America; Deutsche, Deutsche Bank; JNJ, Johnson & Johnson; TYEKF, Thyssenkrupp; and VW, Volkswagen becoming innovators or disruptors, there was a high level of ambition among companies that increased their level of climate activity.

Capturing when and how momentum gathered during the 2010s, Table 6.1 demonstrates that there was a 37% increase in companies' cumulative score between periods 1 and 6. The conventional wisdom holds that the December 2015 Paris Conference was a watershed for the private sector reckoning with climate change in a more serious manner; however, Table 6.1 underscores that corporate climate activity gained significant traction prior to that event. Specifically, from periods 1 through 4, encompassing pre-Paris activity, companies achieved approximately half of the total gains realized over the 2010–2017 timeframe.

Examining evidence that companies increasingly adopted a particular set of practices that came to be recognized as a new dominant design, or standard of behavior with which they had to align themselves to prepare for an anticipated future, Fig. 6.1 presents as a percentage the number of companies out of 34 meeting a certain threshold of action in each period, for each of the three metrics.

As Fig. 6.1 captures, rates of participation in *product* and *investment* were consistently high, never dropping below 71% and 80%, respectively, with *investment* increasing from 80% to 95%; the most significant change concerned *alignment*, which saw a 60% increase between periods 1 and 6. Increasing participation in *alignment* signifies that more companies became confident in a low-carbon future; many of the industry-specific practices encompassed by this metric are especially significant in that they alter a company's incentive to change its behavior in the "here and now" in anticipation of a future in which carbon carries a cost (i.e., the logic of internal carbon pricing). Further, *alignment* practices can have significant second-order impacts (especially salient in the context of addressing supply chain emissions, as many corporations have supply chains involving hundreds or even thousands of other companies). Capturing that the most considerable gains in *alignment* occurred in the pre-Paris Conference context (in 2012–2014 and 2013–2015), Fig. 6.1 conveys that more companies were becoming confident in a low-carbon future and beginning to behave accordingly before the event that has widely been assumed to be a turning point for the private sector appreciating the shortening shadow of a low-carbon future.

While Fig. 6.1 provides a snapshot of how broadly companies were participating in the practices encompassed by the three metrics, Fig. 6.2 captures their level of commitment to these practices, or how deeply

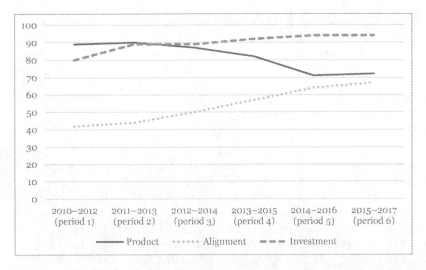

Fig. 6.1 Percentage of companies adopting specific climate practices, 2010–2017 (*Source* Author. *Note* The percentage of companies receiving a score for addressing their emissions [*product*], making current activities more coherent with a low-carbon future [*alignment*], and allocating resources to support a low-carbon future [*investment*])

they were participating in them. It shows as a percentage the number of companies receiving over half the available points for their performance on each metric.

As Fig. 6.2 demonstrates, companies became more deeply committed to all three metrics of action; the most significant change related to *alignment*, with the percentage of companies deeply invested in this type of action increasing by 77%. Considered alongside the results shown in Fig. 6.1, the key finding is that not only were more companies becoming confident in a low-carbon future but they were deepening their commitment to such a future.

Depending on the industry, different metrics are more or less significant in terms of what they indicate about a company's level of climate ambition, as certain practices are more or less important depending on the main sources of the industry's climate impacts (the appendix details the rationale for which metrics were deemed most significant for each industry). Over time, the percentage of companies receiving over half

6 THE EMERGENT CORPORATE CLIMATE CONSENSUS   183

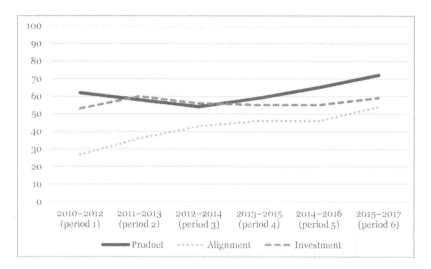

Fig. 6.2 Percentage of companies deeply invested in specific climate practices, 2010–2017 (*Source* Author. *Note* The percentage of companies receiving over half the available points for addressing their emissions [*product*], making current activities more coherent with a low-carbon future [*alignment*], and allocating resources to support a low-carbon future [*investment*])

the available points on the most heavily weighted metric for their respective industries increased nearly 135%, from 23% in period 1 to 54% in period 6—significant progress in a short period of time. The two earliest inter-period changes (between periods 1 and 2 and periods 2 and 3) were the most appreciable (with "deep participation" increasing 39% and 38%, respectively). In short, companies adopted potentially high-impact behaviors early in the decade—not simply in the pre-Paris Conference context and prior to any fillip for action it may have provided, but soon after Copenhagen and amid reverberations from the Great Recession when prospects for corporate climate action appeared especially dim.

* * *

Data showing how 34 companies behaved from 2010 to 2017 captures change in their climate performance, with 28 companies becoming part of the process ultimately producing a new pattern of corporate climate activity, and 17 altering their approach to such a degree as to transition to

184   C. HULME

a higher type. Once the company cohort advanced in terms of overall level of activity, it never regressed; a certain understanding about the "rules of the game," or the kinds of behavior necessary for success in a changing environment, took hold.[1] In addition, more companies adopted two out of three types of climate-relevant behavior, with companies demonstrating a deeper commitment to all three. Part II turns to consider aggregate data on why companies altered their behavior, demonstrating that as they coalesced around new practices, the crucial variable was declining confidence that states would provide an effective response to this issue of transnational importance. Part II also discusses how a key alternative explanation for the private sector's behavior did not gain purchase, as companies did not perceive intensifying consumer-driven pressure to change course.

PART II: PRIVATE SECTOR RESPONSES TO STATE ABDICATION OF LEADERSHIP

Chapter 1 proposed that in coalescing around certain climate practices during the 2010s, companies behaved much like a flock of geese, sensing "some shift in conditions and sensing each other's intuitions," and changing course (Brooks 2020). This analogy is fitting given that the collective outcome of a new corporate standard of climate action did not reflect the individual interest sets of the companies contributing to its realization. The key "shift in conditions" that contributed to this development was diminishing expectations of a robust response by states in the climate change issue area—one long considered as falling within their remit.

Figure 6.3 presents aggregate CDP data on companies' outlook for high-impact material risks and/or opportunities tied to climate change, separating data capturing their overall outlook (encompassing regulation, changing consumer behavior, and, for certain industries, physical effects), from that concerning regulation and changing consumer behavior, specifically.[2]

---

[1] As Fig. 6.1 shows, the only exception to the pattern was the number of companies participating in the practices captured by the product metric.

[2] The perception data in this chapter excludes 2017 due to changes in the CDP disclosure questions that compromise the comparability of the 2017 responses with those of previous years. Thus, there is perception data only for periods 1 through 5. Separate

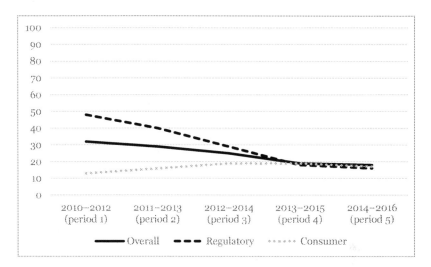

Fig. 6.3 Perceived high-impact risks and opportunities related to climate change, 2010–2016 (*Source* Author. *Note* Among 34 companies, the percentage of climate-related risks and opportunities that were perceived to be a high-impact material concern. If all companies perceived that climate change entailed high-impact risks and opportunities, the "y" axis would register 100)

The company cohort's perception that climate change presented high-impact material effects, whether opportunities or risks, declined by 45% between periods 1 and 5, with the outlook for high-impact regulation declining by 67%. Meanwhile, the outlook for significant changes in consumer behavior increased by 31%, although what appears to be a considerable development represents only a four percentage-point increase, from 13% to 17%. The finding that changing consumer behavior became only marginally more relevant belies the conventional wisdom about the growing importance for businesses of consumer demand for low-carbon, climate-friendly goods and services. In a 2018 interview for this book, a London-based Shell representative summarized the limited significance of climate-driven changes in consumer behavior: "If you ask

perception data concerning the physical effects of climate change is not presented as this category only pertained to select companies in the sample set, including banks, insurers, and oil and gas companies.

186   C. HULME

people whether they think climate change is important, they'll all tell you it is. But if you ask them to change their lifestyles, then they don't" (London, November 8, 2018).[3] Likewise, an expert for Berlin's Stiftung 2 Grad observed, "It's not clear yet in all business sectors that people are really willing to pay more to have climate protection. It's a very difficult question. When people make business decisions, whether to buy a product or not, climate protection and sustainability is not always the biggest factor in it, even if we wish it to be" (Berlin, November 13, 2018).

Figure 6.3 would not present a major puzzle if there had been no meaningful changes in how the private sector approached climate change. As discussed, however, 82% of the company cohort, or 28 out of 34 corporations, made demonstrable progress in their climate performance. Meanwhile, 50%, or 17 out of 34, altered their approaches to a sufficient degree to transition to a higher type (i.e., becoming an evolutionary, innovator, or disruptor). Given the significant increase in the overall level of climate action, the data on companies' perceptions of the material importance of climate change establishes the emergent quality of the new corporate climate consensus. The critical condition spurring such an unexpected development was declining corporate confidence in prospects for bold state action on an issue that by the 2010s had gained increasing international recognition not simply as one global challenge among many, but as one likely to be a defining feature of the twenty-first century landscape.

The decline in corporate confidence in prospects for concerted climate action by states supports Chapter 2's core proposition, namely, that misinterpreted signals and intentions were a critical feature of the landscape in which the private sector became a key climate actor. While states, seeing an unmistakable arc of progress from the 2009 Copenhagen Conference to the 2015 Paris Conference, had a favorable image of their behavior in the climate change issue area, others did not share that image. To some of the most globally significant of these "others"—leading corporations—the key message of developments from Copenhagen to Paris was that states had abandoned efforts to arrive at an effective climate approach marrying ambition with accountability. Their behavior merely confirmed that states still did not agree on how to ensure that all the

---

[3] This Shell representative also underscored that in the 2016 political debates in the United Kingdom and the United States, "energy and climate change didn't get a mention whatsoever. It's a non-issue" (London, November 8, 2018).

critical players cut their emissions sufficiently to achieve the shared goal of limiting global warming to 2°C, much less 1.5°C, above pre-industrial levels, and, even more importantly for corporations, that all key players were invested in establishing clear, enforceable "rules of the game" for a low-carbon future. Whatever ambitious targets states committed to in the Paris context, they needed to be supported by adequate regulatory muscle and accountability to render them meaningful in practice. Corporations saw neither. Indeed, whereas in 2010–2012 companies were moderately confident in prospects for high-impact climate regulation, by 2014–2016, during the Paris period—including the run-up to the conference when most states were announcing their Intended Nationally Determined Contributions (INDCs), the conference itself, and the ratification of the Paris Agreement—they had become much less confident.

States, which were confident that what to them was the unmistakable pattern of progress in their behavior would be equally obvious to others, did not fully appreciate that the climate game was changing. Historically, given their dominant position as the pivotal player shaping the most relevant global security issue areas, states assumed that the message they sought to convey to others about an issue like climate change would be received as intended. Yet, the striking disjunction between how states saw their climate behavior in the 2010s—as clearly on an upward trajectory, evincing a new level of commitment—and how some of the most influential corporations interpreted that behavior precipitated the arrival of a different dynamic in the international system, one to which states were inadequately attentive.

Figure 6.4 presents a snapshot of the book's findings concerning the development of the emergent climate consensus, underscoring the divergence between how companies perceived the material importance of the climate issue and how the cohort behaved. It draws together data concerning companies' adoption of certain practices ("breadth of action") and deepening commitment to those practices ("depth of action") with that concerning their perception of regulation and changing

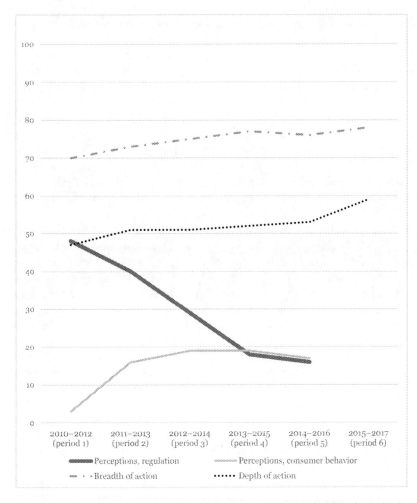

Fig. 6.4 Divergence between companies' climate action and perceptions, 2010–2017 (*Source* Author. *Note* Comparison of companies' adoption of, and commitment to, climate practices, on the one hand, and perception of climate-related regulation and changing consumer behavior as high-impact material concerns, on the other. Perception data for 2015–2017 is not presented due to changes in the 2017 CDP disclosure questionnaire that compromise the comparability of the 2017 responses with those of previous years)

consumer behavior as serious material concerns.[4] As Fig. 6.4 captures, companies were adopting new climate practices and becoming more deeply committed to them as their perceptions of climate change as a high-impact material concern—especially their outlook for regulatory action—declined significantly.

Why did the gap between corporate climate perception and action widen during the 2010s? In Chapter 1, Hypothesis 1 (H1) proposed that the less the international landscape is characterized by prospects for concerted climate action—a proxy for states' willingness to address an issue calling for a transnational response—the more the private sector will behave as a climate actor. The logic is that corporations seek predictability in the international environment. Becoming more certain that the world was headed toward a low-carbon future due to climate-related pressures, they would have been inclined to act more assertively in the issue area the clearer it became that states' pivot from the top-down, Kyoto-style model of climate action to the bottom-up approach of Paris would not produce the type of commitments necessary to establish "rules of the game" for a low-carbon future.

Addressing H1, Fig. 6.5 captures change in the degree of correspondence between the new consensus position and the attitudes of individual members of the cohort, or where the climate issue ranked relative to other priorities in individual companies' interest sets. For each period, the figure shows the relationship between the cohort's climate performance (the proxy for consensus) and its underlying "strength of perception," or the prevalence among individual companies of the view that climate change posed pressing material risks or presented significant material opportunities. Numbers above 1 on the y-axis capture emergent consensus; the higher the number, the less the correspondence between the company cohort's behavior and companies' underlying attitudes.[5]

---

[4] Part I considered the breadth and depth of participation for the three metrics (product, alignment, and investment) separately, for each period. Figure 6.4 combines the data for the three metrics for each period. Thus, for example, "breadth of action" for period 1 shows the average participation for *product, alignment,* and *investment.* Figure 6.4 does not include data on perceptions pertaining to the physical effects of climate change given that this category only pertained to select companies in the sample set, including banks, insurers, and oil and gas companies.

[5] These numbers represent ratios capturing the relationship between strength of climate action and strength of perception. If the number is 1, this indicates that for every "unit" of perception there was a "unit" of action, showing a non-emergent pattern of behavior.

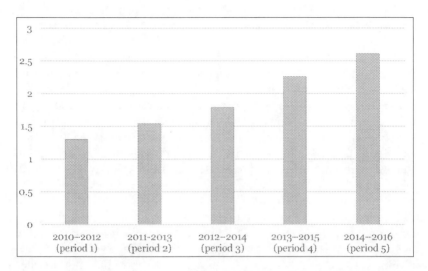

Fig. 6.5 Emergent climate consensus by time period, 2010–2016 (*Source* Author. *Note* For five time periods, the relationship between companies' climate performance and perception that climate change was a high-impact material concern. A score above 1 captures emergent action)

As H1 anticipates, Fig. 6.5 shows that an emergent climate consensus gained strength during the 2010s; in fact, it doubled. Data from interviews conducted in 2018 affirms, consistent with CDP data, that H1 anticipates why this was the case. The increase in climate activity was grounded in companies' waning confidence in states' likelihood of leading effectively in the climate change issue area. Interviewees from London to New Delhi expressed that the Paris Conference was yet another disappointment in the bleak history of international climate meetings. Asked if the Paris Agreement had any impact as of 2018, a UK-based representative for E.ON, one of Europe's largest power companies, noted, "Not really, if I'm honest." He explained that in the United Kingdom and parts of Europe, "there's a perception that we're out front, and Paris is about getting everyone else to catch up. It's about getting the US on board, for example. Good luck with that." From his perspective, "Paris was almost

Meanwhile, if the number is below one, this indicates that action lagged behind what would be expected given the perceived material importance of climate change.

a coordination exercise to get everyone pointing in the right direction, but we're not doing anything in the UK that we weren't doing before as a result of Paris, as a company or as a country" (London, November 12, 2018). Notably, E.ON was one of the case-study companies that became most climate active, transitioning to the disruptor type in 2014–2016.

Speaking from the policymaking sphere, a European Parliament staffer for climate and energy issues characterized Paris as "quite a vague agreement." Since "it's not legally binding and has no real commitments in it, it's a nice paper to look at, and everyone can be behind it a bit. Paris is fine, but nothing was reached if in the end [EU] Member States don't take drastic actions, which I don't think they are doing. Even in Germany [this interviewee's home country], we aren't reaching our own targets" (Telephone conversation with author, October 12, 2018).

Oil and gas company representatives were especially pessimistic about Paris. As an interviewee from BP in Germany, an external affairs expert, observed, "It looks like the Paris goal will not be met—we [in Germany] already are off track" (Telephone conversation with author, November 1, 2018). The Shell representative previously cited reported that the company was "absolutely" unsure about the political and social feasibility of the global energy transition—and that Paris did nothing to address those uncertainties:

> I don't know how anybody could be sure given that the sum of the INDCs do not add up to anywhere near enough to deliver the Paris Agreement. And many countries basically almost ridiculed the IPCC's [Intergovernmental Panel on Climate Change] latest report as being too aggressive. (London, November 8, 2018)

Given that oil and gas companies were among the least climate active of the 34 case-study corporations, their perspective is especially valuable for appreciating the landscape and context in which others *were* becoming increasingly active.

192   C. HULME

Interviewees in India shared similar sentiments about the limits of Paris. A regulatory expert for Tata Steel saw India's ambitious commitments as untethered to realities on the ground.[6] Unconvinced that countries' commitments in international forums "really provide any mileage," he stressed that they are "political statements that the governments of these countries are making, but then to translate them into action, it takes a hell of a lot of effort" (New Delhi, August 7, 2018). Notably, Tata Steel transitioned from the BAU to innovator type in 2015–2017. A C-Suite executive from Tata Power, meanwhile, observed that while "the talk about the Paris Agreement was bold, on the ground some of the things they agreed to have not happened." For example, the "so-called hundred billion dollars every year from 2020 onward"—funding that developed countries pledged to support a low-carbon transition in developing countries—"we don't see that" (Mumbai, August 14, 2018). The conference "was a great photo opp," said a New Delhi-based entrepreneur in clean technology. "I think the intention was great, but if there's no execution, eventually it just means nothing" (New Delhi, August 4, 2018).

During the 2010s, companies' actions increasingly outpaced their outlook for climate-related regulation or changes in consumer behavior. The evidence suggests that companies that became more climate active were not motivated by the perception that Paris was a watershed for international climate efforts—quite the opposite—and that for those that were not climate active, Paris did not help to alleviate uncertainties about a potential low-carbon transition's viability or urgency, whether politically, societally, or economically.

* * *

Contrary to intuitive expectations, this cohort of 34 of the world's largest corporations increased its climate performance and transitioned to a more climate-active approach in the context of diminishing confidence that states would lead in the issue area. Corporate leaders from Europe to India perceived that developments surrounding the Paris Conference may have indicated the overall direction in which states wanted to head, but they were not convinced that states were prepared to undertake the

---

[6] For example, prior to the Paris Conference, India announced that by 2030, 40% of its total energy generation capacity would come from non-fossil fuels. It also pledged to cut the emissions intensity of its economy by up to 35% by 2030 (Vaughan 2015).

ambitious policies or enact the bold regulations necessary actually to move in that direction. To appreciate fully the significance of the considerable increase in climate action during the 2010s, reflecting the private sector's orientation toward a more climate-active approach, the interpretive key is companies' loss of confidence that states would provide "rules of the game" for a low-carbon future in a concerted, ambitious, and timely fashion.

PART III: CORPORATIONS' CLIMATE ACTION AND AMBITION

Which companies became integral to the process by which the new climate consensus took shape and a new pattern of response developed? Which not only recognized the need for a new approach to the issue area but seized the initiative and assumed a new role? The following sections address two hypotheses about factors that may help explain why, in specific cases, companies adopted a new climate approach prior to perceiving strong material incentives to do so.

Hypothesis 2: Industry Type

In Chapter 1, Hypothesis 2 (H2) proposed that companies whose business models are less dependent on the fossil fuel-centered status quo are more likely to be shapers of what developed into the new corporate climate consensus. Being less tightly entwined in the status quo, they are more likely to adopt the kind of practices that came to be recognized as the new standard of climate behavior despite themselves not perceiving strong material pressures or incentives to alter their approach. H2 anticipates that there will be a higher prevalence of such behavior in technology companies and a lower prevalence among companies in the energy-intensive, automotive, and finance industries. Figure 6.6 shows the extent of emergent action in each industry group. The y-axis reflects the relationship between action and perception; the higher the number, the higher the prevalence of emergent action, or the more companies' behaviors outpaced their assessments of the material impacts of climate change.

Figure 6.6 shows that while all industry groups behaved in an increasingly emergent manner over time (between 2010–2012 and 2014–2016, emergent action increased 82% in energy-intensive industries, 99% in

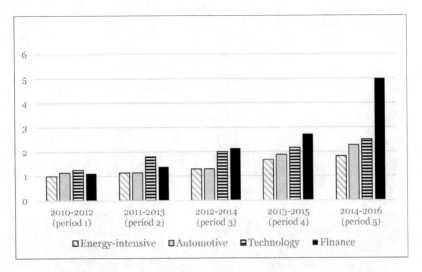

Fig. 6.6 Prevalence of emergent action by industry, 2010–2016 (*Source* Author. *Note* Among four industry groups, the relationship between companies' climate performance and perception that climate change was a high-impact material concern. A score above 1 captures emergent action)

automotive, 100% in technology, and 350% in finance), technology was earliest in distinguishing itself as an emergent actor (from period 2 onward), while finance followed shortly thereafter (from period 3 onward).

While all industry groups ultimately behaved in an emergent fashion, what spurred the technology and finance industries to undertake such behavior sooner than others? Because they have such expansive reach, not only in terms of their geographic footprint but also given their widespread involvement in various areas of the economy and society, these industries arguably are better positioned to glimpse the future and respond earlier than companies whose vision is more narrowly focused on their specific industries, as well as to exert a higher degree of extra-industry influence than automakers or companies in energy-intensive industries. But the nature of the extra-industry influence of technology and finance companies differs in important respects, which helps to explain why the former also were among the strongest climate performers, while the latter were the weakest.

Technology companies have unparalleled societal ubiquity; as Chapter 4 discussed, Apple has an active installed base of 1.65 billion devices and 620 million subscribers on its platform (Nellis 2021), while Google has seven products with over one billion monthly users and processes two trillion Internet searches annually (Balakrishnan 2017). Meanwhile, the key feature of finance companies' extra-industry influence pertains to their industry not just being one among many with deep ties to the fossil fuel-centered status quo, but rather embodying the "old world" as the linchpin of the high-carbon economy. Whereas technology companies have extra-industry influence and are weak incumbents, or have relatively weak bonds to the status quo, finance companies have extra-industry influence and, as enablers of all other industries, are strong incumbents with tight bonds to the status quo. In short, when a company, by the nature of its business model, has both a high potential to exert extra-industry influence, offering a better vantage point to glimpse the future, and relatively weak bonds to the status quo, the conditions are especially ripe for its behavior not only to follow a pattern of emergent action but also to demonstrate a high level of ambition.

Hypothesis 3: Headquarter Country

According to Hypothesis 3 (H3), the behavior of companies headquartered in countries where the national government historically has not been inclined toward high levels of climate activity or leadership primarily should account for the overall phenomenon of emergent climate action in the private sector. A record of limited activity by the state on an issue that a company believes will inform future global trends may lead it to act, regardless of current perceptions of its material salience. By contrast, for companies headquartered in historically climate-active countries, the expectation is for the state's continued activity in, and "ownership" of, the issue area. H3 assumes that a company's assessment of the state is relatively "sticky"; in other words, if a company perceives that the state historically has demonstrated a certain level of ownership vis-à-vis the climate change issue, that perception will strongly color its present-day expectations for state action.

As Chapter 2 explored, the case-study headquarter countries have different records of activity in, and ownership of, the climate issue area; Germany is at the high end of the activity/ownership spectrum, and India and the United States at the low end. If H3 correctly anticipates the relationship between a country's record of climate activity and emergent corporate climate action, the implication is that in the industries for which they are represented in the sample set, there should be a higher absolute level of emergent action among US and Indian companies than among German companies. Figures 6.7–6.10 capture the extent to which headquarter country may have influenced corporations undertaking climate activity that outpaced their expectations for state climate action.

The first implication of Figs. 6.7–6.10 is that H3 correctly anticipated that US companies would account for a significant share of the overall amount of emergent action. US-based energy-intensive, technology, and finance companies acted in a significantly more emergent fashion than their German and Indian counterparts. As the empirical chapters explored, US corporations increased their climate activity even as they became much less confident in prospects for high-impact climate action by states, including, most importantly, by their headquarter country. Consistent with Chapter 2's argument about the perennial misalignment between what select presidential administrations have done

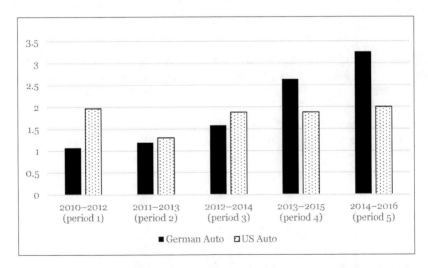

Fig. 6.7 Country comparison of emergent action in the automotive industry, 2010–2016 (*Source* Author. *Note* Comparison of the prevalence of emergent action by automakers based in Germany and the United States. A score above 1 captures emergent action)

on the international stage to position the United States as a climate leader, on the one hand, and their weak domestic basis for action, on the other, during the 2010s, corporations did not give much credence to periodic efforts by the Obama administration (particularly surrounding the Paris Conference) to convey a certain message about US climate leadership. In short, an important factor in the US landscape was corporations failing to receive the government's message as intended, a failure rooted in the state's historical record of inadequate action in the issue area.

H3 was partially incorrect, however, in its expectations concerning Indian companies. As Figs. 6.8 and 6.9 show, respectively, Indian energy-intensive companies' behavior reflected the logic of emergence in periods 1 and 2, but from period 3 onward their behavior came more closely into alignment with their expectations for state action; in the technology industry, meanwhile, Indian corporate behavior did not follow an emergent pattern. For energy-intensive companies, beginning in the period (2012–2014, or period 3) when New Delhi adopted ambitious climate-related targets and began implementing policy pushes related to its renewable energy objectives, companies increasingly perceived that climate change (specifically, regulation) posed significant material impacts; compared to periods 1 and 2, there was relative consistency between companies' actions and perceptions.[7] Importantly, however, companies did not dramatically increase their climate activity amid registering a changing policy landscape; rather, they essentially continued doing what they already were doing, while acknowledging that New Delhi was "getting in the game" more seriously in terms of climate-related policy.

Chapter 2 proposed that while New Delhi believed that the development-driven motivation for its climate-related activity was unimportant, to the private sector its policy rationale potentially mattered. The chapter argued that a development-driven renewable energy campaign that ran alongside an enduring commitment to coal-fired power plants would not necessarily have indicated, in the private sector's mind, a

---

[7] The government of India's renewable energy push began in 2013, when Prime Minister Singh's government crafted the ambitious target of achieving 100 gigawatts of renewables by 2022 (representing a revision of the previous target of 22 gigawatts), and gathered momentum in 2014, when Prime Minister Modi actually announced it. During the 2012–2014 period, the prevalence of emergent action among Indian companies declined by 36%. From period 1 through period 5, among Indian companies, there was a net 22% decrease in the prevalence of emergent action.

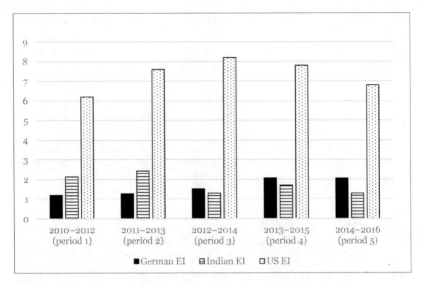

Fig. 6.8 Country comparison of emergent action in energy-intensive (EI) industries, 2010–2016 (*Source* Author. *Note* Comparison of the prevalence of emergent action by energy-intensive (EI) companies based in Germany, India, and the United States. A score above 1 captures emergent action)

commitment to paving the way toward a low-carbon future. But the findings do not reveal strong support for this argument. While companies did not substantially increase their climate activity following the government's climate-related policy pushes (in contrast to what might have been expected and what New Delhi may have anticipated), they did increasingly expect high-impact policy and regulation in the climate issue area, even if it was underpinned by the development-focused rationale. The government assumed that its push on renewable energy would be interpreted in a particular way, as indicating a new level of climate activity and commitment, and the corporations examined in this book generally appeared to interpret it as such.

Figures 6.7–6.10 also highlight H3's failure to anticipate changing rates of emergent behavior; assuming a certain degree of immutability in how corporations viewed a state's likelihood for robust climate action, the hypothesis expected that Indian and US companies consistently would register higher rates of emergent behavior than German companies. Yet,

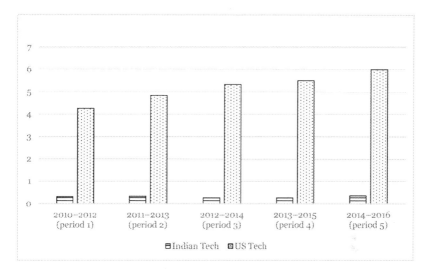

Fig. 6.9 Country comparison of emergent action in the technology industry, 2010–2016 (*Source* Author. *Note* Comparison of the prevalence of emergent action by technology companies based in India and the United States. A score above 1 captures emergent action)

the figures point to emergent behavior unfolding in a more dynamic fashion, particularly among German companies. While early on they either behaved in a non-emergent fashion or behaved emergently to a limited extent, their rate of emergent behavior accelerated over time. Figure 6.11 captures the trend in emergent action in each headquarter country, showing the respective contributions of German, Indian, and US corporations to the overall upward trend. The y-axis shows the cumulative percent change, or the change between the amount of emergent action in period 1 and in each subsequent period.

Figure 6.11 shows emergent action declining and then remaining steady among Indian companies, increasing and then remaining steady for US companies, and dramatically and consistently increasing for German companies. In short, while US corporations were the major contributors to the absolute level of emergent behavior (as Figs. 6.7–6.10 demonstrate), German corporations were the main drivers of the upward trend in such behavior.

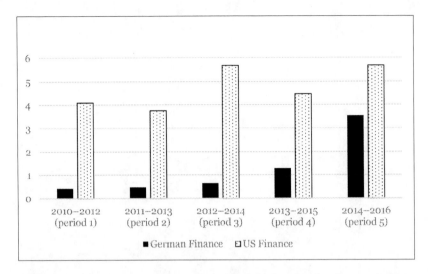

Fig. 6.10 Country comparison of emergent action in the finance industry, 2010–2016 (*Source* Author. *Note* Comparison of the prevalence of emergent action by finance companies based in Germany and the United States. A score above 1 captures emergent action)

What explains this unanticipated development? As Chapter 2 explored, while Berlin has long been active in climate policymaking, during the 2010s there may have been a widening gap between how the government tended to view itself (as climate active, consistent with its longtime approach) and how corporations interpreted its behavior (as indicative of the government having become less climate active, or less effective in its ownership of the issue area). Figure 6.11 points to Germany-based companies, long accustomed to operating in the context of state action and initiative in the issue area, altering their assessment of their environment and pursuing more independent action. This finding, while undercutting H3's expectation concerning the importance of the state's historical record of climate activity and leadership, supports Chapter 2's arguments about the importance of misaligned perceptions during the 2010s. While the German government continued to view itself as climate active and serious about paving the way toward a low-carbon future, to corporations the facts on the ground increasingly conflicted with this image. In short, in the German context, companies' image of the

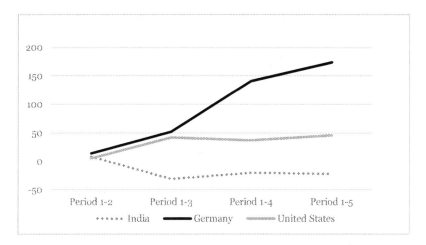

Fig. 6.11 Cumulative change in emergent action by headquarter country, 2010–2016 (*Source* Author. *Note* For three headquarter countries, the cumulative change [i.e., between period 1 and each subsequent period] in companies behaving in an emergent fashion, where climate action outpaced the strength of the perception that climate change posed significant material impacts)

state as climate actor was more dynamic and less sticky than anticipated; companies were more sensitive to change in their environment than expected.

* * *

Clearly, certain kinds of corporate actors have an especially strong potential to help reshape the landscape in the context of a transnational challenge like climate change—including by taking action prior to perceiving strong material incentives to do so. Analyzing the trajectory of emergent action demonstrated that while US companies were pivotal contributors to the overall high level of emergent behavior during the 2010s, German companies were key drivers of the upward trend in such behavior (with the prevalence of emergent action increasing by 46% among the former and 172% among the latter). While US companies were consistently strong emergent actors, German companies, having long operated in the context of strong state leadership in the climate change issue area, gradually came into their own as climate actors amid diminishing perceived prospects for bold government action. For most companies, this was a matter of perceiving, amid the growing gap between government rhetoric and Germany's climate performance, that while Berlin understandably had long enjoyed a reputation as climate active, it recently had become less firmly committed to making and enforcing "rules of the road" for a low-carbon future.

Meanwhile, early on Indian companies were undertaking action that outpaced their perception of the material relevance of climate change, but with New Delhi embarking on its renewable energy push from 2013 onward, their actions increasingly aligned with their perceptions. Importantly, however, the government's climate-related push did not spur Indian companies to significantly increase their climate activity; they simply sustained what they already had started to do prior to the government's mid-2010s "turnaround" on the climate change issue.

Inadvertent Change in the Climate Game

During the 2010s, while states perceived that they were undertaking bold climate approaches after decades of gridlock, the private sector perceived the climate issue area as one in which states were increasingly unlikely to play an effective role. It was in this context that select corporations came to the fore, assuming new roles as climate actors and, in certain instances, as leaders. States thought that between 2009 and 2015, they had made substantial progress toward changing the climate game, assuming that the Paris Agreement supplied the private sector with an unmistakable signal that the international community was poised for concerted action that would nurture a global low-carbon transition. Yet, with certain corporations interpreting their behavior very differently, states inadvertently precipitated a change in the climate game, with its defining players and dynamics appreciably altered by the turn of the 2020s compared to the previous three decades.

This book is concerned with a specific class of private sector "rule-makers": companies in the top ranks of the Fortune Global 500, with resources and reach outstripping that of the vast majority of states. During the 2010s, they shaped, and were shaped by, an ongoing process of forging a new consensus about climate change and a low-carbon future. This consensus has begun to diffuse among a broader cross-section of the private sector. Indeed, in the 2020 release of its annual survey of global CEOs, PricewaterhouseCoopers pointed to the onset of the second wave of the developments this book traced and analyzed, announcing, "The tide has turned on climate change. Organisations worldwide are starting to recognize its risks and even its potential opportunities. Compared with ten years ago, CEOs today are far more likely to see the benefits of going 'green'" (PricewaterhouseCoopers 2020). Viewed in the context of the data presented in this chapter and in light of this book's core argument, the implication is that once the most powerful corporate actors begin behaving as if they have a different role to play in an issue area, others may begin to reconsider their own role and willingness to wait on states to take action on some of the most pressing global challenges. Others not only can come to appreciate more fully the possibility of behaving in new ways—they also may come to perceive the *necessity* of doing so.

REFERENCES

Balakrishnan, Anita. 2017. Here's how billions of people use Google products, in one chart. CNBC. May 18, 2017. https://www.cnbc.com/2017/05/18/google-user-numbers-youtube-android-drive-photos.html.

Brooks, David. 2020. Biden's rise gives the establishment one last chance. *The New York Times*, March 5, 2020. https://www.nytimes.com/2020/03/05/opinion/joe-biden-2020.html.

Francis, David. 2016. The top 25 corporate nations. *Foreign Policy*, March 15, 2016. https://foreignpolicy.com/2016/03/15/these-25-companies-are-more-powerful-than-many-countries-multinational-corporate-wealth-power/.

Green, Jessica. 2013. *Rethinking private authority: Agents and entrepreneurs in global environmental governance*. Princeton, NJ: Princeton University Press.

Infosys. 2012. Sustainability report 2011–2012. https://www.infosys.com/sustainability/documents/infosys-sustainability-report-2011-12.pdf.

Nellis, Stephen. 2021. Apple posts record profit as iPhone sales surge in China. *The Economic Times*, January 28, 2021. https://economictimes.indiatimes.com/tech/tech-bytes/apple-posts-record-profit-as-iphone-sales-surge-in-china/articleshow/80490035.cms.

PricewaterhouseCoopers. 2020. Navigating the rising tide of uncertainty. 23rd Annual global CEO survey. https://www.pwc.com/gx/en/ceo-survey/2020/reports/pwc-23rd-global-ceo-survey.pdf.

Stevens, Pippa. 2019. Behind Walmart's push to eliminate 1 gigaton of greenhouse gases by 2030. CNBC. December 15, 2019. https://www.cnbc.com/2019/12/15/walmarts-project-gigaton-is-its-most-ambitious-climate-goal-yet.html.

Stimage, Kaityn. 2018. The world's largest employers. World Atlas. https://www.worldatlas.com/articles/the-world-s-largest-employers.html.

Vandenbergh, Michael, and Jonathan Gilligan. 2017. Why private "actors" are taking center stage on climate change. GreenBiz. December 9, 2017. https://www.greenbiz.com/article/why-private-actors-are-taking-center-stage-climate-change.

Vaughan, Adam. 2015. India unveils climate change plan. *The Guardian*, October 2, 2015. https://www.theguardian.com/world/2015/oct/02/india-pledges-40-percent-electricity-renewables-2030.

Walmart. 2010. 2010 Annual report. March 30, 2010. https://www.annualreportowl.com/Walmart/2010/Annual%20Report.

———. 2011. 2011 Global responsibility report. https://corporate.walmart.com/global-responsibility/global-responsibility-report-archive.

———. 2013. Walmart announces new commitments to dramatically increase energy efficiency and renewables. April 15, 2013. https://corporate.walmart.com/newsroom/2013/04/14/walmart-announces-new-commitments-to-dramatically-increase-energy-efficiency-and-renewables.

———. 2014. 2014 Global responsibility report. https://corporate.walmart.com/global-responsibility/global-responsibility-report-archive.

———. 2016. 2016 Global responsibility report. https://corporate.walmart.com/global-responsibility/global-responsibility-report-archive.

CHAPTER 7

Superpowers, Inc.: Lessons on World Order

INTRODUCTION

The corporate climate action phenomenon offers a window on a new world—one that the pioneers of the field of transnational relations writing in the 1970s did not fully glimpse, and most states have not yet fully grasped. This chapter presents four lessons on world order from this book's findings about how and why select companies with "more power than governments" (Khanna 2016, 58) recognized in the 2010s that the climate and low-carbon game was changing and began to play a different game. These lessons focus on what corporate climate behavior reveals about some of the actors, issues, and dynamics that have the potential to recast the international system in the twenty-first century.

LESSON 1: CORPORATIONS MAY BE BETTER THAN STATES AT RECOGNIZING NEW "GAMES"

In a 2018 interview in which he discussed progress toward a global low-carbon transition, Amory Lovins, physicist and co-founder of the Rocky Mountain Institute, explained the grounds for his optimism that such a transition was not far off by pointing out that in looking at a photograph of Fifth Avenue in New York in 1900, "you must look hard for the first car. Just 13 years later, you must look even harder for the last

© The Author(s), under exclusive license to Springer Nature   205
Switzerland AG 2023
C. Hulme, *Corporate Climate Action, Transnational Politics, and World Order*, Environmental Politics and Theory,
https://doi.org/10.1007/978-3-031-34115-1_7

206   C. HULME

horse." Immense technological change frequently occurs in a non-linear fashion; as Lovins pointed out, in economic history it is common to see instances in which "the value of old businesses deflates very rapidly, while the output of the old technology stagnates and starts to fall, even when the replacement technology is only at the few percent level." The private sector is a critical driver of such change, given that "both customers and investors can see these big shifts coming and start to adopt them rapidly if it makes sense and makes money. Capital markets in particular keenly sniff out disruption, and if they catch its scent – if they think that an old industry is already in or headed for the toaster – they don't wait for the toast to get done before they decapitalise the old and invest in the new" (Amelang 2018).

This book explored how in the early 2010s, the landscape and context of the climate change issue area was much like Fifth Avenue in 1900, defined by certain actors, practices, and "rules of the road." States, as they had been for decades, were understood to be the pivotal climate players. A low-carbon future was up for debate; as described in an interview by the former strategy director for a major European power company, there were "a variety of views as to where the energy system was going in the long term," owing largely to differing perspectives on the significance of climate change (London, November 12, 2018). To the extent that select corporations were engaged on climate issues, a small number had adopted practices, like internal carbon pricing, indicating that they anticipated "an environment where greenhouse gas emissions carry a price" (CDP 2017). But by the late 2010s and turn of the 2020s, the field of play had been recast. Climate change was an issue of importance to any serious global actor (those refusing to rethink old approaches seemed like the last horses on Fifth Avenue in 1913); alternatives to a low-carbon future appeared increasingly unlikely to the private sector; and some corporations over-shadowed states in their level of climate activity and ambition. The game had changed.

This book explored how select "corporate nations" (Francis 2016) recognized that the game was changing in the 2010s and adopted a new sensibility toward the climate issue area. Behaving as if a "business as usual" approach was untenable, they appeared to have "sniffed out disruption" and to have sensed that the old game was "headed for the toaster." The book also demonstrated that what precipitated this recognition was less climate change per se having become a more urgent material concern, and more the need for a new approach to an issue that states appeared unlikely to address in an effective fashion. In other words, the driving concern of companies that became increasingly climate active was not mitigating climate change; rather, it was reducing uncertainty and unpredictability in their environment by identifying some "rules of the new game," or rules for a low-carbon future, specifically in a context where states were failing to provide them and where they lacked confidence that states would provide them in the near future.

Why did corporations recognize a new future on the horizon whereas most states appeared to miss significant changes occurring around them? In "Hypotheses on Misperception," Jervis noted that there is "overwhelming" evidence from psychology and history that decisionmakers "tend to fit incoming information into their existing theories and images. Indeed, their theories and images play a large part in determining what they notice. In other words, actors tend to perceive what they expect" (Jervis 1968, 455). States did not readily perceive changes in their environment or recognize the significance of corporations becoming more active in that environment, interpreting developments through preexisting lenses and according to old assumptions. They tended to view the landscape through the prism of the twentieth century, an era in which states both were the unrivaled centers of gravity in the global landscape and unmatched in having the resources and the interest to act as leaders on transnational issues. Capturing such a mindset, in an interview in which he recounted his leading role in negotiating the Paris Agreement, a US diplomat, when asked about the surge of interest in the Paris "moment" concerning the role of non-state actors in the climate change issue area, remarked, "I don't think there's anything in the Paris Agreement per se that envisions anything particular about non-state actors." Asked about what sort of input, if any, the United States solicited from major US companies prior to the Paris negotiations, he recounted, "We knew there was a lot of kind of progressive business support.... We knew that if we brought back the wrong kind of agreement, we would have trouble with business." But it was "like that, at a general level," with no specific consultation with individual companies. In a telling remark, he explained that such a lack of consultation was "not because we were ignoring" companies, but rather "because over the course of the years we had developed a pretty good feel" for the private sector's position on climate-related issues (New Haven, Connecticut, November 13, 2017).

Fitting "incoming information" into its "existing theories and images" (Jervis 1968, 455) about the different actors in the climate issue arena and their respective roles and positions therein, the United States government perceived what it expected. It failed to appreciate that the issue had become relevant for any serious global actor, not simply "progressive" businesses, and that many corporations no longer were content to wait and see what kind of a deal states "brought back" from international climate negotiations, but rather were forging their own understanding of the rules of the new climate game.

States also tended to overlook or misunderstand the significance of changes in their environment given *how* developments unfolded, in an emergent fashion. By nature, emergent change is difficult to predict *ex ante* given the relationship between inputs and outputs; incremental developments and seemingly insignificant inputs can set in motion a process leading to the transformation of the environment. During the 2010s, some of the key inputs that ultimately led to the reshaping of the climate change issue area—individual companies adopting new climate practices—often would have appeared to states as incremental and even insignificant given the breadth of the issue and complexity of the problem. States were apt to dismiss these inputs as unlikely to indicate that companies were assuming fundamentally new roles, much less that their behavior foreshadowed significant change in the issue area. As Jervis noted,

> Actors can more easily assimilate into their established image of another actor information contradicting that image if the information is transmitted and considered bit by bit than if it comes all at once. In the former case, each piece of discrepant data can be coped with as it arrives and each of the conflicts with the prevailing view will be small enough to go unnoticed, to be dismissed as unimportant, or to necessitate at most a slight modification of the image (e.g., addition of exceptions to the rule). When the information arrives in a block, the contradiction between it and the prevailing view is apt to be much clearer and the probability of major cognitive reorganization will be higher. (1968, 465–466)

If corporations had set out to behave as climate change mitigators or had sought to displace states as the leaders of the issue area, states may have interpreted their behavior differently and grasped its significance sooner; such a "block" of new information about the private sector would have made much clearer "the contradiction between it and the prevailing view," and there would have been a higher "probability of major cognitive reorganization" on the part of states. But precisely because the driving concern of those corporations that became more climate active was not the lofty aspiration of seizing the mantle of climate leadership, but rather the less conspicuous objective of reducing unpredictability in their future environment, states could cope with "each piece of discrepant data" as it arrived, treating "each of the conflicts with the prevailing view" either as unimportant or as necessitating "at most a slight modification" of their existing image.

If states misperceived changes in their environment because they were too incremental to force a fundamental rethinking of old assumptions and mental models, the climate change issue acted as a forcing function for other players to emerge and assume new roles. Corporations recognized that the game was changing amid their growing confidence that climate issues were poised to push the world toward a low-carbon future, and the perception that they were operating in an environment in which states had abdicated leadership on providing clear and enforceable "rules of the game." In a *Harvard Business Review* article, "Why Your Company Needs a Foreign Policy," John Chipman, Director-General of the International Institute for Strategic Studies, asserted that corporations no longer can assume, "in any region of the world, that the strategic status quo will be sustained by neat balances of power or unbreakable promises of foreign policy assistance from superpower states" (2016), echoing one strategist's observation that in the twenty-first-century landscape, there are "new challenges to the relationships and structures that provided stability in the past" (Yarger 2006, 25). In "this new reality," Chipman advised, "the most successful multinational companies will be those that make expertise in international affairs central to their operations, adopting what can best be described as a corporate foreign policy." A foreign policy in the traditional sense requires, among other things, "that a country define its interests ... and cultivate an environment conducive to its success"; today, Chipman argued, companies "have to, in effect, 'privatize' foreign policy" (2016).

This book demonstrated that select corporations essentially "privatized" their approach to the climate issue area amid their declining confidence in states' willingness and/or ability to provide the rules necessary to "cultivate an environment" conducive to their long-term success. In a striking illustration of how states could not settle on the climate "rules of the game," casting companies into costly uncertainty, in 2018, a UK-based representative for E.ON reflected on how in the mid-2000s, there was a view in his company that "there was some kind of future for coal-fired power stations." As a result, "there was a serious amount of money that was spent on upgrading [these assets] ... to meet newer EU emissions regulations. Not long after we made that investment, all the rules changed, and suddenly that investment didn't look like a very good use of money" (London, November 12, 2018).

In coalescing around a new set of practices, companies did not eliminate unpredictability surrounding the climate issue. But by coming to agree on some rules of the new game, or the kinds of behavior necessary for navigating a changing environment, they generated *more* predictability, as actors became increasingly confident about where others thought they were headed and how they planned to get there. In terms of the climate change issue, which may be the canary in the coal mine for other unconventional issues, the system became less vertical, with rules flowing from states to private actors, and more horizontal, as private actors themselves began devising some of the rules.[1]

The COVID-19 pandemic offers an illustrative example of another unconventional issue area perceived by some corporate and other non-state actors to be lacking effective state-led responses and calling for more horizontal rule-making. It also demonstrates how some observers still apply an obsolete lens to analyzing the relationship between state and non-state actors in terms of their respective roles in responding to transnational issues. Capturing such a conventional approach, in early 2020, a *TIME* article, responding to President Trump's decision to mobilize US companies to produce medical supplies in response to the pandemic, observed, "One aspect of the history is clear: when business has successfully stepped up for national-security purposes, the federal government and the military have played a key role in coordinating the effort" (Waxman 2020). Several months later, a CNN contributor saw a much different lesson from the pandemic, articulating the dynamic that this book explored. Arguing that an incoherent US national response was "not stopping Walmart—along with Kroger, Kohl's, and city and state leaders and officials—from making the tough decisions that the President has shirked," he noted "growing indications ... that such centers of authority across the country are no longer waiting for cues from an indifferent President" (Collinson 2020).

---

[1] The distinction between domestic and international law offers an apt analogy. While domestic legal systems are vertical, with governments making the rules and the subjects (constituents) following them, in international law the system is horizontal, with the subjects (states) making the laws that they themselves have to follow.

7 SUPERPOWERS, INC.: LESSONS ON WORLD ORDER   211

A fruitful avenue for future research is examining to what extent corporate or subnational actors that have become increasingly assertive on the global stage, or more independent as "rule-makers," in the context of challenges like climate change and pandemic disease become key players shaping other emerging issue areas. Recent work by Hedgecock (2021) highlights the especially critical domain of cyberspace, examining limits to the US government's ability to defend businesses against cyber-attacks and pointing to a crucial underlying question: whether, in light of new challenges, governments no longer are able to perform their historical function of providing security to citizens and other actors (including corporations) falling under their sovereign authority.

LESSON 2: CORPORATIONS CAN SHAPE NEW ARENAS FOR STATE BEHAVIOR, INCLUDING GREAT POWER COMPETITION

During the 2010s, the private sector perceived key states as having absented themselves from concerted and ambitious climate action. Today, some of these same states have begun to behave as if they must "catch up" to, and align themselves with, a new reality, one not of their own making. This book explored how the private sector helped to usher in that reality by shaping one of its central ideas, which is that due to climate change-related pressures the low-carbon future has been "pulled forward" in time. Indeed, although the notion that the world is headed toward such a future is treated today as a foregone conclusion, it was up for debate as recently as the turn of the 2010s; serious actors, including in the private sector, imagined alternative energy futures or expected that a low-carbon future, even if likely, was a distant concern.

Nowhere is the phenomenon of states striving to catch up to a new reality more apparent than in the United States. Beginning in the transition period following the 2020 presidential election, the Biden team indicated that climate change would be considered across virtually every facet of US interests and across all elements of national power. By the end of his first two months in office, President Biden had appointed the first National Climate Advisor (Ludden 2020), created a cabinet-level position of Climate Envoy (Friedman 2020), established a Climate Committee of the Federal Reserve, assembled a Climate Task Force of 21 federal agencies and departments "to enable a whole of government approach to combatting the climate crisis" (The White House 2021), directed the Secretary of Defense and Chairman of the Joint Chiefs of Staff to include climate risk assessment in the 2022 National Defense Strategy (Guy and Sikorsky 2021), and unveiled a three trillion dollar infrastructure package with "record spending on mitigating climate change and accelerating a nationwide transition to clean energy" (Newburger 2021).

If this book's first main lesson is that corporations recognized that the climate game was changing whereas states misperceived their environment, the second is that some late-to-the-game states arrived to find that new players had staked out the field of play. "Corporate nations" can shape new arenas and recast the context for state behavior, even for Great Power competition.

In forging a consensus about the climate issue area, the private sector helped set the global agenda during a decade when key states abandoned their traditional agenda-setting role. When President Trump did not attend the climate session of the 2019 G-7 summit, for some observers his empty chair at a multilateral meeting seemed an apt metaphor for US foreign policy under his administration (Sheth 2019). But the incident captured a deeper lesson, namely, when states, even the most powerful, opt out of their place at the table, the conversation continues without them, offering others an opportunity to lock in a new agenda.

Beyond shaping the global agenda, by pulling forward in time a low-carbon future the private sector helped to forge "rules of engagement" for the twenty-first century, or an understanding among global actors about how to play the geopolitical and economic game in the most effective fashion. For example, although today there is a widespread view that investing in a low-carbon future is a winning strategy to promote economic growth, until recently the conventional wisdom was the opposite; as Chapter 1 considered, as recently as the early 2010s, even among enterprising US business leaders, "building economic growth while tackling climate change at its source" was a strategy that was "unheard of," as the president of the World Resources Institute put it (Steer 2014). But during the 2010s, the private sector played a pivotal role in rewriting the script. By 2016, even Saudi Arabia, whose petroleum exports accounted for 25% of its GDP and 77% of its total export earnings (Organization of the Petroleum Exporting Countries 2016, 8), had embraced the idea that low-carbon investment was a key to future economic success; at the center of its *Vision 2030* plan was the target of producing 60 gigawatts of clean energy by 2030 (Collins 2021). In 2018, it partnered with a

Japanese company, SoftBank, to launch "the world's biggest solar power generation project" (DiChristopher 2018); in 2021, announcing that by 2030 Saudi Arabia would generate 50% of its energy from renewable sources, Crown Prince Mohammed bin Salman stated, "We reject the false choice between preserving the economy and protecting the environment. Climate action will enhance competitiveness, spark innovation, and create millions of high-quality jobs" (Lo 2021).

In getting out front in defining what it will take to be successful in the twenty-first century, corporations not only shaped future possibilities, constraining states' menu of choices, but also helped cast a new arena for Great Power competition. Indeed, the full significance of the Biden administration's push to embed climate change in national security and foreign policy reflects the reality that the issue area has become a Great Power battleground, and the recognition that the United States must compete therein. Particularly striking is that this new battleground developed during a decade in which major states, including, most importantly, the United States, were perceived to have "left the room" on the climate change issue; others, including the private sector, played pivotal roles in defining and influencing the arena in their absence.

In new Great Power battlegrounds like climate change, competition is not only or even primarily about engaging other Great Powers. The states that are most successful at competing in these arenas will be those that treat unconventional actors, including corporate and subnational heavyweights, as the influential and ambitious global players that they are, and that do not just add new issues to a list of existing priorities or embed new practices within existing processes, but rather invest in innovative partnerships with these players.

In the 2014 US-China Joint Announcement, in which both states unveiled their Intended Nationally Determined Contributions (INDCs) to the Paris Conference, Presidents Obama and Xi, recognizing "the potential for local leaders to undertake significant climate action" (The White House 2014), committed to "cooperate at the subnational level and, specifically, to hold a cities summit the following year" (Gallagher and Xuan 2019, 6), apparently recognizing the growing significance of non-state actors in the climate arena. Yet, whereas China has proven adept in practice at forging relationships with these actors and leveraging those relationships in its competition with the United States, the United States consistently has failed to appreciate their growing climate role.

214   C. HULME

For example, in 2017, President Xi invited Governor of California Jerry Brown to Beijing to discuss climate cooperation, breaking established protocol by meeting with "a sitting governor and not a national head of state" (Gardels 2018). China also has maneuvered at the city level of the climate "battlespace." As a climate adviser in the office of the mayor of New York City observed in 2021, in the context of the climate issue, "all the action has been happening in cities for four years. So really ... diplomats ... need to know that China sends people from the city level to New York and to [various] cities all the time." This adviser became "a sort of local climate diplomat, meeting with environment ministers from half a dozen countries—without guidance from the State Department." As she described it, "We just figured it out on our own" (Kelemen 2021).

Meanwhile, the Trump administration's climate disengagement policy resulted in 300 US cities, 10 states, and 4000 businesses joining We Are Still In, a group seeking to fill the void left by the US withdrawal from the Paris Agreement. In fact, in the context of the 2019 Madrid Climate Conference, We Are Still In announced that "the American public's voice on climate" would best be represented not by State Department negotiators but rather by "US subnational and non-state actors," who would "meet with foreign governments and international counterparts" to advance US interests (We Are Still In n.d.). There appears to be a slow-dawning realization in the United States concerning the importance of such actors; in 2022, the first Special Representative for Subnational Diplomacy was named, taking the helm of a new State Department office created to "leverage the international engagement of cities and states to benefit U.S. foreign policy" (Pipa and Bouchet 2021).

Considering climate change as a Great Power battleground highlights change not only in the actors but also in the modes and means of competition. As Nye has observed, in a century in which many of the most pressing challenges are not amenable to military solutions, "victory may sometimes depend not on whose army wins, but on whose story wins" (2014, 20). In the climate issue area, whose story wins has proven to be a key dynamic of competition, one whose relevance the United States has underestimated, but for which China has shown a clear appreciation. By deciding to withdraw from the Paris Agreement, for example, the Trump administration underestimated the extent to which doing so would cede the story ground to China. Leaving China "alone in the room" for four years supported a powerful narrative that while the United States is a climate laggard, China is a leader in addressing climate change and standing up a low-carbon future (United Nations 2018). This narrative has proven remarkably resilient to contradictory facts on the ground; for example, while coal represents 17% of the US energy mix, it constitutes 60% in China, which uses over half of the world's coal and has bankrolled coal-fired power plants worldwide (Gallo and Jiang 2021; Quartz n.d.). US disengagement from international climate action under the Trump administration also empowered China to act as the main gatekeeper in the issue area; indeed, during a 2021 White House climate summit, a spokeswoman for Beijing remarked that the US return to the Paris Agreement "is not the return of the King, rather it's a truant getting back to class" (Ni 2021). Narrative becoming an important tool in US-China climate competition highlights how unconventional battlespaces can change how Great Powers understand the most potent ways to compete.

Inherently complex and uncertain, climate change has a high potential to produce second-order effects in other spheres of Great Power competition. For example, even skeptics about the relevance of climate change per se for US national security should be concerned about its potential second-order effects for US interests in a country like India, which is both strategically vital in the Indo-Pacific region and highly vulnerable to climate change (Kugelman 2020). Climate-driven instability, whether stemming from "climate refugees" from neighboring countries like Bangladesh, or from human and economic losses tied to extreme weather events in the coastal megacity of Mumbai (which represents $960 billion of wealth, equivalent to 33% of India's GDP), may spur historically inward-looking India to maintain its domestic focus, undercutting its capacity and appetite for regional balancing against China (Sharalaya 2018).

Future research should analyze distinct elements of Great Power competition impacted by this new arena, one shaped so significantly by non-state actors. Indeed, new actors and the issue areas they help stand up are not just creating additive change in the competitive environment (i.e., simply adding additional arenas for competition to those that already exist). Rather, they are potentially changing the nature of competition itself by altering how states compete in other arenas, affecting the perceived relevance of allies and adversaries, influencing which resources are mobilized and how, and recasting the geostrategic significance of particular regions and states (Colgan 2021).

Lesson 3: Corporations Have the Potential to Become Grand Strategic Actors

The corporate climate action phenomenon points to an underappreciated category of player in the international system: corporate grand strategic actors. As a new era of Great Power competition dawns, there has been a resurgence of interest in grand strategy, an intellectual project pioneered in the interwar period to understand how states, and specifically Great Powers, align the elements of national power across policy contexts to advance their highest aims, especially in the international security arena. Yet, while the landscape in which Great Powers must compete has evolved significantly since the mid-twentieth century, the field of grand strategy largely has failed to adapt; its overarching concern remains state behavior in response to conventional risks (i.e., those that are military in nature and often centered around Great Power dynamics), and its conceptual north star a bygone era in which it was natural to define grand strategy in terms of elements of *national* power that *national* leaders marshaled to secure *national* interests. Indeed, more striking than the oft-noted lack of consensus about how best to define grand strategy is that for a century, regardless of their definitional approach, scholars consistently have considered grand strategy as the special province of states and national policymakers. To the extent that they have treated the private sector in the domain of grand strategy, typically states and their grand strategies remain the primary concern (van Apeldoorn and de Graaff 2016; Narizny 2007).

The rising global influence of the private sector, coupled with the mounting importance of unconventional challenges that states cannot address alone through their national security apparatuses or other traditional instruments and mechanisms of grand strategy, is driving the need to reconceptualize the field. There is a need to widen the aperture on the actors that count as "Great Powers" in the global landscape, given that select non-state actors, whether corporate behemoths or subnational heavyweights, have more resources and exert greater global influence than most states, including some of the most powerful. This book implicitly examined certain longstanding assumptions about which actors act at the grand strategic level, or which belong in the realm of grand strategic thought and action. While some scholars argue that even the world's smallest states can "do" grand strategy (Briffa 2020), and while some assert that all states "inevitably engage in grand strategy" (Brands 2012, 6), the classic understanding of the grand strategic level is that it is the field of play specifically of Great Powers—those rare states with the resources, reach, and scope of interests making it plausible to aim to "impose a preferred state of order on the future," or strive to order the global environment according to a desired organizing principle (Layton 2012, 59). Such an understanding underpins Martel's observation that only states "with a global reach can truly have grand strategies" (2015, 34), and Murray's claim that grand strategy is the purview of "great states and great states alone" (2010, 1).

This book demonstrated that states' perceived abdication of leadership on climate change (notably, an issue long neglected by the field of grand strategy) helped to pull a new set of actors into the grand strategic level of action, or into the field of play classically conceived as the domain of Great Power states. It showed that early in the 2010s, 48% of a sample of Fortune Global 500 companies were confident in the outlook for bold state-led climate action but that by the mid- to late 2010s, only 16% expressed such confidence. In this same context, 82% of companies improved their climate performance, with 50% making significant decisions to align their activities more closely with a low-carbon future. Those decisions helped to mold and reinforce a global consensus about climate change as an issue of importance to any serious actor, altering the context for state behavior, even for Great Power competition. In recognizing that the climate game was changing, select corporations, behaving as grand strategic actors, began to stake out the field of play according to certain organizing principles; in arriving at rules of a low-carbon future they framed a "preferred state of order" for that future.

Importantly, only certain corporations explicitly recognized their potential to behave as grand strategic actors or framed their behavior in these terms. As the empirical chapters explored, only select companies perceived the significance of their climate behavior not simply in terms of their particular businesses or industries but specifically in the context of their potential to shape the global landscape, whether by influencing the energy system in China (Apple 2016, 5–6), altering the calculus of developing countries choosing which kind of development pathway to follow (Infosys 2013, 10), or spurring global capital to move away from the high-carbon status quo and toward a low-carbon future (Allianz 2015, 21). A key lesson of this book is that all "corporate nations" should recognize that they belong in the Great Powers' field of play and have

218   C. HULME

the potential to become grand strategic actors shaping outcomes in the global arena, including, crucially, in the international security landscape.

The corporate climate action phenomenon not only highlights the limitations in prevailing thinking about which actors have the potential to behave as grand strategic actors, but also underscores the need to consider the potential for grand strategy without a grand strategist. The evolution of the modern concept of grand strategy reflects its essential meaning as the integration and synchronization of multiple strategies to advance the overarching objective of a state at a certain time. This characterization assumes grand strategy as being deliberate and coordinated by some coordinator. It is precisely due to the assumption about the centralized provenance and calculated nature of grand strategy that some scholars have called into question its utility in explaining real-world outcomes. Betts, for example, observing that the "grand" descriptor "conjures up unrealistic images of sweeping and far-seeing purpose, ingenuity, direction, and adroitness," contends that grand strategy more often is a "description imposed by observers on the record of statesmen ... or a claim made in hindsight rather than a conscious and coherent plan of an administration in advance of action that is actually implemented" (2019, 7).

Even if Betts overstates the barriers to "doing" grand strategy given real-world constraints, he is correct in pointing to the fact that even the most powerful states face appreciable challenges in executing grand strategy, conventionally understood. Thus, drawing on work by management scholars Mintzberg and Waters, who pioneered the idea of "emergent strategy" to capture how "patterns or consistencies" can be "realized despite, or in the absence of, intentions" (1985, 257), Popescu presented emergent strategy as a policymaker's alternative to grand strategy (2017). Likewise, one scholar of UK strategy, observing approvingly the "contours of an emergent theory of action" taking hold in the British strategic policy community, advised "wariness of grand strategic narratives or hegemonic notions of the national interest" amid "contemporary dynamics of global complexity" (Edmunds 2014, 539).

The "grand" and "emergent" strategy paradigms initially appear diametrically opposed; most significantly, whereas grand strategy places a premium on identifying and pursuing ultimate ends and overarching objectives, in emergent strategy reacting and adapting to changes in one's environment—and even, if necessary, altering one's overarching goal mid-course—have pride of place. Treating the paradigms as antithetical, however, sidesteps a key question: whether, through an emergent process, uncoordinated global actors can achieve a grand strategic outcome. This book in essence asked, and offered one answer to, that question. The development of a new corporate climate sensibility was both a grand strategic effect—one that reshuffled the decks for Great Powers—and represented an emergent process. The corporate climate action phenomenon underscores that some scholars' perception of an incompatibility between what grand strategy purports to do—namely, arrange various lines of effort across discrete contexts into a coherent whole to advance an overarching objective—and what realistically is possible given the complexity of the international environment today stems from a failure to fully appreciate that grand strategy itself is a system, or what Layton describes as a "set of interdependent elements where change in some elements... produces change across the system, and the entire system exhibits properties and behaviors different from the constituent parts" (2012, 13). Classic thinking tends not to view grand strategy this way, leading us to believe that there should be a relatively linear relationship between inputs and outputs; as Betts articulates, a "conscious and coherent plan" is supposed to articulate a "sweeping and far-seeing" path toward the attainment of a certain overarching objective (2019, 7).

The grand strategic level can be thought of as the plane or field of play where global actors "encounter" each other in interactions that shape how they perceive their interests and order their interest sets. In tracing how uncoordinated corporations, dispersed across diverse industries and headquarter countries, came to reprioritize the climate issue in their interest sets in such a way as to achieve collective behavior (as conceptualized by the threshold model, described in Chapter 1), this book captured how, in the absence of a centralized coordinator or actor behaving as the grand strategist, interactions at the grand strategic level can serve as the missing coordinator, setting in motion a process ultimately producing a grand strategic effect in the international system.

In short, the corporate climate action phenomenon sheds light on how grand strategic outcomes can be achieved even as the field of play for Great Powers becomes populated by new players that do not fit the old mold of grand strategic actor. Irreducibly a system, the grand strategic level always has been fertile ground for emergence, even if academics and practitioners often have overlooked this reality or underestimated its importance. The corporate climate action phenomenon suggests that if grand strategy is to remain relevant for thinking about the pathways that

220   C. HULME

produce consequential outcomes in the international arena, the private sector stands to be foremost among the unexpected players forcing a new look at old assumptions.

Lesson 4: Corporations Have the Potential to Outperform States in Tackling Twenty-First Century Problem Sets

While select corporations were out front in terms of recognizing what it would take to respond successfully to certain changes in the twenty-first century environment, playing a vital role in shaping the climate and low-carbon arena during a decade in which key states were perceived as absent from this agenda-setting process, whether they will remain leaders is an open question. While latecomers missed out on shaping rules of the playing field, they still can catch up and "play the game" successfully, marshaling the particular resources and ideas needed to meet new challenges.

On the one hand, relative to states corporations are in an advantageous position to shape new arenas like climate change that are marked by complex new challenges, which call for nimble, creative, and coherent responses, typically difficult for states to muster. While states historically have proven relatively capable when it comes to mounting responses to traditional challenges (primarily military in nature), which may manifest differently but require essentially similar responses, they often struggle to mount effective responses to fundamentally different challenges using the most appropriate tools. In federal systems, particularly, by design it is hard for the state to act boldly; as Krasner observed, pointing to India and the United States as especially clear examples, in states where central institutions are weak the "system makes obstruction easy, positive action difficult," and transformational change rare (1978, 302). In short, national governments generally are ill-suited to respond to the non-traditional problem sets of the twenty-first century, challenges that call for new thinking, tools, and approaches. Indeed, even bracketing the question of their response capacity, states may fail to perceive accurately the nature of new problem sets to which they are ill-equipped to respond, consistent with Maslow's famous observation that "it is tempting, if the only tool you have is a hammer, to treat everything as if it were a nail" (cited in Shorrock 2013).

7 SUPERPOWERS, INC.: LESSONS ON WORLD ORDER   221

The private sector enjoys a greater freedom of action to respond to new challenges given that it does not have to contend with the complex web of political constraints tending to bind decisionmakers to "business as usual." As a European Parliament staffer interviewed for this book observed, companies can change course in their climate behavior with relative ease compared to states facing voters whose livelihoods are affected by a potential low-carbon transition:

> Whenever you hear a minister in Germany [this interviewee's home country] talk about [climate action], they talk about it as an [economic] opportunity . . . but then at the same time, we open a new coal power plant. Then it's a bit contradictory sometimes. There are some success stories, but the overall magnitude of these success stories is still limited compared to hundreds of thousands of jobs linked to coal. It's easier for a company to switch and say that we are going to profit from this [low-carbon behavior]; for a country it might not really work. (Telephone conversation with author, October 12, 2018)

Multinational corporations are accountable to a smaller array of "constituents" than national governments, which helps to explain why, like subnational actors, they are in a relatively advantageous position to undertake climate action. As one journalist noted optimistically amid the flurry of local-level climate discussions occurring on the margins of the foundering 2009 Copenhagen Climate Conference, "local governments are run more like companies. Their mayors act more like CEO's [sic] than other elected officials, and they are in closer contact with their constituencies, making them directly accountable for the health and prosperity of the towns over which they preside" (Burkart 2010).

On the other hand, however, despite certain advantages as climate actors, reflected in their role in spurring a "game change" during the 2010s, it remains an open question whether the kind of corporate heavyweights that this book examined will be better than states at playing the long game, avoiding becoming bureaucratized and slow to respond to changes in their environment. Although the private sector is in a better starting position than most states to respond to complex global challenges in a nimble fashion, even those agile companies behaving as "disruptors" today are vulnerable to stagnating, succumbing to inertia, clinging to "business as usual" (BAU), and even disappearing, tomorrow. Indeed, when the Dow Jones Industrial Average (DJIA) was created in 1896, it comprised 12 titans of US industry, representing "the biggest and most influential corporations of the day," each a "giant in its sector." But only one, General Electric, stayed in business (remaining continuously on the DJIA until being removed in 2019); the others were "broken up, taken over, dissolved, or relegated to subsidiary status over the years" (Investopedia 2021).

Just as today's innovators and disruptors can become tomorrow's BAUs, the opposite is true; as this book has demonstrated, in a short period even a seemingly committed BAU can start to accept that the game is changing and begin to alter its behavior. The lesson is that even status quo-oriented actors—whether companies or countries—should not yet be counted out of the climate and low-carbon game. One such case of a longstanding BAU that appears potentially poised to alter its approach and that could reshape the playing field is Australia, which, as the world's highest per-capita emitter and a leading fossil fuel exporter, consistently "opted out" of the new climate game under the leadership of Prime Minister Scott Morrison, in office 2018–2022. For example, as of 2021, while every Australian state and territory had "committed to the 2050 net-zero [emissions] target," as had "an increasing number of large corporations" (including AGL, Australia's largest emitter), Morrison refused to support such a commitment at the national level, even as Treasurer Josh Frydenberg warned that "Australia faced stiff financial consequences if the country was perceived as 'not transitioning in line with the rest of the world'" (Miller 2021). Yet, the tide appears to be turning. In 2022, under Morrison's successor, Anthony Albanese, Australia committed to its first legally binding emissions reduction target (a 43% reduction from 2005 levels by 2030) as part of a broader legislative package. As the Associated Press reported, entrenching the target in law "has made it more difficult for any future government to reduce the target." It also sent important signals to clean energy investors; as Climate Change and Energy Minister Chris Bowen described it, "The message to investors is that Australia is open for business" (AP News 2022).

It remains to be seen whether, when, and to what extent other key BAU states respond to developments in the climate and low-carbon game; indeed, as this book showed, even amid profound changes in their environment, some corporations, from Chevron in the United States to Reliance Industries in India, remained firm BAUs even by the late 2010s. Russia exemplifies a state apparently not budging from its status quo stance; while climate change is set to impact its strategic future, it is not yet a serious player in the climate arena, missing even easy shots (Conley 2021). For example, in Climate Action Tracker's December 2021 analysis of states submitting new Nationally Determined Contributions (NDCs) to the Paris Agreement, Russia was one of 12 to have submitted a new NDC without even a modestly stronger target (Climate Action Tracker 2023). Russia also is failing to address its greatest climate-related vulnerability: in a world increasingly looking to clean energy sources, oil, gas, and coal account for 65% of its export earnings, according to the latest data from the Observatory of Economic Complexity (n.d.). It remains to be seen whether Russia, despite its potential, ultimately "lacks the political will to grow into a renewable energy superpower of the future," as some experts contend (Safonov 2021). But today it is failing to appreciate how new actors are carving out positions in the climate arena in ways that might constrain its future choices. For example, while industry remains a culprit of Russia's thin domestic climate policy, some leading corporations, including in the oil and gas sector, are "moving ahead of the government to cut emissions and address sustainability issues," according to an expert with the Center for Strategic and International Studies (Conley 2021). To what extent they will push ahead without Moscow's support remains to be seen—but leading industrial players worldwide, from Europe to India to the United States—have shown what is possible.

The lesson for future world order is that although the corporate climate action phenomenon points to the potential for transformative change in the dynamics of the international system, the die is not yet cast. It remains to be seen whether corporations and other centers of global power and influence ultimately spur what Khanna has described as a shift "from a state-based order to a multi-actor system" (2016, 30). A core premise of this book is that it has become increasingly plausible to talk about a "changing of the guard" in terms of the actors with the potential to behave as Great Powers in the global landscape; while states remain of critical importance, they no longer are predominant in setting the global scene, or shaping conditions for decision-making and outcomes, in all of the most important domains. Exploring the case study of corporate climate action, this book has demonstrated that these new actors *can* behave as Great Powers; it does not follow, however, that they *will* in the future, whether in terms of the climate change issue area or other domains. In a world in which 70 of the 100 wealthiest entities are corporations, it would seem as though the international system is on a trajectory toward deep change (Inman 2016); it is easy to assume that different

224   C. HULME

pivotal players will produce different outcomes in the long-term. But this remains an open question. The developments that this book explored offer an inkling of what is possible; future research should take up the task of exploring whether what today is a glimmer of epochal change in the international system gains momentum.

Conclusion

At the dawn of the 2010s, with the world reeling from the most profound economic upheaval since the Great Depression, with climate change issues becoming much less of a priority even for historically climate-active governments, and with a potential low-carbon transition appearing a distant possibility at best, it was hard to imagine that within a decade, Volkswagen would "stak[e] its future on a new line of electric cars" (Ewing 2021); New York State ban the sale of gas vehicles by 2035 (Kolodny 2021); leading corporate climate laggards be "rocked" by "unprecedented investor revolt over climate change" (Toscano 2021); Saudi Arabia envision becoming "another Germany when it comes to renewables" (Collins 2021); and the United Kingdom, the cradle of the Industrial Revolution, force closure of the last coal-fired power plant by 2025 (Vaughan 2016).

Tracing the emergent process by which some of the actors most invested in the status quo became more deeply committed to behaviors with the potential to disrupt it, this book explored how in a short period of time, despite the immense hurdles to overcoming the inertia of the status quo and breaking free of locked-in practices oriented toward a fossil fuel-based economy (Unruh 2000), what seemed an "immutable trajectory" began to bend toward "a new landscape" (Struck 2020). "Corporate nations" proved themselves to be foremost among the new players with the ability and ambition not just to act in new landscapes but to define them, and not just to be supporting actors in states' drama but to be lead authors in writing the story of this century's defining issue areas. The burden is on states, which no longer can take for granted their place as the star turn of the global stage, to adjust to this new reality.

REFERENCES

Allianz. 2015. Sustainability report 2014. March 13, 2015. https://www.allianz. com/content/dam/onemarketing/azcom/Allianz_com/migration/media/ responsibility/allianz_sustainability_report_2014.pdf.

Amelang, Sören. 2018. Disruption caused by energy transition is unstoppable— Amory Lovins. *Clean Energy Wire*, October 17, 2018. https://www.cle anenergywire.org/news/disruption-caused-energy-transition-unstoppable-amory-lovins.

van Apeldoorn, Bastiaan, and Nana de Graaff. 2016. *American grand strategy and corporate elite networks: The open door since the end of the Cold War*. New York: Routledge.

AP News. 2022. Australia enshrines in law 43% greenhouse gas reduction aim. September 8, 2022. https://apnews.com/article/australia-congress-climate-and-environment-government-politics-b998f2eaa0e3e9c5d8988f0b21ae7115.

Apple. 2016. Environmental responsibility report: 2016 progress report, covering Fiscal Year 2015. April 11, 2016. https://www.apple.com/environment/ pdf/Apple_Environmental_Responsibility_Report_2016.pdf.

Betts, Richard. 2019. The grandiosity of grand strategy. *The Washington Quarterly* 42 (4): 7–22. https://doi.org/10.1080/0163660X.2019.1663061.

Brands, Hal. 2012. The promises and pitfalls of grand strategy. Carlisle, PA: US Army War College Strategic Studies Institute.

Briffa, Hillary. 2020. Small states and the challenges of the international order. In After disruption: Historical perspectives on the future of international order, eds. Seth Center and Emma Bates, 50–59. Washington, D.C.: Center for Strategic and International Studies.

Burkart, Karl. 2010. Richard Branson's war on carbon. *Forbes*, February 23, 2010. https://www.forbes.com/2010/02/22/carbon-climate-copenhagen-technology-ecotech-branson.html?sh=683ad84e1d36.

CDP. 2017. More than eight-fold leap over four years in global companies pricing carbon into business plans. October 12, 2017. https://www.cdp. net/en/articles/media/more-than-eight-fold-leap-over-four-years-in-global-companies-pricing-carbon-into-business-plans.

Chipman, John. 2016. Why your company needs a foreign policy. *Harvard Business Review*, September 1, 2016. https://hbr.org/2016/09/why-your-com pany-needs-a-foreign-policy.

Climate Action Tracker. 2023. CAT climate target update tracker. Updated February 6, 2023. https://climateactiontracker.org/climate-target-update-tra cker-2022/.

Colgan, Jeff. 2021. Climate change, grand strategy, and international order. Wilson Center. July 23, 2021. https://www.wilsoncenter.org/article/climate-change-grand-strategy-and-international-order.

Collins, Leigh. 2021. "We will be pioneering": Saudi Arabia reveals 50% renewables goal by 2030, but is that realistic? *Recharge News*, January 29, 2021. https://www.rechargenews.com/energy-transition/we-will-be-pionee ring-saudi-arabia-reveals-50-renewables-goal-by-2030-but-is-that-realistic-/2-1-954094.

Collinson, Stephen. 2020. As Trump refuses to lead, America tries to save itself. CNN. July 16, 2020. https://www.cnn.com/2020/07/16/politics/donald-trump-coronavirus-leadership/index.html.

Conley, Heather. 2021. Climate change will reshape Russia. Center for Strategic and International Studies. January 13, 2021. https://www.csis.org/analysis/climate-change-will-reshape-russia.

DiChristopher, Tom. 2018. SoftBank and Saudi Arabia are creating world's biggest solar power generation plant. CNBC. March 31, 2018. https://www.cnbc.com/2018/03/27/softbank-and-saudi-arabia-ann ounce-new-solar-power-generation-project.html.

Edmunds, Timothy. 2014. Complexity, strategy, and the national interest. *Royal Institute of International Affairs* 90 (3): 525–539. https://doi.org/10.1111/1468-2346.12125.

Ewing, Jack. 2021. Demand from China drives a rebound in Volkswagen sales. *The New York Times*, May 6, 2021. https://www.nytimes.com/2021/05/06/business/demand-from-china-drives-a-rebound-in-volkswagen-sales.html.

Francis, David. 2016. The top 25 corporate nations. *Foreign Policy*, March 15, 2016. https://foreignpolicy.com/2016/03/15/these-25-companies-are-more-powerful-than-many-countries-multinational-corporate-wealth-power/.

Friedman, Lisa. 2020. With John Kerry pick, Biden selects a "climate envoy" with stature. *The New York Times*, November 23, 2020. https://www.nyt imes.com/2020/11/23/climate/john-kerry-climate-change.html.

Gallagher, Kelly Sims, and Xiaowei Xuan. 2019. *Titans of the climate: Explaining policy process in the United States and China*. Cambridge, MA: MIT Press.

Gallo, William, and Jesse Jiang. 2021. China vows to stop building coal plants overseas, but what does that mean? *Voice of America News*, September 27, 2021. https://www.voanews.com/a/china-vows-to-stop-building-coal-plants-overseas-but-what-does-that-mean/6246911.html.

Gardels, Nathan. 2018. Jerry Brown's next role as elder statesman on climate. *The Washington Post*, September 10, 2018. https://www.washingtonpost.com/news/theworldpost/wp/2018/09/10/climate-change/.

Guy, Kate, and Erin Sikorsky. 2021. A blueprint for the Department of Defense's strategic assessment of climate change. *War on the Rocks*, March 12, 2021. https://warontherocks.com/2021/03/a-blueprint-for-the-depart ment-of-defenses-strategic-assessment-of-climate-change/.

Hedgecock, Kathryn. 2021. Deciphering the implications of state sponsored cyber operations for IR theory. Doctoral dissertation, Stanford University. https://searchworks.stanford.edu/view/13884257.

Infosys. 2013. Sustainability report 2012–2013. https://www.infosys.com/sustainability/documents/infosys-sustainability-report-2012-13.pdf.

Inman, Phillip. 2016. Study: Big corporations dominate list of world's top economic entities. *The Guardian*, September 12, 2016. https://www.theguardian.com/business/2016/sep/12/global-justice-now-study-multinational-businesses-walmart-apple-shell.

Investopedia. 2021. What were the original Dow Jones Industrial Average (DJIA) companies? March 19, 2021. https://www.investopedia.com/ask/answers/100214/who-were-original-dow-jones-industrial-average-djia-companies.asp.

Jervis, Robert. 1968. Hypotheses on misperception. *World Politics* 20 (3): 454–479. https://doi.org/10.2307/2009777.

Kelemen, Michele. 2021. State Department should be more diverse and engaged across U.S., report says. NPR. March 3, 2021. https://www.npr.org/2021/03/03/972493656/state-department-should-be-more-diverse-and-engaged-across-u-s-report-says.

Khanna, Parag. 2016. *Connectography*. New York: Random House.

Kolodny, Lora. 2021. New York law phases out most gas-powered vehicles by 2035. CNBC. September 9, 2021. https://www.cnbc.com/2021/09/09/new-york-law-phases-out-most-gas-powered-vehicles-by-2035.html.

Krasner, Stephen. 1978. *Defending the national interest: Raw materials investments and U.S. foreign policy*. Princeton, NJ: Princeton University Press.

Kugelman, Michael. 2020. Climate-induced displacement: South Asia's clear and present danger. Wilson Center. September 30, 2020. https://www.wilsoncenter.org/article/climate-induced-displacement-south-asias-clear-and-present-danger.

Layton, Peter. 2012. The idea of grand strategy. *The RUSI Journal* 157 (4): 56–61. https://doi.org/10.1080/03071847.2012.714193.

Lo, Jo. 2021. Saudi Arabia aims for 50% renewable energy by 2030, backs huge tree planting initiative. *Climate Change News*, March 31, 2021. https://www.climatechangenews.com/2021/03/31/saudi-arabia-aims-50-renewable-energy-2030-backs-huge-tree-planting-initiative/.

Ludden, Jennifer. 2020. Biden announces climate team, including 1st-ever national climate adviser. NPR. December 20, 2020. https://www.npr.org/2020/12/20/948315477/climate-czar.

Martel, William. 2015. *Grand strategy in theory and practice: The need for an effective American foreign policy*. New York: Cambridge University Press.

Miller, Michael. 2021. Australia, a climate laggard, leans toward 2050 net-zero target as election looms. *The Washington Post*, September 24, 2021. https://www.washingtonpost.com/world/asia_pacific/australia-climate-net-zero-morrison/2021/09/24/47d2f918-1c1f-11ec-bea8-308ea134594f_story.html.

Mintzberg, Henry, and James Waters. 1985. Of strategies, deliberate and emergent. *Strategic Management Journal* 6 (3): 257–272. https://doi.org/10.1002/smj.4250060306.

Murray, Williamson. 2010. Thoughts on grand strategy and the United States in the twenty-first century. *Journal of Military and Strategic Studies* 13 (1): 75–88. https://jmss.org/article/view/57938/43602.

Narizny, Kevin. 2007. *The political economy of grand strategy*. Ithaca, NY: Cornell University Press.

Newburger, Emma. 2021. Here's how Biden's infrastructure package will likely tackle climate change. CNBC. March 29, 2021. https://www.cnbc.com/2021/03/29/biden-infrastructure-bill-what-to-expect-on-climate-change.html.

Ni, Vincent. 2021. Compete, confront, cooperate: Climate summit test for Biden's China watchwords. *The Guardian*, April 22, 2021. https://www.theguardian.com/world/2021/apr/22/compete-confront-cooperate-climate-summit-test-for-bidens-china-watchwords.

Nye, Joseph. 2014. The information revolution and power. *Current History* 113 (759): 19–22. https://doi.org/10.1525/curh.2014.113.759.19.

Observatory of Economic Complexity. n.d. Russia. https://oec.world/en/profile/country/rus#:~:text=Exports%20The%20top%20exports%20of,and%20Italy%20(%2416.7B).

Organization of the Petroleum Exporting Countries. 2016. OPEC annual statistical bulletin. https://www.opec.org/opec_web/static_files_project/media/downloads/publications/ASB2016.pdf.

Pipa, Anthony, and Max Bouchet. 2021. Partnership among cities, states, and the federal government: Creating an office of subnational diplomacy at the US Department of State. Brookings. February 17, 2021. https://www.brookings.edu/research/partnership-among-cities-states-and-the-federal-government-creating-an-office-of-subnational-diplomacy-at-the-us-department-of-state/.

Popescu, Ionut. 2017. *Emergent strategy and grand strategy: How American presidents succeed in foreign policy*. Baltimore, MD: Johns Hopkins University Press.

Quartz. n.d. The Belt and Road's decarbonization dilemma. https://qz.com/1760615/china-quits-coal-at-home-but-promotes-the-fossil-fuel-in-developing-countries.

Safonov, Georgy. 2021. Back to the future? Russia's climate policy evolution. Center for Strategic and International Studies. March 1, 2021. https://www.csis.org/analysis/back-future-russias-climate-policy-evolution.

Sharalaya, Nandan. 2018. Taking India's climate migrants seriously. *The Diplomat*, August 10, 2021. https://thediplomat.com/2018/08/taking-ind ias-climate-migrants-seriously/.

Sheth, Sonam. 2019. Trump never made it to the G7 climate meeting, and world leaders say they are giving up on bringing the US back into the Paris accords. *Business Insider*, August 26, 2019. https://www.businessinsider.com/trump-skipped-g7-climate-change-meeting-empty-chair-2019-8.

Shorrock, Steven. 2013. Maslow's hammer: How tools bias attention and straightjacket thinking. *Humanistic Systems*, December 18, 2013. https://humanisticsystems.com/2013/12/18/maslows-hammer-how-tools-straightj acket-thinking/.

Steer, Andrew. 2014. Seeing U.S. business opportunity in a low-carbon economy. World Resources Institute. October 14, 2014. https://www.wri.org/ins ights/seeing-us-business-opportunity-low-carbon-economy.

Struck, Doug. 2020. Power pivot: What happens in states where wind dethrones king coal? *Christian Science Monitor*, August 21, 2020. https://www.csmonitor.com/Environment/2020/0821/Power-pivot-What-happens-in-states-where-wind-dethrones-King-Coal.

Toscano, Nick. 2021. Investor revolt rocks AGL as climate demands intensify. *Sydney Morning Herald*, September 22, 2021. https://www.smh.com.au/business/companies/investor-revolt-rocks-agl-as-climate-demands-intensify-20210922-p58tos.html.

United Nations. 2018. Secretary-General, at chairmanship handover ceremony, hails Group of 77 as central pillar in defending multilateralism, achieving 2030 agenda. January 12, 2018. https://press.un.org/en/2018/sgsm18853.doc. htm.

Unruh, Gregory. 2000. Understanding carbon lock-in. *Energy Policy* 28 (2): 817–830. https://doi.org/10.1016/S0301-4215(00)00070-7.

Vaughan, Adam. 2016. Britain's last coal power plants to close by 2025. *The Guardian*, November 9, 2016. https://www.theguardian.com/enviro nment/2016/nov/09/britains-last-coal-power-plants-to-close-by-2025.

Waxman, Olivia. 2020. The U.S. government has mobilized private companies to face crises before. Here's what to know. *TIME*, March 24, 2020. https://time.com/5808389/coronavirus-mobilization-war-industry-history/.

We Are Still In. n.d. US climate action center at COP25 in Madrid, Spain. https://www.wearestillin.com/us-climate-action-center-cop25-madrid-spain.

The White House. 2014. U.S.-China joint announcement on climate change. Office of the Press Secretary. November 12, 2014. https://obamawhiteho use.archives.gov/the-press-office/2014/11/11/us-china-joint-announcem ent-climate-change.

The White House. 2021. Fact sheet: President Biden takes executive actions to tackle the climate crisis at home and abroad, create jobs, and restore scientific integrity across federal government. January 27, 2021. https://www.whiteh ouse.gov/briefing-room/statements-releases/2021/01/27/fact-sheet-presid ent-biden-takes-executive-actions-to-tackle-the-climate-crisis-at-home-and-abr oad-create-jobs-and-restore-scientific-integrity-across-federal-government/.

Yarger, Henry. 2006. *Strategic theory for the 21st century: The little book on big strategy*. Carlisle, PA: US Army Strategic Studies Institute.

Appendix

Part I of this appendix addresses the methodology for coding corporate climate practices and creating the company typology. Part II addresses the methodology used to code and analyze CDP disclosures concerning corporate perceptions of climate-related risks and opportunities.

Part I: Climate Practices and Company Typology

Data sources

The main sources of data were corporate disclosures, including annual reports, sustainability reports, and CDP reports.

Summary of Scoring and Classification Methodology

For each year from 2010 to 2017, each company received a score out of 20 points based on its performance across three metrics: *product*, capturing the extent to which it addressed its emissions; *alignment*, gauging the degree to which it made its activities more coherent with a low-carbon future; and *investment*, assessing its allocation of resources to support a low-carbon future. Using a rolling average technique to smooth the data, for each company an average score for each three-year period (2010–2012, 2011–2013, 2012–2014, 2013–2015, 2014–2016,

© The Editor(s) (if applicable) and The Author(s), under exclusive license to Springer Nature Switzerland AG 2023
C. Hulme, *Corporate Climate Action, Transnational Politics, and World Order*, Environmental Politics and Theory,
https://doi.org/10.1007/978-3-031-34115-1

231

232 APPENDIX

and 2015–2017) was calculated. Based on their average score in each period, companies were classified as one of four types. The types and corresponding point ranges are as follows: *business as usual*: 0–8 points; *evolutionary*: 9–12 points; *innovator*: 13–15 points; and *disruptor*: 16–20 points.

Presented below is how the 20 possible points were distributed among the three metrics, which varied depending on the industry, as well as the industry-specific practices used to gauge performance. Each metric is listed in bold, along with the maximum points possible for that metric in a given industry; the industry-specific practice for the metric is italicized. Next follows a list of the points allocated for different levels of the indicator practices.

Industry Category 1: Automotive
Product (10 points): *electrifying fleet*[1]

10: plans to electrify entire fleet
8: progressively more ambitious plans for battery-powered electric vehicles (EVs)
6: going "all-in" on hybrids as low-emission option or developing a sub-brand dedicated to EVs
5: offering limited number of EV models
4: offering limited number of hybrid models
3: developing an EV
1: developing a hybrid

Alignment (5 points): *internal carbon pricing*

5: internal initiative to put a price on carbon emissions
2: carbon pricing using existing prices of an external initiative (e.g., the EU Emissions Trading System)

---

[1] Weighted most heavily as tailpipe emissions represent the key culprit of automakers' emissions, constituting, according to McKinsey, approximately "75 percent of all carbon emissions from mobility" (2020).

APPENDIX   233

0: no carbon pricing

Investment (5 points): *low-carbon R&D spending*

5: low-carbon R&D classified by CDP as a driver of "emissions reduction activity" (ERA); main focus electrification of fleet
4: low-carbon R&D classified by CDP as a driver of ERA; hedging on focus (e.g., targeting EVs alongside other low-emission technologies)
2: low-carbon R&D classified by CDP as a driver of ERA but limited details about focus; or low-carbon R&D not classified by CDP as a driver of ERA but emphasis on EVs
0: low-carbon R&D not classified by CDP as a driver of ERA; no emphasis on electrification

Industry category 2: Energy-intensive industries
Cement
Product (10 points): *addressing emissions intensity*[2]

10: annual decrease >1.6%
8: annual decrease $\geq$0.8% but $\leq$1.6%
6: annual decrease <0.8% but >0
3: annual increase $\geq$0 but <1.6%

---

[2] Weighted most heavily given that the emissions produced through the cement production process account for the majority of cement companies' emissions. Points calibrated based on the International Energy Agency's analysis in 2020, which noted that to align with the Sustainable Development Scenario, the CO_2 intensity of cement production needed to decline 0.8% annually to 2030. Throughout the appendix, for all industries for which the yearly change in emissions intensity was calculated, total Scope 1 emissions (i.e., direct emissions from sources owned or controlled by a company) and Scope 2 emissions (i.e., indirect emissions from sources tied to energy that a company purchases) were divided either by tons of product generated or by annual sales, depending on the industry.

234 APPENDIX

0: annual increase $\geq 1.6\%$

Investment (6 points): *low-carbon R&D spending*[3]

6: low-carbon R&D classified by CDP as a driver of ERA; low-carbon emphasis in R&D
3: low-carbon R&D classified by CDP as a driver of ERA but no low-carbon emphasis in R&D; or low-carbon R&D not classified by CDP as a driver of ERA but low-carbon emphasis in R&D
0: low-carbon R&D not classified by CDP as a driver of ERA; no low-carbon emphasis in R&D

Alignment (4 points): internal carbon pricing

4: yes
0: no

---

[3] For all energy-intensive industries, to evaluate whether there was a low-carbon emphasis in a company's overall R&D approach, whenever possible, specific data was gathered from CDP about whether the company spent $\geq 1/3$ or $< 1/3$ of its research budget on low-carbon projects. If companies did not supply such specific information but provided figures (either in their CDP disclosures or annual reports) on low-carbon research expenditures as well as on their entire research budget, these amounts were evaluated to determine whether low-carbon initiatives represented a progressively greater share of the budget.

APPENDIX 235

Chemical

Alignment (8 points): *addressing Scope 3 emissions, with a focus on the supply chain*[4]

8: robust supply chain sustainability and emissions reduction strategy executed
5: supply chain sustainability strategy announced
3: reporting Scope 3 emissions
1: studying Scope 3 emissions

Product (8 points): *addressing emissions intensity*

8: annual decrease >3%
6: annual decrease ≤3% or annual increase ≤0.5%
4: annual increase >0.5% but <3%
0: annual increase ≥3%

Investment (4 points): *low-carbon R&D spending*

4: low-carbon R&D classified by CDP as a driver of ERA; low-carbon emphasis in R&D
3: low-carbon R&D not classified by CDP as a driver of ERA; low-carbon emphasis in R&D
2: low-carbon R&D classified by CDP as a driver of ERA; no low-carbon emphasis in R&D
0: low-carbon R&D not classified by CDP as a driver of ERA; no low-carbon emphasis in R&D

---

[4] The product and alignment metrics are weighted equally for the chemical industry. According to the International Energy Agency, the "chemical sector is the largest industrial energy consumer and the third largest industry subsector in terms of direct CO_2 emissions" (2022), which are addressed by the product metric. In contrast to certain other industries in the energy-intensive industry category, given chemicals' centrality in nearly all manufactured products, Scope 3 emissions (i.e., those outside of a company's direct control, including those tied to suppliers and end-users) are especially key in the chemical industry; in fact, an estimated two-thirds of the industry's emissions worldwide are Scope 3, addressed by the alignment metric (Together for Sustainability 2022).

236 APPENDIX

Oil and Gas
Alignment (10 points): *addressing Scope 3 emissions, with a focus on the supply chain*[5]

> 10: robust supply chain sustainability and emissions reduction strategy executed
> 8: year-on-year progress reducing Scope 3 emissions
> 5: supply chain sustainability strategy announced
> 3: reporting Scope 3 emissions
> 1: studying Scope 3 emissions

Product (6 points): *acquiring/developing renewable energy (RE) businesses; reducing methane flaring*[6]

> 6: acquiring/developing new RE businesses
> 4: significant spending on RE projects
> 1: initiative to reduce methane flaring
> 0: no RE initiatives; no progress on reducing methane flaring

Investment (4 points): *low-carbon R&D spending*

> 4: low-carbon R&D classified by CDP as a driver of ERA; low-carbon emphasis in R&D
> 1: low-carbon R&D not classified by CDP as a driver of ERA; low-carbon emphasis in R&D
> 0: low-carbon R&D not classified by CDP as a driver of ERA; no low-carbon emphasis in R&D

---

[5] Weighted most heavily as Scope 3 emissions (which include supply chain emissions) account for approximately "85% of total emissions that result from the use... of fossil fuels, particularly oil and gas" (Holland 2022).

[6] According to the International Energy Agency, "15% of global energy-related GHG emissions comes from the process of getting oil and gas out of the ground and to consumers" (2020), and reducing methane leaks is a crucial way in which the industry can address these emissions. Yet, for the purpose of this project, an oil company acquiring a new RE business or investing in RE projects was treated as a more significant action, given its potential impact on a global low-carbon transition away from fossil fuel-based energy businesses.

APPENDIX 237

Pharmaceutical

Alignment (8 points): *addressing Scope 3 emissions, with a focus on the supply chain*[7]

8: robust supply chain sustainability and emissions reduction strategy executed
5: supply chain sustainability strategy announced
3: reporting Scope 3 emissions
1: studying Scope 3 emissions

Product (8 points): *addressing emissions intensity*

8: annual decrease >3%
6: annual decrease ≤3% or annual increase ≤0.5%
4: annual increase >0.5% but <3%
0: annual increase ≥3%

Investment (4 points): *low-carbon R&D spending*

4: low-carbon R&D classified by CDP as a driver of ERA; low-carbon emphasis in R&D
3: low-carbon R&D not classified by CDP as a driver of ERA; low-carbon emphasis in R&D
2: low-carbon R&D classified by CDP as a driver of ERA; no low-carbon emphasis in R&D
0: low-carbon R&D not classified by CDP as a driver of ERA; no low-carbon emphasis in R&D

---

[7] The product and alignment metrics are weighted equally for the pharmaceutical industry. The emissions intensity of the pharmaceutical industry, addressed by the product metric, eclipses that of even the automotive industry by 55% (Belkhir and Elmeligi 2019). Like the chemical industry, Scope 3 emissions, addressed by the alignment metric, are especially central to the pharmaceutical industry; in fact, a 2021 report found that Scope 3 emissions for the industry "are 4.7 times larger than Scope 1 and 2 emissions combined" (My Green Lab 2021, 10).

238 APPENDIX

Power
Product (12 points): *coal's share in generation portfolio*[8]

12: no coal
9: <20% coal
6: 20–34% coal
3: 35–49% coal
0: ≥50% coal

Investment (5 points): *low-carbon R&D spending*

5: low-carbon R&D classified by CDP as a driver of ERA; low-carbon emphasis in R&D
3: low-carbon R&D not classified by CDP as a driver of ERA but low-carbon emphasis in R&D
2: low-carbon R&D classified by CDP as a driver of ERA but no low-carbon emphasis in R&D
0: low-carbon R&D not classified by CDP as a driver of ERA; no low-carbon emphasis in R&D

Alignment (3 points): *internal carbon pricing*

3: yes
0: no

Steel
Product (10 points): *addressing emissions intensity*[9]

10: annual decrease >5%
8: annual decrease ≤5% but ≥2.5%

---

[8] Weighted most heavily given coal's contribution to greenhouse gas emissions as the highest-emitting fossil fuel.

[9] Weighted most heavily as the direct emissions produced through the steelmaking process account for the vast majority of steelmakers' emissions. Points calibrated based on the International Energy Agency's analysis in 2020, which noted that to align with the Sustainable Development Scenario, the CO_2 intensity of crude steel needed to decline an average of 2.5% annually between 2018 and 2030.

APPENDIX   239

6: annual decrease <2.5% but annual increase <2%
3: annual increase $\geq$2% but <5%
0: annual increase $\geq$5%

Investment (6 points): *low-carbon R&D spending*

6: low-carbon R&D classified by CDP as a driver of ERA; low-carbon emphasis in R&D
3: low-carbon R&D classified by CDP as a driver of ERA but no low-carbon emphasis in R&D; or low-carbon R&D not classified by CDP as a driver of ERA but low-carbon emphasis in R&D
0: low-carbon R&D not classified by CDP as a driver of ERA; no low-carbon emphasis in R&D

Alignment (4 points): *internal carbon pricing*

4: yes
0: no

Industry Category 3: Technology
Hardware-Focused Companies
Alignment (10 points): *addressing Scope 3 emissions, with a focus on the supply chain*[10]

10: robust initiative targeting supply chain emissions reductions
8: year-on-year progress reducing Scope 3 emissions
5: supply chain emissions reduction goal articulated, index for suppliers concerning emissions performance created, or supplier requirement to report emissions enacted
3: considering supply chain sustainability issues

---

[10] In contrast to companies focused primarily on software, supply chain emissions account for the majority of emissions of hardware-focused companies; thus, the alignment metric was most heavily weighted for the latter.

240 APPENDIX

2: Scope 3 emissions reported or initiative to enhance product efficiency (i.e., address end-user emissions) launched

Product (6 points): *addressing emissions intensity*

6: annual decrease >5%
4: annual decrease ≤5% but >0
3: annual increase ≥0 but <1%
0: annual increase ≥1%

Investment (4 points): *investing in renewable energy (RE)*

4: investment in RE projects aligned with the additionality principle (i.e., enabling projects that otherwise would not have been built)
1: investment in RE projects for offsetting conventional power usage (e.g., purchasing Renewable Energy Certificates)
0: no reported investments in RE projects

Software-Focused Companies
Product (10 points): *addressing emissions intensity*[11]

10: annual decrease >5%
8: annual decrease ≤5% but ≥3%
6: annual decrease <3% but >1%
2: annual decrease ≤1% or annual increase ≤1%

---

[11] In contrast to companies focused primarily on hardware, most of the emissions of software-focused companies stem from their own operations (e.g., the energy used to power data centers); thus, the product metric was most heavily weighted for the latter.

APPENDIX   241

0: annual increase >1%

Alignment (6 points): *addressing Scope 3 emissions, with a focus on the supply chain; internal carbon pricing*[12]

6: robust initiative targeting supply chain emissions reductions
4: supply chain emissions reduction goal articulated, index for suppliers concerning emissions performance created, or supplier requirement to report emissions enacted
3: considering supply chain sustainability issues or implementing internal carbon price
0: no participation in an initiative addressing supply chain sustainability issues; no implementation of internal carbon price

Investment (4 points): *investing in renewable energy (RE)*

4: investment in RE projects aligned with the additionality principle (i.e., enabling projects that otherwise would not have been built)
1: investment in RE projects for offsetting conventional power usage (e.g., purchasing Renewable Energy Certificates)
0: no reported investments in RE projects

Industry Category 4: Finance
Insurers
Product (10 points): *acknowledging climate-related risks or integrating climate-related standards into underwriting policies, with a focus on coal exclusion*[13]

10: exclusion of underwriting for all coal projects/companies with coal operations

---

[12] In contrast to hardware-focused companies, software-focused companies rely on fewer suppliers and thereby have a comparatively higher degree of influence over the degree to which their activities align with a low-carbon future. For software-focused companies, therefore, a secondary indicator practice for *alignment*—internal carbon pricing—also was considered.

[13] Weighted most heavily given that "coal projects [representing the dirtiest fossil fuel] cannot be financed, built or operated without insurance" (Kollewe 2019).

242 APPENDIX

7: reducing underwriting for all coal projects/companies with coal operations
4: restriction of underwriting for select coal power/mining projects
1: climate-related risks acknowledged
0: no acknowledgment of climate-related risks

Alignment (6 points): *proprietary investments in coal*

6: complete divestment from coal-based businesses
4: divestment from coal-based businesses, with 30% threshold for defining coal-based
2: divestment from coal-based businesses, with 50% threshold for defining coal-based
0: no standard for proprietary investments in coal-based businesses

Investment (4 points): *investing in renewable energy (RE) projects*

4: significant investment in RE projects
3: emphasis on de-risking RE projects to support renewables industry
0: no investment in RE projects; no emphasis on de-risking RE projects

APPENDIX   243

Banks
Investment (10 points): *coal financing policy*[14]

10: BankTrack grade: A
9: BankTrack grade: A–
8: BankTrack grade: B+
7: BankTrack grade: B
6: BankTrack grade: B–
4: BankTrack grade: C+
3: BankTrack grade: C
2: BankTrack grade: C–
1: BankTrack grade: D+

[14] Weighted most heavily given that among fossil fuels, coal is the biggest contributor to emissions. To score companies' coal financing policies, an average was calculated from the coal mining and coal power grades they received from BankTrack and partner NGOs. Collins et al. (n.d.) graded companies for 2013–2015; see pages 6–7 for a bank grades summary and pages 10–25 for methodology and scoring concerning coal mining and coal power. Kirsch et al. (2019) graded companies for 2016–2018; see pages 14–15 for a bank grades summary and pages 68–83 for methodology and scoring concerning coal mining and coal power. In the 2010–2012 period (i.e., prior to the years reported by BankTrack and partners), banks were scored for this book based on whether they monitored the carbon intensity of their lending and/or accounted for future potential costs of emissions in applying risk standards to clients in emissions-intensive sectors; in 2010 and 2011, companies received a score of 1 for reporting such monitoring and/or accounting and a score of 0 if they did not. For 2012, a score was estimated based on their 2013 BankTrack grade.

244 APPENDIX

0: no coal policy

Alignment (6 points): *extreme oil financing policy*[15]

6: BankTrack grade: A/B range
4: BankTrack grade: C range
2: BankTrack grade: D range
0: no extreme oil policy

Product (4 points): *expanding investment in renewable energy (RE) and underwriting or issuing green bonds*

4: financing of renewable energy/issuing proprietary green bonds
3: financing green initial public offerings or underwriting green bonds; no proprietary green bonds
1: significant climate-related investments
0: no evidence of investment in limited RE or other green projects

[15] Companies' scores for extreme oil policies were calculated from the grades they received from BankTrack and partner NGOs. Collins et al. (n.d.) graded companies for 2013–2015; see pages 6–7 for a bank grades summary and pages 26–33 for methodology and scoring concerning extreme oil. Kirsch et al. (2019) graded companies for 2016–2018; see pages 14–15 for a bank grades summary and pages 28–35 for methodology and scoring concerning tar sands oil (note that in this edition, BankTrack and partner NGOs separated the elements of "extreme oil" that previously were treated together; thus, for this book the focus was on grades for tar sands oil, as opposed to Arctic oil and gas or another element of "extreme oil" that Kirsch et al. treat separately). In the 2010–2012 period (i.e., prior to the years reported by BankTrack and partners), banks were scored for this book based on yearly change in their total financing for fossil fuels (Schücking 2013); in 2010, companies received a baseline score of 0, and for 2011, they received a 1 if their fossil fuel financing declined compared to 2010 and a score of 0 if it did not decline. For 2012, a score was estimated based on their 2013 BankTrack grade.

APPENDIX   245

PART II: CORPORATE PERCEPTIONS
OF CLIMATE-RELATED RISKS AND OPPORTUNITIES

Data Sources

CDP disclosures from 2010 to 2016 were the principal data source for evaluating corporations' perceptions of the likely risks and/or opportunities of climate-related developments.[16] CDP disclosures from 2017 were excluded due to changes in the disclosure questions that compromise the comparability of the 2017 responses with those of previous years.[17] Complete access to all CDP disclosures is available through subscription; contact the author for information about any of the disclosures referenced in this book.

Summary of Methodology

For each year from 2010 to 2016, the starting point was identifying whether each company identified risks and/or opportunities related to climate-related regulation, changing consumer behavior, and, for oil and gas companies and finance companies, physical impacts—and if so, on what time horizon, with what degree of certainty, and with what anticipated level of material (financial) impact.[18] Excluded categories of risk and opportunity included reputation (treated by CDP separately from changing consumer behavior, despite that companies often treated reputational concerns within the consumer behavior category), uncertain market signals (as this was often discussed and incorporated within the regulation category), and socioeconomic/humanitarian factors (which were wide-ranging and not well-specified).

---

[16] Contact the author for information about supplementary data gathered from confidential interviews with corporate representatives and industry experts: hulmecharlottej@gmail.com.

[17] For instance, in contrast to prior years, in 2017, companies were asked to report about "relevant risks" (as opposed to simply "risks") and, separately, about risks that stood to have a financial and/or strategic impact.

[18] Finance and oil and gas belong on a relatively short list of industries poised to be significantly impacted by climate change per se, that is, by its physical implications (Duva 2014).

246 APPENDIX

Actual and Anticipated Material Impact of Risks and Opportunities
For each company, for each year, the total number of risks and opportunities that were reported as "high impact" (in material terms) was tallied. Risks and opportunities that were reported as "low impact" or "medium impact" were excluded.

Likelihood and Time Horizon
Second, only those high-impact risks and opportunities that were assessed as "virtually certain," "very likely," "likely," or "more likely than not" were counted. High-impact risks and opportunities that were assessed to be "as likely as not" were included *only* if the identified time horizon either was in the short or medium term (i.e., for most companies, defined as current, 1–3 years, or 3–6 years) *or* was described as "unknown time horizon" (i.e., if a company identified a risk or opportunity as "as likely as not" but explicitly only on a long term [6–10 or >10 years] time horizon, then it was excluded).

Calculating "Perception Strength" by Year and Period
For each year, the strength of the perception (first at the level of individual companies and then for each industry group) that climate-related factors presented high-impact costs and/or opportunities was calculated.[19] Presented below is an example of a calculation for one industry group (technology), in one year (2012). A column is marked with a "+" to indicate that the company reported the relevant risk or opportunity and that it met the "high impact" threshold, as well as the likelihood and time horizon parameters for inclusion (as outlined above). An "x" indicates that it did not report the given risk or opportunity or that the reported risk/opportunity did not meet the impact, likelihood, and time horizon requirements for inclusion. Regulatory is abbreviated reg., and changing consumer behavior, CCB.

---

[19] If a company did not respond to CDP, they were treated as reporting no risks or opportunities.

Company	Reg. risk	Reg. opportunity	CCB risk	CCB opportunity
Apple	x	x	x	x
Google	x	x	x	x
Microsoft	x	x	x	x
Infosys	+	x	x	x
Samsung	+	+	x	+
Total	2/5	1/5	0/5	1/5

Thus, for the technology industry, for 2012, the average perception strength across the four categories of climate-related risk and opportunity was 1/5, or 20%. Consistent with the approach laid out in Part I, an average for each three-year period spanning the timeframe of interest was calculated and a rolling average technique used to smooth the data. As the average perception strength for the technology industry in 2013 and 2014 was 1/4, or 25%, the three-year rolling average in 2012–2014 was 23% (as presented in Table 4.3 in Chapter 4).

INDEX

A

Additionality principle, 133, 142, 240, 241

Affordable Clean Energy rule, 70

Agenda setting, 5, 212, 220

AGL, 222

Agora Energiewende, 51

AIG, 149, 154–156, 158–160, 164, 180

Albanese, Anthony, 222

Alignment, 9, 90, 93, 102, 106, 107, 111, 127, 131, 136, 153, 155, 157, 178, 181, 182

Allianz, 149, 153–167, 179, 180, 217

Amazon, 123, 126

Ambition mechanism, 44, 47

Amelang, Soren, 52, 206

American Clean Energy Security Act, 67

Andhra Pradesh, 61

Annex I countries, 36

Apple, 19, 22, 125, 126, 128–131, 133, 134, 136–140, 142, 179, 180, 195, 247

Arctic, 151, 244

Associated Press, 222

Australia, 222

Automotive industry, 53, 85, 88, 94–96, 116, 177, 237

Autonomous vehicle, 88

Avant, Deborah, 7, 23

AXA, 157

Ayres, Alyssa, 56, 57

B

Bang, Guri, 66

Bangladesh, 215

Ban, Ki-moon, 45

Bank of America, 149, 152, 155, 156, 160, 161, 167

Bank of England, 149

Banks, 150, 151, 153, 155–161, 163, 167

© The Editor(s) (if applicable) and The Author(s), under exclusive license to Springer Nature Switzerland AG 2023
C. Hulme, *Corporate Climate Action, Transnational Politics, and World Order*, Environmental Politics and Theory, https://doi.org/10.1007/978-3-031-34115-1

249

250 INDEX

BankTrack, 11, 150, 158, 160
Barra, Mary, 88
BASF, 53, 103, 104, 114, 179
Battery electric vehicles (BEV), 86–88
Bayer, 104, 179
Berlin, 2, 49–54, 72, 87, 89, 94, 95, 115, 116, 167, 186, 200, 202
Betts, Richard, 218, 219
Biden, Joe, 88, 211, 213
Biofuels, 101
BlackRock, 1, 147, 148, 162
Bloomberg, Michael, 147
Bloomberg New Energy Finance, 133
BMW, 86, 88, 91–94, 98, 179
Bodansky, Daniel, 37–39, 41
Bowen, Chris, 222
BP, 1, 191
Branson, Richard, 40
Brazil, 22, 38
Breetz, Hannah, 68
Bremmer, Ian, 39
British Thermal Unit [BTU] tax, 65
Brookings, 40, 43
Brown, Jerry, 214
Bulkeley, Harriet, 4, 5
Bush, George H.W., 64, 65
Bush, George W., 37, 67
Business as usual (BAU), 2, 11, 88, 90, 91, 94, 98–100, 102, 104, 111, 112, 115, 128, 129, 140, 149, 153, 154, 161, 163, 167, 175, 180, 192, 206, 221, 222
Byrd-Hagel Resolution, 65

C
California, 4, 13, 19, 22, 88
"California's Foreign Policy", 22
Canada, 42
Cancun Agreements, 40
Cap and trade, 67, 69
Carbon Brief, 44

Carbon Disclosure Project (CDP), 4, 9–11, 20, 96, 107, 109, 116, 126, 134, 141, 142, 161, 184, 190, 206, 231, 233, 234–239, 245, 246
Carbon labeling, 5
Carbon market, 5
Carbon negative, 123, 141
Carbon neutral, 6, 140, 141
Carney, Mark, 149–151
Cascade effect, 3
Cement, 4, 19, 84, 102, 107, 108, 127, 233
Center for Strategic and International Studies, 223
Ceres, 148
Certification standards, 5
Chemical industry, 235, 237
Chevron, 104, 180, 222
China, 22, 36–38, 42, 43, 47, 58, 59, 66, 68, 70, 86, 87, 89, 95, 131, 141, 152, 213–215, 217
Chipman, John, 209
Chrysler, 88, 91, 180
Chubb, 150
Citigroup, 149, 152, 154–157, 160, 164, 167, 180
City of London Corporation, 22
Clean power purchasing, 125, 126, 140, 174
Climate action breadth, 93, 107
Climate action depth, 14
Climate action momentum, 2, 66, 110, 112, 115, 178
Climate Action 100+, 147
Climate Action Tracker, 44, 223
Climate Analytics, 52
Climate change adaptation, 36
Climate change mitigation, 36, 46, 55, 60, 124, 207, 208, 212
Climate negotiations, 44, 56, 208
Climate Pledge, The, 123

INDEX 251

Climate refugees, 215
Clinton, Bill, 37, 64–66, 70, 71
CNBC, 152
CNN, 210
Coal exclusion policy, 153, 156, 159
Coal financing, 158, 161, 163
Coal mining, 157, 158, 160
Coal power, 52, 158, 160, 163, 221
Coal underwriting, 150, 159
Cold War, 21
Collective action, 3, 48
Collective outcome, 15, 111, 176, 184
Common but differentiated responsibilities (CBDR), 36, 37, 41, 43, 56
Consensus steering mechanism, 14
Constructivist scholarship, 10
Consumer behavior, 26, 87, 96–99, 109, 110, 112–115, 134–136, 161–163, 166, 177, 184, 185, 189, 192
Consumer demand, 20, 84, 85, 185
Consumer pressure, 20
COP3, 65, 66
COP16, 40, 41
COP17, 41, 42
COP21, 43, 141
COP26, 3
Copenhagen Accord, 38, 39
Copenhagen Climate Conference, 3, 16, 37, 221
Corporate citizenship report, 140
Corporate climate action, 2, 3, 7, 16, 20, 24–26, 84, 109, 175, 183, 196, 205, 216, 218, 219, 223
Corporate climate consensus, 2, 7, 12, 14, 15, 18, 20, 25, 108, 134, 175–177, 186, 193
Corporate grand strategic actor, 216
"Corporate nation", 23, 83, 125, 173, 206, 212, 217, 224

Corporate social responsibility, 8
CO_2, 4, 43, 49, 52, 86, 100, 165
Council of Europe, 38
Council on Foreign Relations, 24
COVID-19, 23, 47, 210
Cutler, A. Claire, 5
Cyberspace, 23, 211

D
Daimler, 85–87, 89, 91, 179
Das, Gurcharan, 62
Das, Tarun, 9
Data center, 123, 124, 132
Delhi, 55, 56, 58–63, 72, 190, 192, 197, 198, 202
Deutsche Bank, 149, 152, 155–158, 160, 161, 163, 166, 167
Developed states, 20, 37, 66, 141
Developing states, 37
Dieselgate, 85, 91, 94, 95, 116, 117
Diesel vehicle, 88
Disruptor, 90, 102, 128, 153, 176, 178
Dolsak, Nives, 124
Dominant design, 8, 87, 89, 94, 99, 101, 115, 116, 126, 134, 148–150, 152, 153, 160, 161, 167, 181
Dow Chemical, 104, 112–114, 179, 180
Dow Jones Industrial Average (DJIA), 221, 222
Duke Energy, 67, 174
Dupont, 67
Durban Platform, 41–43

E
Earth Summit, 35
EDF+Business initiative, 143
Electric vehicle (EV), 86–90, 92, 93, 232, 233

252 INDEX

Emergence, 14, 111, 112, 114, 115, 127, 135, 136, 138, 174, 177, 197, 219
Emergent action, 149, 161–163, 166, 193, 195, 196, 199, 201
Emergent consensus, 17, 99, 189
Emergent outcome, 12, 14
Emergent steering mechanism, 110
Emergent strategy, 218
Emergent system, 12
Emissions intensity, 57, 62, 102, 107, 108, 127, 131, 133
Emissions reduction, 2, 6, 34, 36, 37, 39–48, 50, 51, 54, 65, 66, 70, 71, 94, 115, 124, 142, 222
Emissions registry, 5
Emissions regulations, 1, 210
Emissions trading, 52, 53, 69
Energy efficiency, 58, 59, 140, 157
Energy-intensive industries, 18, 52, 53, 57, 83, 100, 102, 107, 109, 115, 116, 143, 148, 193, 194
Environmental Defense Fund (EDF), 67, 143
E.ON, 53, 100, 103, 104, 112–114, 179, 190, 191, 209
Europe, 50, 87, 100, 141, 167, 190, 192, 223
European Investment Bank, 157
European Parliament, 191, 221
European Union Council (EU Council), 95
European Union Emissions Trading Directive, 53
European Union Emissions Trading System, 53
European Union (EU), 37, 49–53, 94, 210
European Union "20-20-20" initiative, 50
Evolutionary, 90, 102, 128, 153, 178
Extreme oil, 153, 155, 158

Exxon, 1, 104, 180

F
Facebook, 124, 126
Falkner, Robert, 20, 46
Farley, Jim, 88
Federation of German Consumer Organisations, 94
Figueres, Christiana, 45
Finance companies, 11, 153, 159–161, 166, 167, 194–196
Finance industry, 149, 152, 153, 166, 193, 194
Fink, Larry, 1, 147–149, 151, 152, 162, 166
First mover, 3, 14, 16, 17
First Utility, 101
Forbes, 23, 40, 123
Ford, 86–88, 92, 93, 98
Foreign Affairs, 22
Foreign policy, 21, 209, 212–214
Fortune Global 500, 9, 202, 217
Fossil fuel, 2, 4, 17, 18, 24, 55, 58, 67, 70, 84, 100, 101, 148, 150–152, 159, 160, 174, 192, 193, 195, 222, 224, 236, 238, 241, 243, 244
Fossil fuel industries, 1, 4, 147, 148, 160
France, 90
Frankel, Frances, 55, 61
Free rider, 48
Frydenberg, Josh, 222
Fukushima Daiichi, 50, 53

G
G-7, 212
G-8, 50
G-20, 4
G-77, 56
Gallagher, Kelly, 43, 213

INDEX 253

General Electric, 67, 222
General Motors (GM), 88, 89, 91, 180
Germany Climate Action Plan 2050, 51, 52
Germany Energiewende, 50, 52
Germany Fifth Climate Policy Programme, 49
Germany First Climate Policy Programme, 49
Germany Integrated Energy and Climate Programme, 50
Germany Red-Green coalition, 50
Gilligan, Jonathan, 2, 4, 6, 13, 25, 124, 174
Glasgow Financial Alliance for Net Zero (GFANZ), 167
Global financial crisis, 50, 51
Global governance, 5, 12
Global Optimism, 123
Google, 19, 124–126, 128, 131–134, 136, 138–140, 142, 143, 195
Gore, Al, 65, 66
Goyal, Piyush, 58
Grand strategic actor, 216–219
Grand strategic effect, 219
Grand strategic level, 216, 217, 219
Grand strategy, 216–219
Granovetter, Mark, 14, 111, 176
Great Power battleground, 213, 214
Great Powers, 23, 24, 26, 212, 213, 215–217, 219, 223
Great Recession, 1, 89, 183
Green bond, 139, 151–153, 156, 157, 161
Green Climate Fund, 40
Greenhouse gases (GHGs), 4, 8, 9, 35, 36, 38, 39, 49, 94, 107, 126, 140, 142, 206
Greenhouse Gas Protocol, 5, 54
Green, Jessica, 4–6
Greenpeace, 126, 131, 140, 141

Green Tech Media, 101
Greenwashing, 10, 11

H
Haas, Richard, 24
Hardware companies, 127, 130, 131, 133, 239–241
Harvard Business Review, 209
Harvard Business School, 142
Haufler, Virginia, 2, 5, 6, 17, 22, 23, 25
Headquarter country, 17–19, 165, 195, 196, 199
Hedgecock, Kathryn, 211
HeidelbergCement, 105, 112, 113, 114
Hewlett Packard, 142
High-carbon economy, 84, 85, 102, 116, 127, 143, 148, 150, 152, 153, 167, 195
Hofmeister, John, 1
Honda, 88
Hovi, Jon, 66
Hybrid vehicle, 89, 93
Hydroelectric power, 60
"Hypotheses on Misperception", 33, 207

I
India air pollution, 60
India co-benefits, 55, 56, 58, 60
India Energy Saving Certificates, 62
India G-77, 56
India hydroelectric power, 60
India Ministry of Forests and Climate Change, 63
India National Action Plan for Climate Change (NAPCC), 56, 57

254 INDEX

India National Mission on Enhanced
Energy Efficiency (NMEEE), 57,
62
India National Solar Mission (NSM),
57
India net metering, 63
India Perform Achieve Trade (PAT),
57, 62
India Public Health Foundation of
India (PFHI), 60
India Renewable Purchase Obligation
(RPO), 62
Infosys, 126, 129, 131, 137–140,
175, 179, 180, 217, 247
Innogy, 100
Innovator, 90, 102, 128, 153, 178
Insure Our Future, 150, 151
Insurers, 150, 151, 153, 155–159,
161, 167
Intended Nationally Determined
Contributions (INDC), 43, 44,
187, 191, 213
Interest sets, 15, 16, 26, 90, 96, 112,
176, 184, 189, 219
Intergovernmental Panel on Climate
Change (IPCC), 34, 35, 191
Internal carbon price, 8, 9, 90, 93,
99, 102
Internal combustion engine, 86, 87
International Energy Agency (IEA),
57, 59–61, 125, 151
International Finance Corporation,
152
International Institute for Strategic
Studies, 209
International law, 210
International Organization for
Standardization (ISO), 6
International organizations, 3, 5
International relations, 5, 10, 25
International security, 3, 22–24, 85,
143, 216, 218

Investment, 9, 90, 102, 107, 128,
136, 153, 159, 160, 178, 181
IONITY, 86, 87

J
Japan, 42, 90
Jervis, Robert, 12, 33, 34, 42, 45, 47,
54, 55, 64, 71, 102, 207, 208
Johnson & Johnson, 105, 108,
112–114, 180
JPMorgan (JPM), 149, 151, 152,
154–157, 160, 164, 180

K
Kahler, Miles, 7
Keohane, Robert, 3, 21
Kerry, John, 45
Khandekar, Nivedita, 62
Khanna, Parag, 21, 22, 205, 223
Kolkata, 60
Konisky, David, 70
Krasner, Stephen, 220
Kuran, Timur, 14
Kyoto Protocol, 36, 37, 40, 41, 49,
53, 56, 64–66, 70

L
Ladrech, Robert, 50
Lake, David, 7
Layton, Peter, 217, 219
Le Prestre, Philippe, 25
Lewis, Joanna, 43
Lieberman, Joe, 67
Lloyd's of London, 149
Lock-in, 131, 134
Lovins, Amory, 205, 206
Low-carbon economy, 2, 62, 141
Low-carbon future, 8–10, 13, 14, 26,
48, 52, 55, 56, 61, 63, 72, 83,
84, 88, 90, 92, 93, 95, 96, 99,

100, 102, 103, 106, 107, 109, 111, 116, 117, 125–127, 141, 142, 149, 152, 165–167, 175–178, 181, 182, 187, 189, 193, 198, 200, 202, 206, 207, 209, 211, 212, 215, 217, 241
Low-carbon game, 89, 94, 205, 222
Low-carbon investment, 151, 166, 212
Low-carbon technology, 67
Low-carbon transition, 13, 18, 24, 34, 46, 48, 58, 71, 72, 83, 89, 102, 117, 138, 151, 166, 167, 177, 192, 202, 205, 221, 224
Low-emission vehicles, 87
Lyon, Thomas, 10, 11

M
Madrid Climate Conference (2019), 214
Market-based initiatives, 4
Martel, William, 217
Maslow, Abraham, 220
Material impact, 12, 95, 96, 99, 110–112, 138, 149, 162, 163, 193, 197
Material incentives, 18, 19, 26, 136, 175, 193, 201
Material opportunities, 18, 135, 177, 189
Material relevance, 7, 84, 96, 99, 109, 115, 127, 149, 202
Material risks, 10, 18, 19, 84, 97, 99, 109, 112, 127, 134, 138, 174, 177, 184, 189
Mathews, Jessica, 3, 21, 22
McCain, John, 67
McKinsey, 89
Merkel, Angela, 50, 53, 95
Meta. *See* Facebook
Methane, 1, 4, 102
Mez, Lutz, 49, 51

Microsoft, 1, 123, 124, 126, 128–131, 133, 138, 140–143, 179, 180, 247
Migdal, Joel, 61
Migration, 23
Mildenberger, Matto, 65, 67–70
Mintzberg, Henry, 218
Misperception, 42, 45, 47, 54, 55, 61, 66, 71, 72
Modi, Narendra, 57
Montgomery, Alexander, 7, 10, 11
Morocco, 35
Morrison, Scott, 222
Multilateral development banks, 4
Multinational corporations, 5, 12, 23, 221
Mumbai, 60–63, 192, 215
Munich Re, 150
Murray, Williamson, 217
Musk, Elon, 86

N
Nadella, Satya, 1
Nationally Determined Contributions (NDCs), 42–44, 46–48, 71, 223
National security, 213, 215, 216
Natural gas, 52, 101
Natural Resources Defense Council, 67
Nature Conservancy, 67
Netherlands, 9
Networks, 7, 60, 103, 125, 175
Net-zero emissions, 123
Newell, Peter, 4
New Energies, 101, 103, 132
New Power Politics, 7
New York City, 22, 214
New York State, 224
New York Times, 46
Non-Annex I countries, 36, 37, 56

256 INDEX

Non-governmental organization
(NGO), 5, 11, 21, 123, 150,
160, 243, 244
Non-state actors, 22, 23, 26, 174,
207, 210, 213–216
Norm, 2, 3, 10, 21, 26, 102
Norwegian State Fund (NSF), 100
Nuclear power, 52, 60
Nyberg, Daniel, 24
Nye, Joseph, 21, 214

O

Obama administration, 67, 69–71,
197
Obama, Barack, 38, 42, 43, 64,
68–70, 213
Oil, 1, 59, 101, 102, 109, 151, 191,
223
Oil and gas industry, 102, 107, 127

P

Pandemic disease, 23, 26, 211
Paradigm of climate action, 127
Paris Climate Agreement, 2, 43, 115,
139
Paris Climate Conference, 16, 34, 91
Peak carbon, 43
Pew Research Center, 21
Pfizer, 103, 104, 112–114, 179, 180
Pharmaceutical industry, 237
Physical impact (climate change), 165
Plug-in hybrid electric vehicles
(PHEV), 89, 93
Poland, 125
Political Psychology Research Group
(PPRG), 67, 68
Political salience, 68
Pope, Carl, 147
Popescu, Ionut, 218
Portfolio Decarbonization Coalition,
165

Power industry, 102
Prakash, Aseem, 124
PricewaterhouseCoopers, 58, 95, 202,
203
Product, 9, 90, 93, 94, 102, 107,
127, 131, 153, 157, 159, 178,
181
Project Gigaton, 174
Public Health Foundation of India
(PFHI), 60
Public Role for the Private Sector, 5
Putnam, Robert, 64

R

Rajamani, Lavanya, 40, 41
Reagan, Ronald, 64
Regime, 4, 5, 17, 37, 39–43, 45, 48,
56, 59, 67
Regulation, 1, 2, 5, 6, 10, 11, 13, 26,
53, 83, 85, 94–99, 102, 109,
110, 112–116, 134–136,
140–142, 161, 163, 166, 174,
175, 177, 184, 185, 187, 192,
193, 197, 198
Reid, Harry, 68
Reliance Industries, 222
Reliance Power, 60
Renewable energy, 2, 52, 54, 55,
57–61, 63, 100–102, 123–126,
128, 130–134, 136, 139–143,
151, 153, 156–158, 167, 173,
174, 197, 198, 202, 223
Renewable energy certificates (RECs),
132, 133
Renewable energy power purchase
agreement, 125, 132–134, 174
Research and development (R&D),
90, 102, 108, 175
Rio Climate Conference (1992), 34,
35
Rocky Mountain Institute, 124, 205
Rosenau, James, 7, 12, 85, 110, 136

Royden, Amy, 65
Ruggie, John, 3, 5, 21
Russia, 23, 42, 222, 223
RWE, 53, 100, 101, 104, 180

S
Salman, Mohammed bin, 213
Samsung, 9, 126, 129, 130, 140–142, 180, 247
Saudi Arabia, 212, 213, 224
Scope 3 emissions, 102, 127, 130, 131, 133, 136
Second-order effect, 15, 112, 215
Self-regulation, 5, 6, 17
Self-reinforcement, 134
Shell, 1, 9, 22, 101, 104, 180, 185, 186, 191
Shell Energy, 101
Sierra Club, 150
Singh, Manmohan, 58
Small Island Developing States (SIDS), 37
SoftBank, 213
Software companies, 131, 133
Solar power, 61, 123, 213
South Africa, 41
South Korea, 126
Sport utility vehicles (SUVs), 86–88
Sprinz, Detlef, 66
State leadership, 10, 20, 25, 84, 85, 111, 117, 175, 201
State system, 3
Steel industry, 174
"Steering mechanism", 7, 85, 99, 110, 136
Stern, Nicholas, 39
Stern Review on the Economics of Climate Change, 39
Stiftung 2 Grad, 2, 116, 186
Stokes, Leah, 68
Subnational actors, 4, 211, 221

Supply chain emissions, 6, 102, 107, 108, 130, 131, 133, 140, 173, 174, 181
Sustainability report, 10, 126, 141
SUVs. *See* Sport utility vehicles
Swiss Re, 150

T
Tata Power, 192
Tata Steel, 62, 103, 192
Technology companies, 124–128, 130, 131, 134–136, 138, 142, 148, 193, 195
Technology industry, 18, 138, 142, 197
Technology Mechanism, 40
Telangana, 61
TERI (The Energy and Resources Institute), 60
Tesla, 86, 89
Texas, 22, 174
The Gambia, 35
Third World, 62
Threshold model, 14, 15, 17, 111, 112, 176, 219
Thyssenkrupp, 53, 103
Toyota, 9, 88, 89, 91, 98, 179, 180
Tragedy of the commons, 3
Transnational actor, 7, 12
Transnational climate governance, 5, 6
Transnational issues, 3, 5, 12, 16, 85, 124, 143, 175, 177, 207, 210
Transnational politics, 3
Transnational relations, 5, 21, 205
Trump administration, 1, 23, 54, 58, 70, 143, 214, 215
Trump, Donald, 70, 88, 128, 210, 212
"Two-level game", 64, 66

U

Ukraine, 23
Ultratech Cement, 103, 112
Unconventional issue, 17, 23, 24, 210
Unilever, 152
Uniper, 103
United Kingdom, 22, 85, 186, 190, 224
United Nations (UN), 4, 35, 36, 38, 39, 44, 45, 62, 166, 215
United Nations Conference on Environment and Development, 35
United Nations Framework Convention on Climate Change (UNFCCC), 35–37, 40, 56, 65, 141
United Nations General Assembly, 143
United Nations Secretary-General, 45, 58
United States Affordable Clean Energy rule, 70
United States Byrd-Hagel Resolution, 66
United States carbon tax, 65
United States Chairman of the Joint Chiefs of Staff, 212
United States Clean Air Act (CAA), 69
United States clean energy mandate, 67
United States Clean Power Plan (CPP), 69
United States Climate Committee of the Federal Reserve, 211
United States Climate Envoy, 211
United States Climate Stewardship Acts, 67
United States Climate Task Force, 211
United States Congress, 65, 67

United States deficit reduction, 65
United States Democrats, 67
United States Department of Defense, 22
United States Department of State, 214
United States emissions trading scheme, 67
United States energy tax, 65
United States Environmental Protection Agency (EPA), 69, 70
United States executive branch, 70
United States Federal Reserve, 211
United States House of Representatives, 67
United States Independents, 67
United States interest groups, 70
United States legislative branch, 70
United States National Climate Advisor, 211
United States National Defense Strategy (2022), 212
United States partisan gap, 67
United States Republicans, 67, 69
United States Secretary of Defense, 212
United States Senate, 67, 69
United States Special Representative for Subnational Diplomacy, 214
United States 2010 midterm elections, 69
United States 2020 presidential election, 211
United States Waxman-Markey Bill, 67
United States White House Summit (2021), 212
UN Race to Zero, 167
US-China Joint Announcement, 43, 213
US Climate Action Partnership, 67

V

Vandenbergh, Michael, 2, 4, 6, 13, 25, 124, 174
Victor, David, 3
Vietnam, 125
Virgin Group, 40
Vision 2030, 212
Volkswagen, 85–88, 91–93, 95, 98, 99, 180, 224

W

Walmart, 6, 22, 173–175, 179, 210
Warner, John, 67
Waters, James, 218
We Are Still In, 23, 214
Wehrmann, Benjamin, 50, 54
Weidner, Helmut, 49, 51
Westerwinter, Oliver, 7, 23
Westphalia, 21, 26
Wetselaar, Maarten, 101
"Why Your Company Needs a Foreign Policy", 209

Wind energy, 124
Wired, 126
World Bank, 101, 151
World Economic Forum, 141
World order, 26, 205, 223
World Resources Institute, 2, 47, 58, 212
World Trade Organization, 22
World Wildlife Fund International, 38
Wright, Christopher, 24

X

Xi, Jinping, 42
Xuan, Xiaowei, 43, 213

Y

Yale Environment 360, 53

Z

Zero-emission vehicle, 88, 90, 99
Zurich, 150, 157

Printed in the United States
by Baker & Taylor Publisher Services